ENEMY

RUTH CLARE

Praise for ENEMY

"Extraordinary memoir." **Booktopia**

"...enormously rewarding and revealing exploration of the effects of war on family life and on the human soul and psyche.... an emotionally charged and thoroughly engaging book." **The Australian**

"...powerful... stories such as Clare's must be read." **Books + Publishing**

"Resembling a novel in its sensory detail and riveting narrative... Ruth Clare's memoir takes us deeper, into the mind of the child and her day-to-day reality, where she is constantly primed for her father's next act of cruelty."
Australian Book Review

"Brilliantly moving" **Annabel Crabb**

"At once angry and violent, forgiving and understanding, chilling at its most dangerous moments... The parallel strengths of this work are the author's ability to reach out to her deeply troubled father with considerable empathy despite the domestic violence, fear and pain that stained her upbringing, and her determination not to let this insidious 'enemy' in her past invade her own adulthood, and her role as a parent." **Judge's comments, Asher Literary Award**

"An extraordinary story by a very gifted writer. Ruth Clare has managed to capture her childhood with High Definition crystal clear vision, before HD was even a thing. I could smell the bread in her father's bakery, feel the oven heat of Rockhampton, see the painfully slow telephone dial in an emergency, taste the salty air on a deserted island, feel the greasy scalp of a bank manager, see the love for her mum, feel each painful blow from her father, and experience the anger, empathy and truth in every carefully recalled experience of Ruth's life story. This is a truly courageous and inspiring story". **Kari O'Gorman**

"This book is the fantastic untold story of the battles fought decades after and thousands of miles from the Vietnam War we think we know. It should be read and shared by all." **Angus & Robertson**

"Ruth Clare brings history into the home with piercing intelligence, unflinching honesty and total, terrifying recall. By drawing a direct line from the violence of war to the brutality of domesticity, Enemy refuses to excuse the tormentor yet tries to understand the legacy of torment. I wanted this book to stop and I couldn't put this book down." **Clare Wright, author of the Stella Prize-winning The Forgotten Rebels of Eureka**

"A brutal, compelling and insightful memoir from an exciting new Australian talent." **Brunswick St Bookstore**

"Beautiful memoir about how our childhood shapes us and the scars it leaves." **Amra Pajalic**

"This book is a must read, seamlessly integrating an adult and child voice as the author simultaneously recalls her abusive childhood and tries to understand why her father was the way he was. Gripping, heart-breakingly sad, and breathtakingly forgiving, it is a story of childhood survived and transcended." **Bec Yule**

"Compelling, profoundly moving, extraordinary memoir. So well-crafted. It just rang true, and as a reader you quickly came to care deeply about Ruth and her mother and siblings." **Caroline Hutton**

"I literally could not put the book down. That we should all be so gracious in the face of adversity." **Sean Kelleher.**

"Deeply moving memoir that drew me in from the very start." **Debbie Lamb**

"A wonderful, sympathetic and very honest account… so worthwhile."
Helen King

Life Lab Books, 2023
First published by Penguin Australia Pty Ltd, 2016

Text copyright © Ruth Clare 2016
ruthclare.com

All rights reserved.

Cover and text design by Matt Clare
monodesign.com.au

Lines from 'I've had this shirt' by Michael Rosen on p. 62 reproduced with permission of United Agents.

Lyrics on p. 127 reproduced with permission of the Seventh-day Adventist Church.

*For Kerstin and David, and the childhood that was
And for Scarlett and Alex, and the childhood that is*

'I am not what happened to me,
I am what I choose to become.'

– Carl Jung

MACHINE GUN CLATTER

I was born into the war still raging inside my father. The DNA he gave me came charged with trauma he didn't know how to process, and as my life unfolded it seemed I was fated to follow in his footsteps. I too learned life should be lived on guard because you never knew when the next attack would come.

Dad came of age in the era of Australia's National Service Scheme. According to the National Archives of Australia, of the 800,000-plus twenty-year-old men who registered during this time, more than 63,000 had their birthdays drawn in the lottery and served in the military. Over 19,000 went to Vietnam.

Douglas Robert Callum was born on 30 January 1946. His birthday condemned him to give up the plans he had made for his own life so he could serve a country that would go on to shun and shame him.

Going to war, watching his mates die, causing the deaths of others shattered his soul. He put the pieces back together again the best he could, but the clatter of machine guns always leaked through the cracks. Most people on the outside would never get to see the damage he fought to hide, but within a family even the best disguises slip.

In 1974, the year I was born, post-traumatic stress disorder

(PTSD) hadn't been recognised as a condition. Even after it was added to the *American Psychiatric Association's Diagnostic and Statistical Manual of Mental Disorders*, in 1980, it was never something spoken about in my house.

When I was growing up Dad rarely mentioned the Vietnam War, or his part in it. No one ever told me the way Dad behaved might have anything to do with a war. No one ever told me it wasn't my fault.

One day, after he had left our family for good, Mum said to me, 'I wish you had known your father before he went to Vietnam.'

I wish I had too.

FIRST MEMORY

My first memory is of Dad hitting me. I was three years old, and hiding under the table in our dining room watching Mum dry dishes in the green-and-brown kitchen of our seventies style two-storey brick house on a quarter-acre block in Strathpine, one of Brisbane's outer suburbs.

I had been spying on her for ages, pretending to be a secret agent. She didn't know I was there. I was an excellent spy.

The front door banged and as Dad's heavy steps came closer I shuffled further back into the darkness under the table. I planned to put him under surveillance as well. His engine-oil smell and hairy legs passed me by, then his shadow came to a sudden stop in front of me.

'Jesus Christ,' he muttered, then yelled, 'Girls!'

His loud voice made my stomach sick and my heart start thumping. I didn't want to get in trouble again. Kerstin's voice drifted from our bedroom. 'Coming, Dad.'

Ten seconds later she skidded to a stop in front of him. 'Yes, Dad.'

Whenever Dad said our names we had to say, 'Coming, Dad!' before the count of five, then drop what we were doing and start running. I knew I would be in big trouble but I couldn't make myself move.

'Where's your sister?'

'I dunno.'

I wriggled back more so she wouldn't see me. 'Ruth!' His yell was louder this time.

My heart raced faster but I managed to get the words out. 'Yeah, I'm here.'

He bent to find me under the table. Not saying anything, he uncurled one finger from the fist of his right hand and jabbed it first at me, then toward the wall, indicating where he wanted me to go.

I didn't move. He stood waiting a moment before his face whipped back into view and his voice came out as a growl. 'Get out of there.'

I started to crawl, but it wasn't fast enough, and his hand shot under the table. He grabbed my arm and swung me up, plonking me down hard on my feet next to my sister. Even once he let go, his fingers still dug holes into me.

Dad formed his words slowly, making sure we heard every consonant. 'Look at me.'

His hair was blond and flopping down over a tanned forehead streaked with grease from the motorbike he was fixing. The yellow t-shirt that stretched tight across his big chest had a dark V in the middle from his sweat.

He turned on his quiet voice, the one that could trick you into thinking everything was going to be okay. 'Come over here.'

Kerstin and I lined up in front of him.

'What's this?' He pointed to a spot on the wall.

My heart dropped down to my toes, taking all the heat in my body with it. He was pointing at the label I had peeled off my box of Tic Tacs and stuck to the wall.

I stood dumbly for a moment, ears thudding. Kerstin leaned in and looked at the sticker and I copied what she did, trying to look innocent. I stared at the curled-up edges and pretended I was seeing it for the first time.

'It's a Tic Tac sticker.' I tried to make my voice sound interested and surprised.

'I know it's a Tic Tac sticker. What I want to know is who put this sticker on my wall?' Dad's voice pretended to be patient.

Kerstin moved a bit closer to me and swayed slightly, giving me a small bump. She was looking at the ground but I knew she wanted me to own up.

Fear raced through my body like a runaway train, shaking my legs and swooshing in my ears as it rocketed through my brain trying to help me come up with the lie that would make this go away.

'Well?' Dad's eyebrows were high on his forehead.

Kerstin was the first to talk. 'It wasn't me.'

I paused. Maybe if we both said we didn't do it then no one would get in trouble. 'It wasn't me.'

Dad's hand disappeared behind his back then shot out as fast as a cobra, striking Kerstin on the shoulder. She knocked into me and I stumbled. Before I could regain my balance, his hand moved back again and he hit me in the ear. I stumbled backward, falling onto the floor.

My ear burned and throbbed and I cried. Kerstin cried too. Her cry sounded like shock and pain. My cry was those things as well, but also horror at myself; my lie was the reason she was hurt.

'Get up!' He moved to pull me upright but I crawled out of his reach and scrambled to my feet before he could touch me again. My ear was screaming for attention but I knew better than to put my hand up to hold it. Dad hated it when you acted like he had hurt you.

I looked up for a moment toward the kitchen and saw Mum standing there, frozen in place. Her cigarette was down low, the smoke curling all around her, turning her into a ghost.

'Now, don't make me do that again.' Dad put his face so close to mine I couldn't take it all in. He jabbed his thick square finger at the wall again and again. 'Tell me who put this sticker on this wall!'

Though he pulled his head back, his up-close face glowed like a camera flash in my mind. The light streaming through the window and bouncing off the wall was bright too. I couldn't focus on where he was pointing. I had to think of a way to stop Kerstin being hit while not getting hit myself, but I couldn't make my brain work.

'I'm going to ask again, who stuck the sticker on the wall?' When his eyes went flat and cold like this he wouldn't be happy until someone had been punished.

'I didn't do it!' Kerstin's words mixed with her sobs.

I tried to own up, but I couldn't make myself. 'I didn't do it either.'

This time I watched for his hands. He hit Kerstin on the side of her head and she screamed. When his hand came for me I managed to swerve out of the way and put my arms up to protect my head. Though I escaped a second blow to my still-ringing ear, the soft underside of my upper arm took its place. I felt the deep pain of a soon-to-be bruise but at least I managed to hold my feet in place. I screamed and my sobbing started again.

Kerstin was standing with her head flopped forward, half whimpering, half sobbing. I chanted silently to myself: *sorrykerstinsorrykerstinsorrykerstin*.

Dad bent down into a squat, grabbing Kerstin's arm in his right hand and mine in his left. His leathery fingers dug deep into our flesh and he pulled us into an orderly line again. He shook us.

'Who did it?'

We didn't speak.

He shook again, harder this time. My teeth snapped together and the world blurred into rainbows as my head rocked back and forth on my neck.

'Who did it?' His shakes were getting harder and I knew I couldn't let Kerstin take any more of this no matter how scared I was.

'I did. Me.'

Dad threw Kerstin into the corner of the room and focused his dead eyes on mine. He kept his hand wrapped tightly around my left arm so I couldn't run away, and got me into a better position.

He began hitting me properly now, using his swings to keep

the beat of his words.

'I (*whack*) am not (*whack*) hitting you (*whack*) because of the sticker (*whack*). I am hitting you (*whack*) because (*whack*) you lied to me!'

I tried to get away but his fingers clawed in further, and I couldn't avoid the hits landing on my legs, my arms, my bottom. Sometimes his hand was open, but sometimes it was a fist, punching, punching.

His face was only inches away and I could feel myself merging with him. The rage pumped out of him, into me, filling me with anger bigger than my body could hold.

A booming voice filled my head. *You're a liar too. You say you are only hitting me because of the lie, but you hit Kerstin too, and she didn't lie. Liar. Liar. Liar.*

Becoming aware Dad had finally let go of my arm, I ran, making it only as far as the lounge room before his footsteps thundered behind me. My eyes felt incredibly sharp and the world slowed into snapshots. Door. Hallway. Bookshelf. Window. TV.

I was scanning for escape, but I couldn't figure out where to go so I dived under the couch, knocking my forehead in the attempt. As I scrabbled toward the back, Dad grabbed hold of my right leg and pulled. The springs underneath the couch caught my hair and a chunk of it was ripped from my head. I screamed.

I managed to grab the leg of the couch but his hand strengthened its grip on my ankle and he pulled me up into the air until I was hanging upside down. I was still holding on but the couch was now tilting as it was lifted into the air with me. He shook me back and forward roaring, 'Let go of it! Let go of it!' I finally lost my grip and was left dangling in the air.

Dad set me down hard on my feet. Blood pounded in my temples, making my ears throb, and my head kept tumbling from being upside down. He started up where he had left off. 'Don't (*whack*) run away (*whack*) from me (*whack*). Listen (*whack*) to what (*whack*) I'm saying!'

I no longer felt his blows land. The beating of my heart and the hissing in my ears were all I knew. I didn't care what he was saying; I had to get away. I ran to my bedroom and scrambled under my bottom bunk, but had barely managed to conceal myself when I felt him grip both my legs.

I was covered in sweat and his hand slipped. Just as he readjusted his hold to allow him to better drag me out, Mum appeared at the door.

'Doug! Stop it!' Her voice was a scream so wrapped in terror it was barely more than a whisper. 'You are going to kill those kids one of these days!'

He stopped, loosened his hold on my legs, then let go completely. I scurried further under the bed, backing against the wall and making myself as small as possible. From my hiding place I saw Dad's legs storm out of the room and Mum disappear down the hall after him. It was finished.

I stayed under the bed, turning around and pressing my face into the wall. Hugging into it, I sobbed in relief at finally being invisible. I wished I could crawl inside this wall: so solid and safe.

As my tears disappeared, leaving their echo in my shuddering in-breaths, I drifted into the blue-flowered wallpaper. I became one with the green leaves and blue dots, and a soft, dreamy fog stole over me. I couldn't tell if I was asleep or awake. I don't know how long I stayed there, but when I became aware of my body again I was shivering and sore where the wooden floor pressed my bruises. I shimmied into the open.

Sitting on my bed, gloriously soft after the hardness of the floor, I scanned my body to see what hurt. My scalp was the sharpest pain, throbbing where the hair had come out, but there was a deep pounding inside my brain and ache at the back of my neck that made me want to cry all over again. My ankle was sore and my arm had red and purple marks that would be bruises by the end of the day. A few hot tears slipped out. *Don't think about it.*

Soft footsteps approached and I quickly lay on the bed and faced the wall again, holding myself still. A moment later, Kerstin's hand was soft on my back. I didn't turn around. I didn't deserve her kindness when it was my fault she had been hurt.

Her hand stayed where it was, lovely and warm. I eventually faced her. The familiarity of her warm brown eyes unravelled me and I buried my head in my fraying blue chenille bedspread, crying and saying, 'I'm sorry,' over and over.

She rubbed my hip gently. 'It's all right.'

I didn't believe her. I was the worst kind of person, sacrificing someone else to save myself.

Turning back to the wall, I shifted slightly away. How could she be nice to me after what I had done? Besides, I needed to be alone if I was going to make myself strong again. 'I'm fine now. You don't have to be nice to me. I just want to lie down.'

She got off my bed without saying a word and climbed onto her top bunk.

A little while later Dad's heavy footsteps stopped outside our room.

'Ruth.' His voice was small and quiet.

I kept facing the wall, pretending to be asleep.

'Ruth.' His tone was more insistent. Not wanting him to get mad again, I turned around. His eyes had gone soft and he seemed smaller somehow.

He stepped into the room with his arms outstretched. 'Give me a hug.'

I stayed where I was.

'Come 'ere.' His voice was teasing, but I could hear the slight impatience underneath. 'Don't be silly.'

I was desperate to say no. I wanted him to know I truly and deeply hated him and would never forgive him, but I didn't want to get into any more trouble. I walked and stood stiffly in front of him, arms by my side.

As he hugged the marble statue I offered him, he murmured into my ear. 'I'm sorry, love. But that hurt me a lot more than it hurt you.'

I boiled with the unfairness of his words, but kept quiet until he let me go. I stayed where I was, looking at the ground and wishing with all my heart he would leave.

'Are we okay?'

As if I had a choice. 'Yes, Dad.' I didn't give him my eyes. 'Good.' He left the room.

To avoid getting in trouble, I spent a lot of time when Dad was home lying still on my bed watching the curtains. As the sun shifted through the lace, people and shapes and animals emerged, whole stories springing forth, keeping me transfixed for hours.

But I couldn't stay still and quiet all the time. Nor could Kerstin. Though we tried our best to remember all the things we weren't allowed to do, we kept tripping up. Any time we stepped outside the tight circle of acceptable behaviours, Dad was there to knock us back in.

Our bodies grew used to a constant lack of respect, aware that at any moment a hand might reach out to slap. Standing by and watching him hit Kerstin made me hurt just as much as when he turned on me. We took it in turns offering gentle comfort, our sibling squabbles put aside as we poured helpless concern onto aches that stretched down to the most vulnerable parts of us. Sometimes it was just a few whacks, but other times he lost control and Mum yet again screamed for him to stop before he killed us.

I didn't want to die. I promised myself if he kept on hitting me, I was going to run away.

ADORABLE CHILDREN

Dad spent most of his life out of the house at work, so Kerstin and I were usually alone with Mum. Brisbane is warm and sunny 260 days a year. The majority of our days were spent in the blue-tarp pool on couch grass in our backyard. Blonde hair turned white, skin coffee.

Once a week we would stand on chairs, crowding Mum as she tipped cake mix and an egg into the Mixmaster, cigarette dangling from her lips. The noise from the machine made my insides vibrate and crunch together. I wanted to make it stop, but I pressed my hands hard on my ears instead, breathing in chocolate powder and waiting for my beater to lick.

Up until I was three, Dad had delivered concrete to builders in the orange-and-green mini-mix truck he owned. After he sold that, his strong arms bulged under the weight of bags of flour instead of bags of concrete. He had bought a bakery only six blocks from our house.

A couple of months after he had set up shop, Kerstin, Mum and I walked down to see him. By the time we had passed through the car park and reached the shade of the shop awning, our faces were bright red from the heat.

'I'll be glad when this baby comes,' Mum said, leaning against the glass of the shopfront and flapping her loose green dress up and down over her beach-ball belly.

Stepping onto the faded squares of red-and-white linoleum inside the shop, I was assaulted by a jet of warm air whipped down by the ceiling fan working frantically above us. The siren call of the display cabinet beckoned me. Careful not to leave fingerprints, I put my face a few inches away from the glass. Lightly toasted buns filled with mock cream and dabs of bright red strawberry jam, rows of symmetrical brown-and-pink neenish tarts, sponge squares of lamingtons dipped in chocolate and rolled in coconut...

'Hello, there.' Dad appeared from the doorway to the kitchen, smiling above his dusty white apron. He pushed the back of his hand against the spreading stain of sweat at the front of the white paper hat he wore. 'C'mon, come out the back.'

I let Kerstin and Mum go first, lingering at the display. If we were allowed to have a treat today I was going to have a custard slice, or maybe a mini apple tart. Just thinking about firm custard escaping its pastry square filled my mouth with saliva. Definitely a custard slice.

I dawdled an extra moment hoping someone might walk into the shop just in time to see I wasn't an ordinary person. I got to go *behind* the counter.

'I'm just making some bread rolls,' Dad said as I joined them in the massive room of the kitchen. He reached down into the shiny machine that looked like a big version of our Mixmaster, pulling out a blob of white dough as big as his chest.

As he banged it down on the stainless-steel counter, a waft of yeast hit the air.

'Can I touch it, Dad?' I asked.

'If you go and wash your hands.' He automatically began folding the stretchy whiteness in on itself.

I hurried to the sink beneath the white tiles covered with receipts, avoiding the metal mop bucket underneath.

'All clean?' Dad asked as he threw flour, with the same flourish I had seen him use on dice, all over the counter. I nodded as I wiped my hands on my red-and-pink striped skirt and positioned myself at his left elbow, just tall enough to see.

The light coating of flour slid my hand effortlessly down the smooth curve of the dough. The warmth made it feel like a living thing. Last time Dad had let me take a small dough ball home as my pet, but by the end of the day the insides went sticky and the outside was a thin, cracked crust. I buried it in a hole I dug with Mum's metal trowel at the back corner of our yard.

'All right. You ready?'

Kerstin and I lined up on the opposite side of the bench. As Dad picked up his blue plastic dough scraper, Mum sank down on the nearby stool to watch as well, her heavy belly forcing out a loud breath.

Dad cut off two pieces, one for each hand. With a few quick circles he conjured two perfect round balls and placed them on the big silver tray I wanted to ride like a sleigh.

Watching Dad roll dough through a mist of flour dust felt like a form of hypnosis. My eyes drooped. But in no time at all thirty-two white balls were lined up like soldiers.

Through the doorway we saw a blonde-haired lady wearing a red dress covered in big white-and-yellow flowers enter the shop. Kerstin and I followed Dad as he moved behind the counter.

'Hello, there.' She smiled her red lips down at me.

I smiled my best 'helping behind the counter' smile back: direct eye contact, not looking away. 'Hello.'

'These are my kids.' Dad put his arms around our shoulders and squeezed us in. His pride pulsed into me, making me taller.

'What adorable children.' She smiled at him.

I lapped up her words, wondering if she really meant them. I wished I could ask her what we were doing that was adorable so I could do more of it at home.

When Dad pulled the browned rolls out of the oven, they were wider and flatter than the balls that had gone in. I put my nose as close to the hot tray as I dared, breathing deeply. They smelled as wholesome as a hug.

Fifteen minutes later, Dad loaded six of them into a bag and tied a brown twist tie around the top. The heat formed an instant mist inside the plastic. 'Want to get the ham?'

Kerstin and I looked at each other and nodded gravely. 'Getting the ham' meant a visit next door to the fat butcher named Phil who smelled like chips.

The bell above Phil's door rang as we entered. As soon as he registered it was us, he let out a huff, reached in and grabbed the pink ham leg with the criss-crossed brown skin. After banging it down on the stainless-steel counter he lifted it to the big, sharp wheel and slowly cut off eight slices. The noise clenched my teeth together and I held my breath to stop the smell of blood getting inside me.

Less than a minute later, without saying a word, he dangled the ham over the counter and snatched the bag of rolls Kerstin held up to him. 'Thank you,' Kerstin and I said together as we rushed out the door. The ten-step journey to his shop was obviously long enough to wear our adorableness off.

Back in the kitchen, the thick slabs of butter Mum had spread melted into the rolls, before she curled the ham on top.

'This is the best taste in the whole world,' Dad said. We nodded along on our makeshift chairs of green-and-blue plastic milk crates, our mouths stuffed with big, greedy bites.

I closed my eyes and wished the way I felt in that moment, lucky and loved, could last forever.

RUNAWAY

The Dad at the bakery was so easy to love, it made it hurt all the more when the other Dad, the one who lived with us, lashed out. Anything could set him off. Spilling a drink. Tripping on my feet. Drawing on the wrong paper. Breaking something.

Now he was a baker, we had to be extra quiet all of the time because he had to go to work in the middle of the night and he needed his sleep. The more tired he became, the longer his list of punishable offences grew. *Don't use that tone. Get that look out of your eye. Walk faster. Don't run.*

Every new rule broken was met with the same emphatic punishment, my body his drum as he drove the message home in rhythm with his words.

Each time he hit me I tried to follow through on running away, but though I had packed my bag a dozen times I never made it further than the end of the hallway.

The day I finally made it out the door, it was warm enough that I wore only a t-shirt and shorts despite it being the middle of winter.

My four-year-old hands were shaking and my arm still

aching as I put two dresses on top of the three skirts I had already packed into the small wooden suitcase with the big hinges Dad had made during his apprenticeship.

Ten minutes before, Dad had tripped over the tricycle I had left in the front yard. He had dragged me by the arm to look at it.

'Is this where this is meant to be?' he asked as he shook me.

'N-n-no,' I tried to get out through chattering teeth.

'Did you want to hurt me with this?'

I didn't answer him quickly enough so he kept on shaking me and shaking me until the colours of the trees and sky twirled into a kaleidoscope. I couldn't remember what answer I was meant to give.

'No? Yes?'

'Don't (*whack*) be (*whack*) smart (*whack*) with me. Put (*whack*) it (*whack*) away.' He shoved me onto the ground next to the bike and stalked up the stairs.

Counting out five pairs of underpants, I argued with him in my head. *I wasn't being smart with you; I was trying to remember the question, Dad.* He couldn't hit me if I wasn't here.

Kerstin leaned against the doorway, watching me with a smirk on her face. 'You're not gunna run away,' she said. Kerstin would never break the rules. She thought being small and obedient was the best way to keep herself safe. I tried that way too, but my daydreaming meant I lost focus and kept making mistakes. The only solution was to leave.

'Am too.'

'Are not. You always say you're gunna do it but you don't.' Just because she was two years older than me she thought she knew everything.

I put my nose in the air and removed from my pocket the three ginger nut biscuits I had stolen from the kitchen.

'You'll get in trouble if Mum sees those biscuits,' Kerstin said. 'No I won't. I won't be here.' As I added them to the pile I gave her a look to tell her how stupid she was for not thinking of this, but she just smiled back at me like I was the stupid one.

Next I packed my favourite necklace of rainbow-coloured wooden beads, and the little plastic game I had got for my last birthday where you flicked a lever and tried to shoot balls into holes. I didn't really want to take it, but I had to; otherwise, Kerstin might play with it.

I walked down the hallway with Kerstin following close behind. Checking around the corner to make sure Mum and Dad weren't watching, I opened the front door.

Looking out into the street made my throat feel tight. I didn't really want to leave. I definitely didn't want to leave Mum. But Kerstin was watching me, so there was no way I could back out. I raised my chin and headed down the stairs.

Every step away from the house made my tummy feel heavier and my suitcase weigh more. My legs felt wobbly under the extra weight and I couldn't seem to make them go forward. I made it to the other side of the massive pine tree consuming most of our front yard before I stopped.

I checked over my shoulder to make sure Kerstin couldn't see me. I was going to go. I just wished I knew where. I looked up and down the street, hoping for an idea. In the distance I saw someone coming. It looked like a man. A stranger.

Don't talk to strangers. Don't take lollies from strangers. Don't hop into cars with strangers. If a stranger tries to grab you, start screaming. My heart raced. This was the 'stranger' my parents had been warning me about. If I didn't get off the street right now he was going to kill me.

I looked back at the house for a moment. I couldn't let Kerstin know I was giving up. I got down on my belly, threw my suitcase deep underneath the pine tree and wiggled in.

The acid pine smell was sharp in my nose and a tree root dug into my back. The branches above me hung inches from my face, trapping me so I couldn't sit up or even get my head off the ground. I worked on making my breathing completely silent, but the thumping of my heart filled up my head. I was sure he could hear it. 'Shh,' I said softly to myself. 'Shh, shh, shh.'

As the seconds ticked by, the flashes of sunshine through the jumble of limbs began to look like hands reaching in to grab me. I wished I had run to the house. But it was too late. If I moved now the stranger would get me.

At the distant sound of footsteps my body acted before my brain had a chance to think. I wriggled out as fast as I could, not caring when a branch scraped across my face. Then I was out in the blinding sunshine running fast up the stairs.

Kerstin was still on the landing so I came to a stop right next to her.

'There's a stranger coming,' I panted out. 'He was going to get me. I had to come back.'

Kerstin and I kept our eyes on the man as he walked past not looking in our direction.

'He didn't even look at you,' she said.

'I can't run away now. He'll be waiting to get me.' 'Why would he want to get you?'

'Because he's a stranger and strangers like to kill kids.' I wanted to impress her with the drama of what had nearly happened.

'He wouldn't kill you.'

'Would too.'

'No, he wouldn't.'

'He would!'

She turned back into the house with a know-it-all smile.

I touched my face where the branch had cut me and looked onto the street to see if more unfamiliar men were coming. My running away plans hadn't taken strangers into account.

It was probably lucky I hadn't gone anyway. I would have been in such big trouble if Dad had needed to go looking for me. The ginger nuts!

I raced down the steps and slid back under the tree, grabbing my suitcase. I checked to make sure no one could see me from the house before opening up the stiff metal clips.

Grabbing out a biscuit, I shoved it into my mouth. If they couldn't find them I couldn't get in trouble.

Later that night I kicked off sheets damp with my sweat, listening to the loud heartbeat thumping in my ears. It was the same dream I had most nights. The shrieking noise of metal on metal, the cold, robotic gears of a machine that changed direction whenever I did, coming after me to grind me into nothing.

I put my feet on the floor and looked into the darkness for a moment. I wanted to feel Mum's warm flesh, to know for sure the machine had not made me die. But I wasn't allowed to go to Mum and Dad's room at night no matter what. No one was allowed to approach Dad when he was sleeping.

'Dad has bad dreams,' Mum had told me when I asked her why. 'If you surprise him he might grab you before he even knows he's awake. He might accidentally grab you round the throat when he doesn't mean to.'

'Has he ever grabbed your throat?' I had asked.

'A couple of times.'

'Did he hurt you?'

'He didn't mean to. He stopped as soon as he knew what he was doing.'

In my head the dream of the machine wrapped itself around the picture of Dad's hands on Mum's throat, and my heart thumped deeper and faster. I had to see her.

Moonlight shone through the window, making pale stripes among the black shadows like a forest of trees where I tiptoed down the hallway. I wasn't scared of the dark, that was Kerstin's job, but my teeth were chattering from the dream.

I stopped at the entrance of their room. My new baby brother, David, born a couple of months ago, slept behind the white bars of his cot in the corner. There were two lumps on the bed. The Mum lump breathed in a soft rhythmic snore. The Dad lump was silent. His face, squashed in sleep, looked out at me from the side closest to the door. He looked relaxed, but I knew how quickly Dad could move when he was mad.

The echoes of the machine still screeched faintly in my head.

I wanted Mum to wrap her soft arms around me and tell me it wouldn't get me. I tried waking Mum up by screaming her name in my mind, but she didn't stir. David, however, let out a sigh. I held my shape like I was playing musical statues, not daring to breathe. I would be in huge trouble if I woke the baby.

I weighed up the risk. Even in broad daylight I was clumsy, always tripping over nothing and smashing my teeth through my lips in a bloody, painful mess. Now it was dark and there was a basket of folded clothes at the foot of their bed. I would have to creep past that if I wanted to get to Mum. If I stumbled I might fall onto the bed and wake Dad up. I watched his chest moving up and down, up and down, imagining hands around my throat.

Holding my breath, I crept quickly over to the washing basket, grabbing Mum's red-and-white striped t-shirt. A couple of pairs of folded underpants dropped to the floor and I squeezed my eyes tight, sure their whispered landing would wake Dad. When no hands choked me, I backed out and ran as quietly as I could to my room.

I hopped into bed and put the shirt over my face, letting the freshly washed smell flush away the pictures from the dream that still clung to the edge of my thoughts. I often spent a portion of my day hiding in Mum's closet, crammed between her overflowing clothes. The soft brush of fabric on my skin as I breathed in her scent was almost like having her there.

DERAILED

When he was two, my son went through a phase where every tiny frustration made him lash out, mostly at me. He went through biting, head-butting, scratching, punching; but the worst for me was the face slapping.

If he fell down, or was unable to remove the lid of a bottle, or if I didn't understand what he was trying to say, he would walk up and slap me across my cheek as hard as he could.

The familiarity of that sting opened up old pathways in my brain that derailed my adult self. All knowledge that my son was exhibiting normal two-year-old behaviour was forgotten as I tumbled backward inside my skin, freefalling to the bottom of a long dark well. Looking up through the eyes of my younger self, my son was not my son; he was my father. I was doing nothing wrong and I had been hit. My hand itched to slap back.

Luckily I understood that though I felt violated, as the parent I was the one with the real power. I would not let myself abuse it. Still, my voice was more a roar than a calm instruction as I told him, 'No! It is not okay to hit. Be gentle with your hands!'

I stumbled to my bedroom, leaned my back against the door and dropped down to the floor, curling in on myself as I cried.

It had been over twenty-five years since Dad had laid a hand on me. Yet some days it still felt like my past dragged behind me like a sack of drowned kittens. I was utterly bored by the tear-soaked drama of it all.

People were always saying you should appreciate every moment when your kids were young because it went by in the blink of an eye. One part of me knew that was true, but another part just wanted to fast-forward a few years to the time when my son was older and more reasonable. I was desperate for his hitting to stop triggering the memories from my own early years.

My son's violence also made me worry there might be some genetic factor at play. Other mothers I spoke to said their sons had gone through stages of hitting as well. 'Don't worry,' they reassured me. 'He'll grow out of it.' But their fathers were not like my father.

Each time my son hit, my mind told me it would go on forever, that he would grow into a violent man, just like his grandfather. When the intensity of the moment passed I grew more rational. This was a stage, not an inherited trait. How could it be?

None of Dad's brothers or sisters were violent. When I spoke to them about their parents and the way they were treated during their childhood, they described their upbringing as 'firm but fair'. All had utmost respect for their parents. But there was one major variation between their lives and Dad's: the Vietnam War.

I had thought about my childhood a lot over the years. Indeed, the memories stayed so fresh, many days it felt like I had never left it. But mostly my viewpoint stayed limited to the tunnel vision of my childhood pain, with Dad cast as the evil villain. It wasn't until I became pregnant with my first child, my daughter, in 2007, that my view on the situation began to expand and I started to give serious consideration to the impact the war had on Dad.

As my body changed to support the life growing inside, a whole new world of emotions started leaking out of me. I cried at the merest hint of sadness. Every person's pain felt like my own. I had never felt more vulnerable, but at the same time I was aware of the fierce protectiveness I felt toward my unborn child.

As the months progressed and the kicks and movements let me imagine my baby more fully, I was filled with a certainty that I would sacrifice everything I had for her. I would kill for this baby. I would die in her place without a second thought.

Filled with these new feelings it struck me as incredibly sad that Dad might never have felt this way toward his own children. Or if he did, these softer feelings came out tainted by the poison of his trauma.

It is one of our deepest biological drives to keep our offspring safe so our genes survive. To cause your children harm goes against the laws of nature. It is no small thing to be so wounded that you subvert the innate urges of your biology.

The new compassion I was feeling for my baby, and the world at large, started seeping into my thoughts about Dad. It wasn't fair that he had been picked. It wasn't right that his brothers and sisters got to continue full lives while Dad's was forever derailed because of a stupid lottery.

With the burden of my upcoming responsibility as a parent weighing as heavily and urgently on me as the baby's head on my bladder, I was filled with the need to know what had happened to Dad.

RED THONG

The rickety fibro walls and high stilts of our newly rented home were shaking like a train on wonky tracks as I jumped over the obstacle course of unpacked boxes. For the last twenty minutes Mum and Dad had taken it in turns to yell out, 'Don't run through the house – you will break something or hurt yourself!' But they had been saying the same thing every day since they had started packing, a month ago, so I didn't listen any more.

Just before I turned five, Dad announced he was selling the bakery and was now going to be a teacher. This meant moving to a different city, 636 kilometres north of Brisbane, called Rockhampton.

While I was surprised to be moving, I was completely shocked to learn Dad was a teacher. I was finally old enough to go to school and had been dreaming of this moment for years, but there was no way I was going if Dad was going to be the one teaching me.

'Are you really a teacher?' I asked.

'Yes. I am going to teach grown-ups at a TAFE college something called fitting and turning . . .'

He kept talking, telling me how bolts and screws need to fit together perfectly for machines to work, but I tuned him out. He wasn't going to be my teacher. That was all I needed to know.

The game I was in the middle of playing went like this: run down the central hall, jump over one box, two boxes, don't slip on the clothes, watch the small step leading onto the built-in verandah, don't trip on the hole in the lino where you can see the floorboards underneath, race to the end near the new washing machine, hit the wall and back again.

I ran over and over the same loop until I tripped and stumbled into the washing machine. My foot came down on a bracket lying on the floor beside it. Cool metal sliced into the arch of my hot left foot in slow motion. My breath caught as I pulled my foot off it. I stared at the five-centimetre stripe left behind, telling myself it couldn't be that bad because there wasn't any blood. A beat later, thick, dark red oozed out and I screamed.

'Mum! Dad! Ruth's cut her foot open!' Kerstin yelled.

The noise of my scream circled back into my ears and made my heart pump in fear. The red was dripping a pool onto the floor. I had never seen so much blood in my life.

The house shook, *boom, boom, boom,* as Dad ran toward the sound of my screams. I looked up expecting to see bandages, but instead I saw fury. He barely glanced down at my foot. His angry eyes locked onto mine as he walked toward me.

Squeezing his fingers deep into my arm, he yanked me around to face him. He hated it when you looked away from him so I didn't dare take my eyes off his, but I could feel my foot slipping in the blood on the floor and it made me cry more.

'I told you not to run through the house.' He shook me. 'This is what happens when you don't listen to me.' He gestured to the dark pool on the floor.

My eyes shifted to the blood still trickling from my foot as Dad continued, 'You'll get no sympathy from me. I'm not taking you to the doctor, and neither is your mother. And you can just walk to school on that foot. Maybe that'll teach you a lesson.'

The amount of blood made it seem worthy of medical attention, so I looked up at Dad again to see if he might change his mind. He just shook his head and strode away, shaking the house as he went.

Pain was shooting up my leg. The rusty metal smell of the blood made my throat start swallowing and my nostrils flare out. I looked down at the dark puddle to make sure it was real. There was a vivid red smear off to the side where I had slipped in it. For some reason looking at that smear made me want to spread the redness all over the walls.

A moment later he was back, carrying an old towel with a faded green flower pattern and a hole where the piping was pulling away. 'Put this around your foot.' He threw the towel at me, then walked off.

By this time I could no longer really feel my foot, or any part of my body. There was a white cloud creeping around the edge of the room that made me feel floaty and soft. I balanced my weight on my good foot, but I needed to grab onto something so I didn't fall into the blood. I hopped toward the dusty windowsill.

Each hop stabbed a knife into the gash. The sharpness of the pain snapped me out of the fog. My crying rose up again and I wiped my snot on my bare forearm. In an instant the hot breeze coming through the rows upon rows of louvres changed it from clear to white. Leaning more heavily on the windowsill, I bent down to try to do something with my foot. I made an attempt to cover the wound but the towel was big in my clumsy little hands and I didn't know what I was doing.

I sat down on the floor, away from the blood puddle, and Kerstin came over and patted me on the head. Somehow it made me feel sadder and my crying went loud.

Mum came in quietly, looking over her shoulder to make sure Dad hadn't seen her. She bent down quickly and wrapped the towel around my foot. It wasn't soft, like you imagine a towel to be, but rough and scratchy. I screamed when it touched the cut. Her eyes shot into me, then looked toward the door where Dad was, letting me know how much trouble she would be in if Dad found her helping me. I squashed my cries back into my lungs for later. Once the foot was wrapped she moved away without looking back.

Kerstin sat down next to me and we watched spots of blood start to come through the towel.

Mum walked past us and I yelled out a whisper. 'Mum. How am I meant to go to school? All the blood keeps coming out. I can't put on shoes.'

She paused a moment, then whispered back, 'You'll have to put on thongs.'

'But it hurts too much to walk on it.'

She shook her head, muttering something I couldn't hear. She looked at my foot for a long moment, then checked the door to see if Dad could see her talking to me.

'I'll take you in the stroller,' she whispered.

'I can't go in a pram, Mum! I'm not a baby. I'm in grade one.'

'Well, it's the best I can think of.' She disappeared down the hallway.

I bowed my head down between my knees and looked at the grain of the floorboards. I had been going to this school for only a little while and now people were going to see me getting pushed to school in a pram, wearing the wrong shoes with a bleeding foot. My underarms prickled and I scratched them, feeling the sweat start to come out.

I wouldn't have minded going to school if I'd had a bandage and crutches, even a wheelchair. But a stroller was *not* a wheelchair.

Mum got my wide blue thongs with the indentations for each toe, and helped me ease my foot into them. It scraped near the cut and I screamed.

'Shh!' She looked angrily at me then checked the door for Dad.

I pulled both my lips inside my mouth and bit down on them as she dragged the pram to the front gate.

Heading down the steps after her, I used the metal pole railing to support as much of my body weight as I could, but the pain felt fresh each time I bounced onto the next step. To distract myself from the sting and throb, I pretended the pole was my crutches and a crowd of concerned people were downstairs waiting to bandage me up, their eyes welling with pride at how brave I was.

When I plonked myself into the stroller, the blue-and-white

striped fabric seat stretched tight around my bum and drooped low between the wheels. With my good foot down on the rubber foot rest, my knee sat up high in the air. I stretched my sore foot out in front of me like they do in hospitals, but it strained my hamstring, so I carefully crossed it on top of the other leg.

Mum picked up David and put him on one hip as she got behind to push the pram. It didn't move. 'Kerstin. Can you push this?' She stepped away and Kerstin took her place.

As she pushed she jerked me forward. The movement stirred the pain and I cried out.

'Sorry,' Kerstin said.

She jostled me again and I screamed and cried. She started crying too. 'Sorry, sorry, sorry.'

'It's not your fault.' *It's my stupid, clumsy fault. Dad told me not to run, but I didn't listen.* I pulled my lips inside and bit down again, letting the tears trickle quietly.

As we made it to the end of the street and turned left onto a busier road, I was sure everyone was staring at me, thinking how stupid I looked. I dipped down, trying to make myself disappear.

With my eyes closer to my foot, I saw most of the cloth strap on my blue thong was now stained red. I tentatively wriggled my toes. The hot breeze had dried some of the ooze, making my foot stick in parts. Trying to dislodge the sole of my foot from the glue of my blood was strangely satisfying.

'My thong's turned red,' I told Kerstin. She moved around to the front of the pram to have a look. Her face was covered in a sheen of sweat from pushing me along.

'Well, red is your favourite colour,' she joked.

I laughed.

'And I always wanted red thongs instead of blue,' I said. We both laughed. Then the laugh swelled up into more laughter and we were cracking up, unable to catch our breath. I was light-headed with relief to find life funny again.

At school, the rest of the day moved in strange time slips. That same white fog I had felt earlier slithered through reality, making it as strange and unreal as a dream. One moment I was at sick bay. Did a crowd of women gather around me tutting and shaking their heads, or had I imagined that? Someone said something about needing stitches, but I couldn't remember who. I was in class with a bandage on my foot. Next I was at home with no recollection of how I got there.

The one flash of clarity that kept cutting through my confusion was the look on Dad's face as he stared down at my cut. Disgust. My suffering revolted him. Each sickening jolt of my foot reminded me how stupid I had been. Dad *had* told me to stop running. If I had just listened to him this never would have happened.

For the next week, my cut continued to bleed through dressings. Each time I put weight on my foot it screamed at me. But I didn't get any stitches. Dad had said no doctors. The pain was my punishment for not doing what I was told.

SUBSTITUTE TEACHER

By the time I started grade two, the cut had faded to an angry red scar. Kerstin told me she now slept each night with her own feet clamped together to keep them safe from harm.

Two weeks before the end of first term, my class was heading out to little lunch. In the bottleneck of the doorway some boys started talking about the substitute teacher who was going to take our class tomorrow.

'Did you hear who it is?' a stocky boy called Jack asked his friend Harry.

'It's Mr Wood, isn't it? He's the one who hit those kids, isn't he?' Harry asked.

'Yeah. I heard he lined a couple of them up in front of the class and whacked them with a ruler.'

Harry and Jack were the boys all the popular girls in class were going to marry when they grew up. They were both good at sport, wore brand-new uniforms and had proper haircuts from a barber framing their handsome tanned faces.

Normally I wouldn't even have looked at them in case they caught me and laughed, but their words had started a pounding in my chest that made me feel brave. I cut into their conversation.

'Is that true?' I asked.

Harry exchanged a glance with Jack and smirked before saying, 'Yeah. My brother had him for a teacher once and he saw him do it.'

'He actually hit kids?'

'That's what I said, isn't it?'

I turned away as they snickered and mimicked my words, 'He actually hit kids.' The blood drained from my face and a deep, clenching feeling gripped the pit of my stomach. I didn't know people who hit kids were allowed in school.

Finding a spot on a bench seat by myself, I pulled the cling wrap off the buttered Country Cheese biscuits Mum had given me. They were normally my favourite, but my appetite had disappeared.

A man who hit was sure to see me through the same eyes my father did. He would find a hundred reasons to want to hurt me. *Know-it-all, show-off, suck-up, liar, smart-arse . . .* The rest of the day passed in a blur as the weight of things this man had to hate pressed down on me.

As soon as my eyes snapped open the next morning and I remembered Mr Wood, I went in search of Mum. She was swiping butter over the sea of bread she had spread out over the kitchen bench.

'Mum, if you send me to school, there's a man coming and he's going to hit me.' My words tumbled out as soon as I walked into the room.

'What?' she asked, looking up at me.

'A man teacher is coming who I've never met, and everyone says he hits kids.'

She moved on to the Vegemite, dabbing small dots, just the way I liked it. 'I'm sure they're just stories —'

'But they aren't. A boy in my class called Harry, his brother saw him do it.'

I stared at her face, trying to hypnotise her into letting me stay home, but she kept on at her task, not looking up.

'You'll be right. Don't worry about it. Go and get ready. I'll walk with you if you like.'

I spent the entire 300-metre walk to school begging Mum not to make me go. A picture of the man's face kept flashing into my mind, his lips curled back, eyes full of hatred. As we neared the gate my feet slowed to a stop.

'C'mon, Ruth,' said Mum, 'we haven't got time for this.'

The other mothers and children swarmed past us. At the sight of the building that housed my classroom, my stomach sank into the bottomless hole that had opened up under my feet. School was meant to be safe. But Dad was a teacher. If people like Dad came here to teach . . . I couldn't move.

Mum walked toward me with her hand stretched out, as if to take my arm and guide me to my classroom. I knew she didn't want to hurt me, but she was willing to send me to someone who would.

I wanted to run, but instead I screamed, 'No! I don't want to go!'

The crowd around us stopped as one and turned to look at me. I didn't care. Mum leaned in close and whispered loudly into my ear, 'Stop this. You're being silly.' She smiled at the other parents and said sorry to them.

'No! No! No!' The screaming wouldn't stop. The curled-back lips of the man in my mind mixed up with pictures of Dad. Somehow, my imagining this man had opened up the door to the terror I had to keep at bay when Dad came after me.

Mum pulled a bit harder on my arm, a frozen smile on her face as she looked around at all the other parents who were now taking a wide path around us. She leaned in close again and hissed out her words. 'You are embarrassing me. Stop this!'

But I couldn't make it stop, and that frightened me more. As she dragged me closer to the entrance, I wrenched my arm free. I ran over and threw myself at the fence, threading my fingers through the diamond shapes of the wire and holding on as tight as I could.

Mum came up behind me, apologising to the people near us. Grabbing me around the waist, she pulled. Unable to dislodge me, she hissed again. 'Stop this! You're being ridiculous!' But I hugged myself tighter into the wire, liking the way it dug into my hands, binding me to it.

The high heels of the vice principal clicked urgently down the steps of the verandah and she walked quickly toward us. My heart pounded harder at the sight of her short red hair and purple suit. I sobbed. Now I was going to be in trouble at school. I had never been naughty before. She was probably going to whip me with the cane.

'What seems to be the trouble?' The vice principal's voice was kind, her face quizzical rather than annoyed.

'Sorry about this,' Mum said. 'I don't know what's gotten into her. She's never like this.'

The vice principal's face pulled into view as she crouched down and talked to me from the other side of the fence. 'Hello there,' she said. 'Is everything okay? Can I help you in some way?'

She had such a nice face. I wanted to talk to her, but I couldn't get the words out around my sobs.

'She doesn't want to go to school today,' Mum said for me.

'Oh.' She leaned further in toward me and angled herself until she captured my eyes. 'Why's that?'

I wasn't sure what to say. Did she know Mr Wood hit kids? I didn't want to get him in trouble if she didn't know.

'Just p-p-lease don't m-m-ake me go,' I managed to get out. I held her gaze for a moment, pleading with her to see everything I couldn't say.

Mum spoke again. 'I think she's scared of the substitute teacher taking her class today. Ruth thinks he's going to hurt her.'

I collapsed into the fence in relief, so glad the words were out there, yet I hadn't been the one to say them.

'Oh no.' The vice principal gripped her hand over mine reassuringly. 'That won't happen. We'd never let a teacher hurt you. Mr Wood's a lovely man.'

She opened her eyes wide, twinkling green sincerity at me. 'C'mon, let's meet him.' She tried to disengage my fingers from the fence.

'Mummy!' I screamed in panic. 'Mummy!' Mum joined in the effort to detach me and I was pulled from the fence, but I grabbed onto Mum's shirt instead, clutching and dragging and pulling to try to get her to take me into her arms. She slipped and dodged, and with the help of the vice principal disentangled herself from me.

The vice principal hugged me into her, gentle but restraining. I breathed in her reassuring mint and musk smell and stopped fighting, though my body kept shaking.

'Say goodbye to your mum,' she said, pressing my back against her legs, her arms over my chest.

'Goodbye, Mum,' I said, tears streaming again.

The vice principal clasped my hand between both of hers and looked deeply into my eyes. 'You'll be all right. I promise. I won't let anything happen to you. Come with me and I'll introduce you.'

She kept my hand and led me past our classroom down toward the oval. I still didn't want to go, but I did feel lucky to have the vice principal holding my hand. I went along quietly, hoping that kids in the classrooms we passed would look out and wonder what made me so special.

My class was in the middle of a game of tunnel ball when we approached. There was a man with them with a large brown beard, wearing long pants and a short-sleeved blue-checked shirt. Mr Wood.

My legs filled with jelly. The vice principal pulled gently on my hand but I couldn't move.

'Stay here for a moment,' she said. I kept my eyes on the man and saw him look over as the vice principal spoke to him and motioned in my direction. They headed to me together and he crouched down and looked at me with kind brown eyes.

'Hello there. I'm Mr Wood.' His voice was as bouncy as a

Play School presenter's. 'What's your name?'

'Ruth.' I spoke quietly and took a small step back.

'I'm not going to hurt you, Ruth.' He showed his hands to me, palms forward, as if letting me check for weapons. 'I promise.'

I froze in shock when I realised he had been told I thought he was going to hit me.

He smiled. 'Really, I won't hurt you.'

A flood of relief unlocked my body and let me step forward again. Instead of being mad about my accusation, he was being nice to me. I felt the block of ice in my stomach begin to melt.

He kept smiling at me as I hiccuped from my earlier crying. There were no twitches or tightness in his face that made me think he was lying.

'Do you think you'll be all right now?' the vice principal asked.

'Yes, miss,' I replied, vigorously nodding my head. I wanted her to know it was all a big misunderstanding.

'Okay, why don't you join that team over there?' Mr Wood gestured to a line of students who were cheering excitedly as they waited for their turn with the ball.

'Okay.' I ran across the browned grass at top speed. I wanted to make it up to him. School was my safe place. They would never let anything bad happen to me. I would start making up for my doubt by doing my best tunnel ball ever.

40/30

The menthol smell of eucalyptus oil still clung to my fingers from where Dad had crushed a leaf for me to smell. I let the pieces flutter into the dead-looking grass at my feet, realising the smell was not confined to my hand – it was all around me, a haze lit golden by the afternoon light.

The patch of bush he had driven us to was densely layered with trees, some of them soaring into the sky in perfectly straight lines, others lying nearly horizontal. Their stillness calmed me, even with the occasional *whoosh* of a car flying past on the road a few metres away.

Dad called over to me. 'C'mon, Ruth. This is a good one.'

My thongs flipped a rhythm on my heels as I crunched through the grass toward his voice. I made sure to make lots of noise as I ran to scare snakes away. 'They're much more frightened of you than you are of them,' Dad always said.

His shirt flashed red and I detoured toward it, brushing the grey-blue leaves of a low-lying branch out of my face without losing pace.

He offered the clump of round leaves in his open hand to me. 'Did you know there are nearly nine hundred species of eucalyptus?'

I looked dubiously at the scraggly leaves hanging in sparse bundles from the trees around us. They all looked pretty much the same to me.

I had been driven past this place hundreds of times on the way back from the beach, but until Dad had pulled the car over at this spot ten minutes ago, I had never really considered it anything more than a backdrop. It felt wrong somehow to break through and enter the scene, finding myself part of the movie I usually watched. It was extra weird to find myself in the bush on a Tuesday afternoon after school, especially alone with Dad.

When I had asked him in passing that afternoon what topic I should choose for my next school lecturette, he had suggested eucalypts. I was willing to nod politely and look around for something easier, but then he had offered to help. It was the first time Dad had been involved with my homework and I jumped at the chance to do something to make him proud.

'C'mon, let's go,' he had said. One minute we were at home; twenty minutes later we were in the bush. It felt like a grand adventure. Just Dad and me.

'Eucalypt trees do look pretty similar but you can tell the difference in a couple of ways. Firstly, there's leaf shape.' He spread out his palm and showed me the pile of fat grey leaves in his hand. 'This is called the silver-leafed ironbark and it comes from this tree here.' He banged his hand on the rough brown bark of the trunk of a tree that soared above our heads. 'It is also called *Eucalyptus melanophloia*.'

I looked at his face in shock. The words sounded so long and clever, I couldn't believe he could even say them, let alone know them off the top of his head. 'How do you know it is called that?'

'I dunno. I remember things like that.'

'Me too.' We shared a small smile and I felt my heart swell to know maybe one day I would know big words the way he did.

'C'mon, put these in your bag and let's see what else we can find.' I put the leaves gently inside the white plastic bag I carried, taking care not to bend or crunch them.

'Will you remember which ones are which, Dad?'

'Yes, love.' He smiled over his shoulder as he went deeper into the bush.

Ripping the end of a branch off another tree, he handed it to me. 'This one's black ironbox.'

The leaves were a glossy green, shaped like tiny crescents, the stems palest pink. A sprig of fluffy white blossoms burst out of tiny green gumnuts like fireworks. 'It's beautiful. I bet fairies would love these.'

'I'm sure they would.'

'Do you know the other name for these ones, Dad?' I wanted to hear those clever words rolling off his tongue again.

'This one is *Eucalyptus raveretiana*.'

'Can we write them down when we get home, Dad? So I can learn them?'

'Yeah. No worries.'

With Dad as my guide I was able to see how things that I'd thought were the same were actually completely different. Moments ago all I had seen was grey. Now I noticed smooth white bark with mottled pink patches. This one had gumnuts;

that one smelled of lemon.

The sun blazed lower on the horizon, touching the forest with pink and orange, signalling a flock of rainbow lorikeets to start landing by twos and threes on a tall tree to our right.

Watching them gather, I got a stick and scratched an 'R' into a smooth white trunk, exposing the green underneath. As soon as I did it, I regretted it. I hugged the tree and whispered sorry, wishing it could grow bark quickly to cover the evidence of my attack.

Within five minutes over fifty birds were screeching above us. I shouted to make myself heard. 'Why do they all go on the same tree?'

'It's safer for them to stay together. C'mon, love, Mum'll have dinner on the table in a minute.'

I checked to make sure our afternoon's work was safe in the bag and hurried after him, following the flattened grass his footsteps made.

That night I lay in bed thinking about our day. He had taken me, by myself, on a special trip into the bush. That must mean something. That must mean he thought I was special, mustn't it? I was going to show him how much I appreciated him. I was going to do the best project ever so he could see his attention had not been wasted. I itched to get to the library to learn those long words so Dad could see I was as clever as he was.

'You must be pretty smart to say those words when you are only seven,' he would say.

'You taught them to me, Dad,' I would say back, chucking him on the shoulder.

I would make Mum take me to the fancy air-conditioned library with the automatic opening doors in the middle of town tomorrow after school.

Moments after his arrival home from work the following afternoon, I pounced on Dad as he was flicking through the mail.

'Let me show you what I got.' I ran to my room, struggling to carry the heavy book on eucalypts I had borrowed back to the kitchen. 'Can you help me find the right names, Dad?'

He breathed cigarette smoke over the kitchen table as he looked up at the clock. 'It's nearly dinner time.'

'Please, Dad? Please?' For once I held Dad's full attention, and I was desperate not to let it go.

'All right. Give it here.'

He helped me find all the Latin names and I wrote them down on a sheet of paper along with some other facts about the trees. But I felt paralysed when it came to writing on the piece of white cardboard we had bought especially for the project. I couldn't afford to make any mistakes. I knew this new thread between us was tenuous. Any moment I could pull in the wrong direction and make it snap.

'What sort of lettering do you think I should do for the title, Dad?'

'I'm not sure.' His eyes were flicking to the newspaper beside him. I was losing him.

'Could you do the lettering, Dad?'

'I'm not very good at lettering. All I can do is block capitals.'

'That's great, Dad. That'd be perfect.'

He got a pencil, a ruler and an eraser then measured up and drew some faint lines in the middle of the white card. When he moved on to the black permanent marker his hand was strong and his letters exact and straight.

In my neatest writing, I transcribed all the information, then glued the leaf samples we had collected. I spent hours and hours practising my talk in front of the chickens, delighting when I finally wrapped my tongue around all the Latin names.

I wanted him to see I was worth talking to. If he saw how hard I was working on this project, he would know once and for all I would do whatever it took to make him love me. Then he could stop hitting me.

The afternoon after my presentation I rode up and down the driveway on a tricycle left over from when we were small, listening for Dad's motorbike. I had to be the first person to see him.

I ran after him as he parked the bike under the house and spoke as soon as the thunder of the engine evaporated and Dad's head emerged from his helmet.

'Guess what I got for our project today, Dad?'

'Hello, Dad. How was your day? Very nice, thank you. How was yours? It was great, Dad, thanks for asking.' His voice was light and teasing.

I put my hand on his arm to stop him. 'No, Dad. You have to guess.'

'Okay. What was it out of?'

'Thirty.'

'Umm . . . twenty out of thirty.'

'No.'

'More or less?'

'More.'

'Twenty-five out of thirty.'

'More.'

'Not thirty out of thirty?'

I shook my head no and let the huge smile I had been holding in all afternoon stretch my lips to my ears. 'Do you want me to tell you?'

'Go on then.' He smiled back at me.

'Forty out of thirty.'

His brow knitted together for a moment. 'You can't get forty out of thirty.'

I felt my smile falter. Had I imagined it? No, the teacher had made me do the presentation in front of another class and go and show the principal. The librarian had asked if he could put it on display in the library. It was real. It was.

'They did say it, Dad. I'm not making it up.' My voice trailed off.

He reached down with the arm not holding his helmet, put it around my shoulder and squeezed. 'I believe you, love. I've just never heard of someone getting forty out of thirty before.'

Joy flooded my body with electric tingles that sent goosebumps down the backs of my arms. 'I know. Me neither. I didn't even know they could do that!' A laugh burst out of me.

He laughed too and pulled me tight into his chest. 'I don't know where you get it from, love. I always hated school. You've always loved it, haven't you?'

Wrapped in his arms, I thought about his perfect lettering and all the Latin names he had known off the top of his head. I knew where I got it from, even if he didn't.

A few weeks later I rode home at double my normal speed, the report card in my bag spurring me on. I was desperate to make sure it didn't vanish before I could show someone.

The air was full of the comforting smell of spray starch when I entered the house. I loved the world of order that spray starch represented. It was a sign. Everyone was going to be amazed by my report card.

Without stopping at the fridge for a drink, I raced through to where Mum stood behind the ironing board in the section of hallway separating our dining room and lounge room. Instead of ironing, she was staring into space, so distant from the present she didn't even look in my direction until I spoke.

'I got my report card today.' I threw my bag on the ground and grabbed it out, checking it hadn't changed on the ride home.

As she took it from me, I went around the side of the ironing board and began pointing, in case she missed anything.

'See here. I got an A for English ... A-minus for maths ... A for social studies ... A-plus for presentations ... B-plus for PE ... A-plus for behaviour. And look here. Look what she wrote: *Ruth is a pleasure to teach. She has achieved excellent results for all of her work this semester.*'

Mum looked at it a moment longer, eyebrows going up as she nodded along. 'That's great, love.' She handed it back to me, then picked the iron out of the wire cradle it rested in.

My hand containing the report lingered in the air. *What, that's all I got?* Some of the kids at school were being paid five dollars per A. If I wasn't getting paid, surely I was owed twenty-five dollars of extreme praise. A dollar a minute seemed about right. Maybe she didn't understood how good an A was. I opened the report and slid my finger slowly down the page.

'Mmm . . . I think there's a code. Ah yes. Here it is. A means excellent, B means very good, but I got a B-plus which is almost like an A. There's one A-minus but I also got an A-plus which is like it's even better than excellent.'

Her eyes didn't move from the brown shirt Dad had worn to the fishing club dinner last Saturday. The flap of the pocket submitted to the heat and pressure, flattening back to crisp lines. She rested the iron on the cradle again and shuffled the shirt to get better access to the creases underneath the arm. Once the position was set she looked at me and smiled. 'You did really well, love.' Her face disappeared behind a cloud when she picked the iron up again.

I ducked around the corner of the kitchen and pressed up against the wall next to the pantry so I could hide what I was doing if anyone came in. I opened the report. The As were still there, but it was just as I'd thought: the little jolt they had given me was gone. When I looked at them now the corners of my mouth turned down. If I didn't know better I would think I was going to cry.

I thought back to the pat on my hand my sparklingly blue-eyed teacher had given me as she passed the report to me and said, 'You did very well, Ruth. Every A on here is down to your hard work. Well done.'

Her words weren't much more than what Mum had said, but when she had looked at me, I'd really felt like she meant it. It couldn't be right that a teacher was more impressed with me than my mum, could it? Thinking about it made my armpits prickle.

I cleared a space in the middle of the junk mail and bills on the kitchen table and left my report there so Dad could see it the second he got in from work.

As I watched a repeat of *Inspector Gadget*, I thought about what Dad would say when he saw my report. 'Haven't you done well. It must have been our eucalyptus project!' Then he would laugh, pull me into his best hug and maybe dance me around the room on his feet. Imagining it brought the charge back to my As.

As soon as the uneven bottom step of the outdoor stairs announced his arrival, I ran toward the back door yelling, 'I got my report card!'

His eyes stayed focused on his feet. I pulled up short then shrank back and blended into a shadow on the wall. We weren't meant to run up to Dad when he wasn't expecting it, especially not if we were yelling.

As he walked past me, still not making eye contact, he said, 'Report card. That's good.' His voice had no bounce. I followed behind him at a distance, skulking into my earlier spot next to the pantry. He put his grey velcro wallet and keys down on the table right next to the pale blue square of cardboard with my school logo on the front cover. Reaching over it, he grabbed the newspaper and flicked it open. *Not that. My report.*

Using my front teeth, I grabbed a ragged strip of skin from

my bottom lip and pulled, then searched with my tongue until I tasted blood. He turned another page, then hunted around and found his cigarette packet. *Not cigarettes. My report.*

I projected my powers onto the blue cardboard, calling him to it. Catching hold of another strip, I pulled.

Using the hand that held his burning cigarette, he turned another page of his newspaper. The movement curled his blue smoke like a genie.

I started at my top lip. Grip. Rip. Grip. Rip. After a thousand years I prompted him. 'It's just there. My report.'

He dragged on his cigarette and picked it up. After a quick glance he nodded. 'Yeah, that's good. Did Kerstin get hers as well?' His voice was as flat as before and he still hadn't looked at me.

I knew it was probably hopeless, but I wanted the magic back. If he could just tell me he was proud, the As would mean something again.

I pushed myself away from the wall and walked nearer to his back. 'Did you see how many As I got, Dad?'

'Yeah.' He rifled through the junk mail, checking for Kerstin's report.

'And did you see the A-plus, Dad?'

'Yep.'

'That's for you as well, you know. For our eucalyptus project.'

He finally gave me his eyes. The green flecks had grown bright with irritation. 'Doing well at school doesn't mean you're smart. I work with a bunch of complete dickheads and most of them have been to university. Sure hasn't made them clever. Your sister has more common sense in her little toe than you have in your whole body. Common sense is what makes you smart.' He reached over and tapped my temple hard three times as he said it, like I was so stupid he needed to point to my brain. '*You* can't even remember to bring your bloody lunchbox home.'

As he turned back to his newspaper, the already thinned membrane of the feel-good bubble I had been floating in since our trip to the bush gave way, and I crashed back to earth. I counted six cigarette butts in the ashtray to distract myself from the air rushing out of my lungs.

I looked down at my feet. The right one was straddling a line in the lino pattern. I stepped off it quickly and put it in an unlined space. *Step on a crack and you break your mother's back; step on a line and you break your father's spine.* If I hadn't been standing on the line maybe he wouldn't be mad at me.

The light in the room suddenly felt dim, the ceilings low. I walked toward my bedroom, trying not to move fast in case it looked like I was responding to his words, but not slow enough that he would think I was sooking.

My throat ached as I lay on top of the purple blanket on my bed. There would be no more school projects together. I turned over and pushed my face hard into my pillow, waiting until I saw spots dancing in front of my eyes before I let myself breathe.

I was such an idiot. What Dad had said was true. When I was in class I was able to tune out every distraction and focus entirely on the lesson. That's why my teachers thought I was clever. But as soon as it was playtime it was like a weird time warp happened. Most days I had no idea where I had been, let alone where my lunchbox had gone. I had begged Mum not to give me any lunch just so I wouldn't have to keep track of what I did with it.

Idiot. Idiot. Idiot. Once I gave one mean voice the stage in my head, the others joined in, talking over the top of each other to tell me how stupid I was. At first it just sounded like the babble of a busy shop, but then each voice became clearer. It was kids at school, and teachers, and Dad. *Can't even look after a lunchbox. Think you're so smart. Nobody likes you. Don't do that again. I don't want to play with you. That's very rude. Go away. Think you're so good.*

The voices started to attach to the form of the person who was talking. A fish-eyed magnifying glass zoomed over each face, making them loom closer as they spoke, before moving on to the next. They grew bigger and bigger, their faces angrier and angrier, as they crowded above me in a circle.

Their weight crushed down on me, making me smaller. The tinier I became, the harder it was to breathe. I had read that the heartbeat of small animals was so fast you didn't even hear the individual beats. I was sure if someone put their head to my chest at that moment, all they would hear was a high-pitched hum.

Just as I became certain I was going to burst from the pressure, in a zooming rush I became a speck of dust. No heartbeat. No body. No Ruth. Just a lovely speck of dust, floating and free.

I was sitting on the floor of the lounge room later that night, brushing my wet hair, as Mum flicked clothes in loud cracks, before folding and arranging them into neat piles in the washing basket.

Gathering my hair in a ponytail over my shoulder, I squeezed a drop of water onto the face of one of the little girls with red hair dotted all over my nightie. The flickering brightness of the TV lit up the drop, injecting it with glowing rainbow magic as it fell.

'Bloody Americans. Such big-noters.' Dad fidgeted in his chair and crossed his feet on the footstool in front of him. I looked at the television, concentrating on the refined drone of the serious man presenting the ABC news. His words washed over me, too boring to grab my attention.

'What does that mean, Dad?'

'A big-noter is a show-off.'

I thought on that for a moment. He was probably telling me I was just like an American for showing off my report card.

He kept his eyes on the TV as he talked, but his gaze was turned inward. 'Did you know we had to fight next to the Americans when I was in Vietnam? They wore these big helmets you could see a mile off. Some of the blokes wore *aftershave*.' He spat the last word out with venom, then shook his head.

'What's wrong with aftershave?' I asked.

Angry eyes flicked to me. 'I'll tell you what's wrong with aftershave. If you're sitting in a stinking hot jungle trying not to get shot you need to be invisible. You can smell aftershave a mile off. If I could smell it, you can bet your arse the enemy could smell it too.

He stared into space for a moment. 'The same with the hats. You want to blend in. Australian hats were soft.' He tapped his head. 'When you crouched down you couldn't see the Aussies 'cause their hats looked like leaves. Those American helmets didn't look like anything except helmets. Some of those dickheads even put flags and things on their hats. Might as well have put a sign on their heads saying *shoot me*.'

He reached over to the coffee table and shook out a Winfield Blue from the packet there, then flicked his lighter and drew back smoke. He breathed out with a puh sound and subtly shook his head, relaxing into his chair as the nicotine hit his lungs.

'Over there the Vietnamese blokes we fought with always said how much they liked fighting with us Aussies because we knew how to be invisible. They said we were good and quiet, just like them. There was nothing quiet about some of those Yanks. You could see 'em coming a mile away.'

He turned his attention back to the screen as the broadcast cut to the weather.

Brushing my teeth, I thought about going back to the lounge room and promising Dad I would be invisible like a good Aussie. I spat into the bowl. Better not. I wasn't sure I could do it.

Last day of school term tomorrow. Maybe I would pick some flowers for my teacher. I looked at myself and mouthed the words in the mirror. *Big-noter.*

PARENT AND CHILD

Five months into my first pregnancy I got in touch with the Vietnam Veterans Association to see if anyone there had known Dad. A man named Tim called and said he might have some photos of him from his time in Vietnam.

My husband and I drove to his outer Melbourne suburb to meet him. Tim greeted us at the door, smaller than I had imagined and so scrubbed clean he was almost transparent. Inside, his unit was immaculate. On the small table in his kitchen he had laid out a plate of Arnott's Assorted Creams in perfect lines: shortbread, monte carlos and kingstons. That plate of biscuits tipped me over the edge and I started to cry.

Tim looked at me, shocked.

'Sorry,' I said to him. 'It's the pregnancy hormones.'

But it wasn't. The effort he had made with those biscuits felt like he was courting my affection. On the phone Tim had told me he was happy to help, pleased that someone wanted to find out about the war. His own kids had never shown any interest. I was flooded with guilt. I had never paid attention to the war before now either. But until I was facing parenthood myself, and wondering how it had all gone so wrong for Dad, the thought had honestly never occurred to me.

I was born two years after Australia's involvement in the war ended. At that time, and for decades after, it was as if society, confronted by televised images of combat, unhappy with our involvement in Vietnam, had made a collective decision to act as if the war had never happened. This determined unwillingness to recognise the Vietnam War was so profound, Vietnam veterans didn't even receive an official welcome-home parade until 1987, fifteen years after the last soldier had returned.

The shaming inherent in this silence certainly did its job on the veterans. Few of them spoke about their involvement in the war. Certainly Dad kept quiet.

In the 4,300 days he lived with us, Dad brought up the Vietnam War only about twenty times, mostly in off-the-cuff remarks. Like many children of Vietnam veterans, I grew up thinking the war he had fought in was not really a big deal. We never learned about it at school. We rarely talked about it at home. How significant could it be?

When I started looking into it I was shocked by the statistics.

For America, the Vietnam War went on for nineteen and a half years, and was the longest war fought in their history. Though Australia wasn't there as long, it was the longest major conflict we had fought in until Afghanistan, lasting ten years, from 1962 to 1972.

Depending on the source, it is estimated that between 800,000 and 3.1 million Vietnamese civilians, 200,000 and 300,000 Cambodians, and 20,000 and 200,000 Laotians died during the conflict.

America sent almost 2.6 million soldiers to the war, 1.7 million of whom were draftees. Over 300 000 were wounded, and 58,220 were killed.

Australia's contribution to the war was smaller, though large given our military history. Almost 60,000 Australians served in Vietnam, 19,000 of whom were conscripted. Over 3,000 were wounded, and 521 died.

As I sat beside Tim while he showed me photographs of young men in khaki holding guns against the backdrop of large-leafed foliage, or clustered in front of tents pulling goofy faces for the camera, it struck me how rarely I had seen images of Australian, rather than American, soldiers in Vietnam.

The lack of helmets was the main difference that caught my eye. Instead of unyielding metal domes, if they weren't bare, Australians' heads were topped with the floppy, small-brimmed hats Dad had spoken about. The Aussie attitude seemed less reverent than the American in images I had seen as well. Or maybe I was just picturing my father among them and infusing his qualities into these unknown, yet somehow familiar, men.

When I was a kid it would have been nice to see my dad marching alongside other veterans of war, so I could have had a chance to be proud of him instead of just confused and frightened by behaviour I didn't understand.

Just as I was preparing to talk to more veterans, life cut in with other plans. My daughter arrived nine weeks prematurely. The extended stay in hospital followed by the shock of first-time parenthood drove out thoughts of war. All my energy was directed into being present, available and responsible for a new human being twenty-four hours a day.

Though Dad sat in the back of my mind, I was too busy washing, cooking and not sleeping to give him much more than a passing thought. No matter what age you are, your parents evoke the child you once were. It makes it hard to see them as real, flawed people who happened to have a baby and tried their best to raise it, instead of the bundle of the fantasies you have projected onto them since you were born. Now I was a parent myself, I finally understood how it felt to be unprepared and unqualified for a role at the centre of someone's universe.

All of my research into the conflict in Vietnam had given me a more rounded picture of Dad. He was not just my father; he was a person who had come back damaged from a war. I liked the new way I thought about him and I was happy to let that be the end of it.

It wasn't until five years later, when my son started hitting me and I felt my father pulsing through his bloodline, that I realised the past wasn't done with me yet.

In abusive situations it is common to identify with the perpetrator. When I was young I focused on Dad, the one with the power, instead of myself, the child being abused. Now, with my son's constant surprise attacks, and me back on high alert waiting for the next assault, it was my childhood all over again. For the first time in decades I fell back into old habits, merging back into Dad to protect myself.

My body grew tight and reactive, descending into the zone that allowed zero tolerance for error. I drove myself insane checking every interaction with my kids to see if I was acting normally or with Dad as my puppet master. Despite this I heard his words muttering themselves under my breath. *Stupid. How many times do you have to be told? Not good enough.*

I needed my son's hitting to stop, but I didn't know how to

make it happen. I needed Dad's voice out of my head, but it kept shouting in my ear. I turned his words over, following them back to the memories from which they sprang, hoping each time that I would finally reach a place of new understanding that would make them quieten down. But it was like pulling at a thread: just as I reached the end of a row, another layer started unravelling in my hand.

One day, a strange thought occurred to me. Could it be possible that all the time I had spent merged with Dad during my childhood meant our histories had become intertwined?

The wounds of war were too profound and too many for any one man to bear. What if I was carrying the residual weight of all he had not been able to process? What if the only way to put my past behind me was in some way to help put Dad's past behind him? For the sake of my ongoing relationship with my son I was desperate enough to give it a try.

Maybe if I brought the Vietnam War out of the shadows once and for all, I might be able to understand Dad's fury and finally let it go. Just because the war had been forgotten by many didn't mean it had to be forgotten by me.

THE TENT

Strains of *The Goodies* filtered through to the bedroom one night as I packed shorts, t-shirts and undies into my pastel rainbow duffel bag in preparation for the school holidays.

Thinking of what else I needed to take, I removed my copy of the poem I had recited for my class earlier in the week from my khaki, woven cotton school bag.

I've had this shirt
by Michael Rosen

I've had this shirt
that's covered in dirt
for years and years and years.

It used to be red
but I wore it in bed
and it went grey
cos I wore it all day
for years and years and years.

> The arms fell off
> in the Monday wash
> and you can see my vest
> through the holes in the chest
> for years and years and years.
>
> As my shirt falls apart
> I'll keep the bits
> in a biscuit tin on the mantelpiece
> for years and years and years.

I had done my best handwriting, decorating the border with a twisting vine of daisies, and practised until I knew every word. Next to the *20/20* and the comment *Wonderful presentation!* was a shiny gold love-heart sticker.

Even if Dad thought school didn't make you smart, it made *me* feel smart. I rocked the paper so the sticker glinted beneath the single sixty-watt globe shining under the dented beige lampshade overhead.

Stickers cost money. This one was made of gold; it was probably the most expensive sticker you could buy. My teacher must think I was worth *something* if she was willing to put gold on my work. I laid it neatly on top of my undies, but after a moment's deliberation took it out again.

Tomorrow we would be camping. School rules would not apply.

Rockhampton is right on the Tropic of Capricorn so it is always sunny, with the winter temperature still reaching the mid-twenties. This makes ideal weather for year-round camping.

Dad loved camping. So we went camping. And as a TAFE teacher, he got almost twelve weeks of holidays each year, so we went camping a lot. Nearly every school break or long weekend we loaded the tent into our blue Kingswood station wagon, hooked up Dad's boat and headed down to Emu Park.

The Easter I was eight was no exception. We had left early to beat the rush, but the first glimpse of the campground revealed blue nylon tents and old people in caravans as far as the eye could see.

As our tyres crunched along the snaking gravel road to our campsite, the reflection off the white sand of the beach burned worm-shaped flashes into my sight that lingered even when I blinked. Still, the beach was close enough to taste the salt, and the sky stretched as huge and blue as midday above. It felt like holidays.

As we reversed the boat into our regular spot among the hive of families, my stomach did little flips. I had almost let myself forget. Before entering the warm, sparkling water or building my first sandcastle, there was the matter of the tent.

Our tent was not like other tents. There was no flimsy nylon for us. We spent our holidays cocooned within the warm embrace of a massive ex-army tent, that could, and had, withstood cyclones without so much as a ripped seam.

When that tent came out, Dad entered military mode. The car had barely come to a stop before he peeled himself off the vinyl seat and moved to the back of the car, releasing the heavy metal tailgate with a loud creak. We rocked in our seats as Dad began manoeuvring the tent out from underneath our sleeping bags and clothes.

Dad was as solidly built as the former rugby league player he was, but the mammoth weight of our tent still tested him. He walked awkwardly to somewhere approximately in the centre of our site and hoisted the tent off his body. It landed with a heavy thud, throwing sandy dust into the air.

I hopped out of the car and rested against my door. No member of the family was allowed to shirk their duty when the tent came out. Even so, I thought God might have more power than Dad so I appealed to Him for help. *Dear God, if you don't make me put up this tent then I will know that you love me and I will be good all the time. Thank you. Amen.*

'Dad, can we go down to the beach first?' I ventured, wondering how quickly God answered prayers.

'First we set up the tent, then we relax.'

God obviously hated me.

Dad unwrapped one layer of canvas then waved us stiffly over. 'Right, you kids get here.' He looked to where Mum was unloading the blue camp stove. 'You too, Barb.'

Over time, Mum had become so scared of putting a foot wrong she had all but given up on making decisions of her own. She took action only when Dad told her to. Most of the time I didn't really think of Mum as a parent at all. It was us against him.

'David, you're on peg duty.' Dad removed the canvas peg bag, handing it to David. The weight was a surprise and the bag dropped to the ground. I immediately moved forward and grabbed one handle, making sure Dad could see that though there was an error, it had been dealt with quickly and effectively: no need for him to intervene.

David and I shuffled over to one of the patches of threadbare grass scattered around the sandy site and released the peg bag with a clang. Unlike the tiny pegs that go with normal tents, our army pegs were about thirty centimetres long, two centimetres thick and covered in rust. No one messed with them, not hard ground, not solid rock, nothing. David opened the bag and started lining them up.

'C'mon, Ruth.' Dad's words had their endings clipped off, the way he talked when he meant business. I walked over to where Dad, Mum and Kerstin were gathered around the tent and grabbed a corner.

'All right. Diagonal walking. Now.' Everyone marched.

I struggled against the weight of the canvas and tightened my grip to keep it from slipping out of my hands.

Dad dropped his corner down and looked up to see me standing in place. 'Walk, Ruth!'

I leaned back with my whole body.

'You're not trying! Pull the bloody thing!'

'I am trying!' My feet scrambled in place for another moment, but finally my section began to unfold and I walked backward with my corner.

Dad stalked toward me then placed his hand roughly on top of mine. 'Pulling. This is called pulling.' In his effort to show me the correct way to pull, he knocked me off balance. I fell to the ground and started crying.

'Don't be silly. I didn't mean to do that.' He pulled me up roughly, grabbed my hand and forced it onto the corner of the tent again.

His big hand crushed down harder on top of mine. As he heaved, his elbow banged into my face. I screamed out and cried some more.

'Stop being such a sook. I didn't do it on purpose.'

Just because it was an accident doesn't mean it didn't hurt, Dad.

He dismissed my sobs, walking toward David as he lectured me over his shoulder. 'Just try harder next time and do what you're told.'

He bent down and grabbed a handful of pegs. Noticing us all standing where he had left us he lifted his eyebrows and rolled his eyes. 'Well.' When we didn't move he spoke slower. 'Everyone grab some pegs and drop them where they need to go.'

We collected our pegs and paced around the perimeter of the tent, but it wasn't fast enough for Dad.

He came up behind us in a low running crouch to get us moving. 'Run! Run! Run!'

We picked up speed, the bell chimes of the heavy pegs making music of our jog. It was still not quick enough.

'Move it! Hut! Hut! Hut!' Dad yelled again. David was only four so he was the slowest. Dad gave him a little shove in the back to get him moving faster. He started crying.

Mum was running with us, dropping pegs as well, when Dad said, 'Barbara, you need to help me tie these ropes.'

Tying the guy ropes to the tent properly was an art. Each

time we went camping Mum got it wrong. I slowed my run and shifted my entire focus to her, willing her to do it right this time.

'Right.' He handed her a rope. 'You remember how to do this, don't you?'

Mum nodded. She grabbed the rope and threaded it through the hole without pause.

'No, Barbara.' His defeated voice told me she had already failed. 'You come in from the top, not underneath.' I was walking now, watching. Her hand shook, making her struggle to thread the rope as instructed.

Dad would hate how weak that shaking made her look. Weak and incompetent: his two least favourite things.

Dad snatched the rope out of her hand and shook it at her, speaking as if she didn't understand English. 'This rope.' He shook the metal eyelet. 'This hole.' He stabbed at the hole and moved the rope in and out. 'Rope go in hole.'

Mum's arms dropped and she looked down at her feet. He grabbed her hand and pushed it back onto the rope. 'C'mon, I can't do everything myself. Tie the rope like I've shown you a hundred times before. Show me.'

She grabbed the rope, twisting it around itself. He moved in until he was almost standing on top of her, the easier for him to pounce when she made the wrong move. He didn't have to wait long. 'Give it to me,' he said in disgust, wrenching it from her hand, 'I guess *I* will do *all* the ropes then.'

Mum stepped quietly onto the small hill where Kerstin, David and I were watching ants race along on the uneven sand. I grabbed her hand and gave her arm a hug, but she pulled away from me gently, opening her eyes wide and tipping her head toward Dad.

I looked over to him. His strong hands moved with quick assurance as he expertly tied rope after rope. He seemed oblivious to the heat, though the back of his yellow t-shirt was darkened with sweat. This was how he wanted us to be. No mistakes. No fumbles. No feeling.

My heart throbbed and I stepped away from Mum so she didn't get in more trouble. No matter if Dad managed to hold his comments in; this was the undercurrent of their entire relationship. He never hit Mum – though in a matter of years he would break that rule as well – instead, he drained her of self-worth: death by a thousand cuts. Snide little comments, rolling eyes and always that tone in his voice, the one that told her how worthless she was.

I wished I was brave enough to tell him not to talk to her like that. I had always known Mum was no match for Dad, but I didn't feel that way. If I was a bit bigger I could protect her from him.

I returned my attention to the ants' movement, wondering what urgent mission made them scurry at such a pace, but my ears were tuned entirely to Dad. The five-second window we normally had to respond to his requests didn't exist when we were setting up the tent. We had to be like runners on a starting block, ready to sprint as soon as the words left his mouth.

From his occasional swearing and the way he kept looking at us and shaking his head I knew he was annoyed we were just standing there, but none of us had any idea what to do that would not end with more trouble.

'At least make yourselves useful and start setting up the beds,' he yelled over to us. Mum ran over to the stack of bed components and dealt them out to us.

Continuing with the army theme, there were no air mattresses; we slept on army-issue hessian beds. They were extremely scratchy but very comfortable to sleep in, even with the creaking noise they made when you turned over. We worked silently, sliding hessian over metal poles until the five beds were constructed.

Dad had moved on to assembling the central pole for the tent. About ten centimetres in diameter and three-and-a-half metres high, it was made of timber and covered with flecks and streaks of yellow paint. Dad was the only one strong enough to manoeuvre it properly.

'C'mon, Barb, give us a hand,' he spat out.

She jogged over and he got down on his tummy and disappeared under the dark underside of the boiling hot canvas, shimmying his way in the dust and sand along to the middle until he inserted the pole's pointed end into the reinforced hole in the centre. He then used all his weight to push the tent up.

As soon as it was erect, Mum ran under and grabbed the pole from him so he could get the support ropes up as quickly as possible. The canvas flapped in her face as she strained to stop the pole wobbling.

'Hold it still!' Dad yelled.

She muttered through gritted teeth. 'I am bloody trying to hold it still.'

Once the tent was basically up, its true size was revealed. It looked like a circus tent. Kerstin, David and I ran inside it.

'Stop running around or you'll hurt yourself... and don't trip over the pegs.' It was guaranteed that at some stage over the next few days we would all trip over the pegs, and Dad would bash us in turn because we should have been more careful.

While Dad continued tightening ropes we dragged our beds into position before moving to the kitchen area. Often we just brought our red folding card table away with us, but this holiday went for a couple of weeks so we had strapped our Laminex kitchen table with the steel legs to the roof of our car. After putting the folding chairs around it, the tent immediately felt like home.

Nearly two hours after we arrived, we were finally set up and ready to start our holiday. 'Right,' Dad said, 'now we can go to the beach.'

The days of our holiday passed in relative freedom and we spent hours building sandcastles, fishing or playing cricket on the beach. But unless Dad went out on a solo fishing trip, it was rarely relaxing. Trapped in a tent with him, I lived outside my body, scouting ahead for the next mistake that would tip him over the edge.

The proximity of people in neighbouring tents kept his violence to a minimum, but sometimes strangers witnessed a slap or a shove. The moment they became conscious of what they were seeing, they averted their eyes and hurried past as if wanting to put distance between themselves and something unclean. That they had seen it, and not tried to stop it, made me wonder if they too thought I deserved to be treated that way. Long after they had gone I felt their eyes on me as hot as a brand, burning the shame of exposure deep into my skin.

On the way home, after a pack-down as stressful as the setup, we stopped at a fruit shop twenty minutes down the highway, loading up on rockmelon and mandarins. Dad bought us each a soft-serve ice-cream in a cone as well. I put the mandarin I had peeled away, not wanting the bitter taste to taint the flavour of the sweet.

ENEMY

STILL BEAUTIFUL

By October, the small stretch of cool days that counted as Rockhampton's winter was long gone and we were back to a consistent thirty degrees. The last Saturday of the month, Mum was lying down on the lounge room floor waiting for her Avon egg mask to set as she listened to 4RO radio play the Best Hits of the sixties, seventies and eighties. I hovered over her, checking every few minutes to see if her face had stopped being sticky and grown its rubbery second skin.

'What does it do again, Mum?'

'It makes your skin look nicer.' Her words came out through welded-together teeth and her lips didn't move as she attempted not to crack the mask.

I laughed, already knowing the answer, just wanting to make her do the funny robot-talking. Her eyes smiled back.

It probably happened only once or twice a year, so when Mum and Dad went out together as a couple, it was a big deal. Usually the extent of Mum's cosmetic routine was a slash of red or orange lipstick on her thin lips before she walked out the door. But when she went out with Dad, I always trailed along behind her as she got ready, breathing in her excitement. Today was no exception.

Once the egg mask was off we moved to the front verandah, where the light was better. Sitting on the top steps she looked into a circular magnifying mirror to tweeze her eyebrows before reaching into her rigid black make-up chest, where her nail polish lived.

'I used to be a buyer for David Jones, you know,' she said as dust from her emery board floated up my nose. 'I got to work in all the departments. The ladies in the salon there showed me how to do a manicure the right way.'

Next was the fashion parade. In the small amount of space around the double bed in her and Dad's bedroom, Mum tried on about five different outfits and I gave her my opinion on them all. Tonight she would be wearing my favourite: cream crepe falling just below the knee crossed over in the front with gold sparkly dots on the lapels. She was already taller than Dad but the super high heels she was going to wear would mean she towered over him, bigger than life.

After she had applied a perfect line of black liquid eyeliner and covered her eyelids in frosted-blue eye shadow from a tube, I told her over and over how beautiful she looked; she just smiled indulgently at me. The words didn't count until they came from Dad's lips.

At 6.13 p.m. he finally came home smelling of grease from his second job selling and fixing boats.

'Hi,' Mum said as he moved toward the bathroom. She smiled and kept one of her legs straight while bending her other leg to show off her high heel.

'Hi.' Dad looked at her for a moment, not seeing. 'I'll just have a shower. We're meant to be there at half past.'

As he turned and left, she brought her legs together again, watching him until he disappeared behind the door of the bathroom. She went back into the bedroom to tidy up the remaining outfits strewn on the bed.

'You'll have fun tonight, won't you, Mum?' I kept my voice chirpy, pretending I hadn't noticed him not noticing her.

'Yeah, it'll be good.' Her words were muffled as she spoke into her small over-stuffed closet. Keeping her back to me, she reached over the still open make-up box on her untidy vanity, grabbed a tissue and blew her nose.

Maybe she wanted to cry in private, but I didn't want her to feel like I was abandoning her. I kept my eyes focused on the black box of secret pockets filled with sample sachets. I brought my wrist to my nose. The scent from the small vial of perfume I had found in the box had faded.

Everything in that box had seemed exciting and mysterious this afternoon. Why did I now want to close the lid and hide it so Dad wouldn't see? I felt my throat ache and knew it was her sadness I swallowed down.

Within three minutes Dad had dressed in the grey slacks and short-sleeved button-up shirt Mum had ironed and laid out for him. He combed his hair with a small blue plastic comb without looking in the mirror.

As he slid his feet into the grey leather lace-up shoes with the slippery bottoms good for dancing, he looked at Mum. 'Are you ready to —'

'Doesn't Mum look beautiful, Dad?' I cut in.

He looked up at her and smiled as he pulled a lace tight. 'You look lovely.'

A deep flush spread under the skin of her cheeks.

As he tied the other shoe he looked at me. 'Did you know your mum was a model? When I met her —'

'Not really. Only a few times for in-store fashion shows,' Mum interrupted, flicking her eyes between him and me while a big smile lit up her face.

'She was. Everyone said how beautiful she was. She looked just like Audrey Hepburn.'

I nodded.

'It's true. Your mum used to be a very beautiful woman.'

I loved when they talked about Mum's other, more glamorous life, so far removed from the picture I had of her mowing the yard, cooking sausages and washing dishes. But I didn't miss the fact he said she *used* to be beautiful. I thought she still was.

HAND OR POCKET

Since we had moved to Rockhampton, four years ago, it had been in severe drought. Rain was so infrequent and water restrictions so tight that huge cracks like portals to the centre of the earth had opened up in a couple of spots in our yard. But one morning a massive thunderstorm hit.

Kerstin, David and I stayed outside in celebration, soaking ourselves to the skin as we gathered up rocks and made dams in the gutters, trying to stop the flow of water. I checked on the cracks, hoping to see them close up as the water flooded in, but all that happened was the dirt walls got slimy and wet.

When the rain slowed, I went upstairs looking for something to eat. My wet feet squeaked on the lino as I twisted on my toes scanning the shelves. Tin of beetroot, tin of corn, tin of asparagus, tin of champignons... where was the real food? Where was Mum anyw—

'What're you doing, Ruth?' Dad said.

I jumped and let out a squeal as I turned to face him. He was only two arm-lengths away. I hadn't even heard him come in. 'Gimme a heart attack, Dad!'

'Did I scare you?'

'Yes!' I closed the cupboard behind me, heart racing.

'Were you looking for something to eat?' He sat at the kitchen table and opened the newspaper.

'Yeah.'

'Find anything?'

'Nah.'

We laughed and I sat down at the table opposite him. Immediately I was hit by the thought I shouldn't be sitting on the chair wearing wet clothes. Maybe he hadn't noticed. The chair was made of vinyl. Maybe it didn't matter. If I got up now it might draw his attention to it. My stomach twisted. I wished I had changed clothes.

A moment later Dad extended a hand full of loose change in his open palm toward me. 'Which one do you pick? Hand or pocket?'

'What do you mean?'

'It's a game. Do you pick hand or pocket?'

'Do I get to keep the money?'

'Yep.'

'Are Kerstin and David going to have a game too?'

He huffed. 'If you are going to make this a pain in the arse just forget —'

'No. No. I won't.'

I counted the silver in his hand. It came to one dollar and forty cents. That was a lot of lollies. Scanning his face, I tried to work out what he wanted me to do.

His eyes were full of fun, but that could mean his pocket was full of dirt, or empty.

'C'mon. A good game's a quick game.'

'Okay ... hand.'

He shook his head, his mouth tightening with disappointment. 'Here you go then.' He dumped the coins into my hand and two ten-cent pieces dropped onto the table. As I picked them up my underarms prickled and my ears got hot.

'Just so you know, Ruth, I had nearly four dollars in my pocket. That's what you missed by going with the safe option.' He jingled his pocket, still shaking his head.

Anger rose to my mouth, wanting to speak. *Maybe if I knew how you were going to act from one minute to the next I could predict what you wanted from me, Dad.*

He pushed his chair back and walked away. Game over.

For weeks after that, the rain kept coming. The park over the road filled with water deep enough to swim in, and a few people began using dinghies to hoon their way down flooded streets. The constant squelching through puddles and sitting in damp clothes kept me hooked into that moment with Dad.

The game played over and over in my mind, with one exception. This time I noticed the playful twinkle in his eye when he gestured to his pocket. This time I chose differently. In my amended reality, he smiled his big smile and pulled me into him saying, *You're just like me. Not scared to take risks.*

That was how it should have gone. I wasn't an expert at much, but I thought I was a master at reading Dad. I knew the secret language of his body better than anything else – the weight of his footsteps, how much he was smoking, the tone of his voice, the pulse under the skin of his neck. All of these things were clues that told me how to behave moment to moment. I should have known he wanted me to take a risk.

One afternoon as I stared out the window of my classroom at the huge brown lake that was once our school oval, I realised why the moment haunted me. I couldn't remember the last time I'd had a spontaneous moment of fun alone with Dad. One where he noticed me. Just me. His daughter. Ruth. The eucalyptus report eighteen months ago may have been the last time.

This moment of fun hadn't been about gambling for a few extra coins. It had been a one-off chance for me to be worthy of access to the door into his heart. But I had failed. And the door had stayed shut.

The pocket! I choose the pocket, Dad. I choose the right door. I choose you.

LUCKY STARS

It was nearly lunchtime, months later, when we walked up the carpeted stairs with swirly flowers leading to the Returned Services League (RSL). I was thinking about the crumbed seafood basket I normally ordered, though Mum had already told me we wouldn't be eating there today.

On special occasions there were two places my family would go to eat: Wah Ha Chinese Restaurant – sweet and sour pork, special fried rice, chicken chow mein, spring rolls and prawn crackers – or the RSL. But not today. We were just here for a drink today.

When we reached the top of the stairs, Mum started up a conversation with the grey-haired man with the purple-veined nose who sat behind the big book she needed to sign to gain entry.

Stale beer and cigarettes seeped from the walls. As she chatted I found a tiger shape in the carpet swirls and jumped from tiger to tiger alongside the stairs that led to the night-time dining area full of white tablecloths and with a large, slippery wooden dance floor. 'You ready?' Mum asked, guiding Kerstin, David and me toward the downstairs bar where we sat during the day.

Most times there were just a few men and some families eating, but today was Anzac Day. It was packed with men. Some of them were in uniform. Some of them were not. All of them seemed to be smoking cigarettes, drinking beer and shouting at each other. The volume crushed into me. I put my fingers in my ears.

I didn't know what we were doing here. Over the last couple of weeks, Mum had started dragging us along on outings to 'surprise' Dad. I had the feeling she was trying to catch him doing something he wasn't meant to, while at the same time reminding him we were his family. She had even said those words in a strange pleading tone after he responded angrily toward us for showing up unannounced at his work. 'We are your family, Doug. Your family. Don't you want to see us?'

Though it was hard to see with so many men packed in, from what I could make out we were the only kids. Except for Mum, I couldn't see any other women either. This was a man-only place. Dad was going to be furious.

Mum led us into the sea of bodies and Kerstin, David and I pulled close together and tried to keep up. We yelled 'Excuse me' and men made way for us, often bumping into other men and spilling their beers to let us through. Sometimes they smiled and patted our heads. Once we were in the middle, little taps on their backs didn't get their attention. I ended up pushing to get through, feeling a panicky need to get out of there so I could breathe.

During the pushing we had lost Mum. Finding a little space near the bar I scanned the crowd looking for her. Instead, I spotted Dad standing a couple of metres away. He was wearing a clean grey polo shirt, navy-blue stubbies and thongs with his hair neatly combed: his usual 'going out' clothes. The man he was talking to was laughing, and I could see by Dad's cheeky grin that he was having fun and being his happiest self.

Mum was in the middle of the crowd. Her bright red lips flashed into a smile, then a laugh, at something the man she was talking to had said.

Dad seemed an easier target so we pushed our way down to him. He spotted us, shocked surprise changing his face. I watched for the ripple of anger sure to come, but instead his face changed into a big smile and he beckoned us over. Joy shot to my fingertips. We were his family. He wanted to see us. He crushed us into him in a big hug. 'Hello, kids. This is a surprise.'

He looked around for a minute, trying to find Mum, but she was talking to the man. Dad looked down at us, still smiling, and asked if we wanted a drink.

Whenever I was in a bar, I liked to order cocktail-like soft drinks – lemon, lime and bitters, double sarsaparilla or pink lemonade – anything to make me seem more grown up. I settled on pink lemonade this time and as we waited for our drinks Dad pulled us in closer to him.

The man he had been talking to leaned in and yelled his beery breath all over me. 'You're lucky to have a dad like yours!'

The happiness I had felt a moment ago disappeared. I stared into the man's pale blue eyes, keeping all the things I wanted to say in check. He kept looking at me as if he expected some sort of response, so I nodded and fake-smiled for him.

'No! I mean it.' He spoke as though he was angry with me. His bar stool was tall and he leaned down close enough for me to see the grey lines of fillings at the side of his brownish teeth. 'He's a fucking great man. You should count your lucky stars every day to have a dad like him! I bet you don't even know what a great man he is.'

He leaned back and grabbed his beer, raising it in a toast and looking at Dad. 'He's served his country. He's always looked after his mates. And none of the bastards, not even his bloody kids, I bet, appreciate it. But we appreciate ya, Dougy. You're a bloody top bloke.'

The man looked at me again, his glass still high in the air. 'He's a great man. Don't you forget it.' He swallowed the rest of the beer and yelled to Dad, 'And I am going to buy this great man another beer!'

Dad looked at him and smiled his good smile, then pulled his arm away from us to wrap it around his friend. Somehow we had failed him. The moment for family had passed. We were not welcome here any more.

The bartender came back with my pink lemonade. The room was air-conditioned, but the number of bodies crammed in, plus the hot day, meant there were already beads of water dribbling down the outside of the glass. I reached up to grab my drink and in the process put my elbow onto the sticky wet bar mat. I pulled my elbow back and sniffed it. Old beer. Gross. I wiped it on my dress at the side of my ribs, then reached for my drink again.

With the amount of raspberry cordial swirling around the glass, it was more red than pink lemonade, and as I drank my first swallow my throat closed against the rush of so much sugar. I coughed. I stirred the ice cubes in the bottom of the glass and took another sip, looking up at Dad. When Mum joined us I asked if we kids could move to somewhere less crowded.

We found a spot in the corner of the room and I began pretending I was here on my own – like I was just wandering down the street and thought I might pop in for a pink lemonade on a hot day.

There was a new orange payphone with push buttons on the wall and I began typing our phone number again and again as fast as I could. 277616. 277616. 277616. After I reached peak speed I made my way over to the cigarette machine.

Holding my drink with one hand and slinging behind me the empty brown leather handbag I was carrying to make me look more sophisticated, I checked the change drawer for money. Nothing. I leaned my back on the machine, surveying the crowd again with what I hoped was a bored adult look, wondering how long it would take someone to notice me.

After a couple of minutes I turned back to study the pictures of the different cigarettes. If I was forced to buy cigarettes, which ones would I pick? I settled on Benson & Hedges because they were in a gold packet, though I did like the tropical island theme of the Alpines as well. I pressed both buttons and checked the change drawer again. Still nothing.

There were a couple more men around Dad now. Everyone was laughing. I kept watching to see what they were doing to make him happy, but it looked like they were just talking. I talked to him all the time. He didn't laugh like that with me.

The man who had said the F-word to me was still there. The skinny legs sticking out of his short shorts didn't match his stupid, ugly moustache that went way down the sides of his mouth nearly to his chin. His laugh was so loud I could hear it over all the other noise. What a show-off.

He was not the first man in a bar to tell me how lucky I was to have a dad like mine. I wanted to tell him, this man who thought he knew Dad so well, that the man Dad was to him was not the man he was to me. *He might smile at us in front of you but when he gets home he is mean and he hates us. Don't you dare tell me I'm lucky.*

I wished he would shut his stupid loud laugh up.

I looked for Mum and saw her rocking back on her heels, laughing at something a different man she was speaking to had said. As she nodded along with the frozen polite look she wore when talking to strangers, her eyes kept drifting over to where Dad was sitting, but he didn't look back at her.

I pushed my way through the crowd, not even bothering with 'excuse me's this time. Dad was with his friends. He didn't want us here. Couldn't she see that?

'Can we go?' I asked Mum.

As we sat down in the boiling car, squinting in the bright sunshine, I imagined wavy stink lines coming off us from the smoke embedded in our clothes. Mum added to the smell, lighting a cigarette of her own. I wound down my window and leaned my head out, sucking in air as we headed back home.

Brushing my teeth that night, I thought about Moustache Man, imagining running into him in the street, asking him what right he had to tell me how I should behave toward my father.

I bet if I told him about some of the times Dad had hit me, he might understand why I didn't appreciate him as much as he thought I should.

I looked down at the thin white line on the arch of my foot where I had sliced it open running through the house. The scar had healed so you could barely tell it was there, but at least it was visible: proof of something. If all the bruises and pain Dad had marked me with over the years had formed a permanent stain as well, people like Moustache Man might shut the hell up about what a great father I had.

CHANGED MAN

Delving into the Vietnam War gave me a concrete task that allowed me to feel I was progressing toward an understanding of what went wrong in my family, so I could make sure I didn't allow it to happen again now I had children of my own.

I began sifting through the personal service documents Kerstin had photocopied and sent down to me from the time of Dad's national service. The first page for 1732937 Private Douglas Robert Callum was a personal data sheet filled out on 28 March 1967. In neat block capitals, the way he was taught in technical drawing class, Dad had written his name, address, educational record and, interestingly, his hobbies: squash, swimming, gardening. Did they imagine he would have free time to pursue his interests in the army?

My breath caught at the familiarity of his handwriting. It was the same lettering style he had used on my eucalyptus report in grade two, but this page had been written when he was only twenty-three years old. Twenty-two days after this form was filled out, he had left the life he knew and entered the military training required by his conscription.

My eyes lingered on the confident, no-nonsense scrawl of his signature – the same one he used until he died. I wondered if this was the last time he had signed something before he went to Vietnam, and if he paused, pen hovering over paper, aware he was marking a moment in time. Did he know that in a few short months his eyes would be opened to the worst humanity had to offer, that his soul was about to be forever tainted by the grief and horror of war?

The next page listed James Cameron Callum, Dad's dad, as his nominated next of kin. I had expected to see Grandma's name instead. But maybe that's because I was a mother now. If Dad had been my son, I was sure it would have been me filling out the form alongside him.

Of course, knowing what I knew, if Dad had been my son, he would never have filled out the form in the first place. If Dad had been my son, I would have dragged him by the hand, dug a hole to the centre of the earth and stayed there with him until the war was finished.

I moved on to the section of the report detailing Dad's basic movements during his time in the army.

The first line read: ENL UNIT For 2 yrs in RAS(NS) as PTE GP 1 3 RTB TS.

Maybe . . . enlisted unit for two years in royal army service national serviceman as private group one . . . ?

Scanning the list, there were some points I could understand. His unit posting was 1RAR, or the 1st Royal Australian Regiment. Another line, written in longhand, said he had negligently handled a rifle and was fined twenty dollars. He would have hated that: both handing over the money, and being deemed negligent.

There was also an entry saying he was admitted to camp

hospital for six days while in training, but there were no details on the reason. Most of the twenty-six other listings summarising his time in the military were abbreviated to the point of impenetrability. Even if they hadn't been, this information was not what I needed.

For me to help close the door on Dad's past, and my own, I needed to know what it was really like over there, and how it was for him when he came back.

If Dad had still been here, I would have asked questions of him. But he was not here. It felt like my only option for understanding was to talk to Vietnam veterans who'd had similar experiences to him. The thought terrified me.

When I had first made contact with Tim, back when I was pregnant with my daughter, I'd understood a lot less about the potential impact talking about the war could have on veterans. But I had done a lot of reading since then. I now knew if they were suffering from PTSD, talking about their time in Vietnam could activate dormant nightmares or cause intense bodily responses: a pounding heart, sweating, panic attacks and worse. The last thing I wanted to do was cause further pain to someone already hurt and bleeding.

But if I was going to exorcise the ghost in the nursery, I had to do something. Before I could crumple under the weight of my anxiety, I got back in contact with the Vietnam Veterans Association.

A woman answered the phone and I told her I was the child of a Vietnam veteran and was interested in speaking to veterans about their war experience. I was especially interested in anyone who had been at the Battle of Coral, the one battle I knew Dad had fought in.

We chatted for a moment and she suggested I get an email together so she could send it out to members and see if there were any responses. Then she threw in, 'My husband, Andy, is a Vietnam veteran as well. He was in the Battle of Coral. You might want to talk to him.'

I gulped in relief that my first call might end in a conversation with a veteran who knew what Dad had been through. 'Yeah, that'd be great.' Before I lost my courage I blurted out, 'Do you guys have any kids?'

'Yeah.'

'Do you think Andy's relationship with his kids was affected by the war?' My voice came out half an octave higher than usual.

'Oh yeah. He was very regimented with the kids. For a long time there they couldn't look sideways without getting in trouble.'

Relief washed through me. I was not alone. This was a pattern. Men went to war. They came back changed. Their families were affected. I had known this intellectually, but having a conversation about it, however brief, with a person who wasn't part of my immediate family made it feel real in a visceral way.

She handed the phone to Andy, whose voice came down the line in a happy bounce. After a quick run-down on who I was, I told him Dad's name and asked if he had known him. Though he had served as a regimental policeman during much of the same period as Dad, Andy didn't think he had ever met him. I asked him about his time in the army.

'I was seventeen when I joined. Four days after I turned nineteen I was told I was heading out.'

'Seventeen. That's young.'

'Yeah, well, my home life wasn't too crash hot so I thought the army might be a better bet. I got out in 1969; 1993 was the last time I worked. I hit the brick wall. TPI [totally and permanently incapacitated].'

'Oh right. How did you find out you had PTSD? Was there a trigger?' I panicked at my blunt question. 'Sorry if this is too personal. You don't have to answer.'

'Nah, I don't mind. It just happens all of a sudden. The way I found out I had a problem, I was fixing a bike. I was just looking at the bike saying to myself, I can't fix this bike. I don't want to fix this bike.

'Anyway, I'll look into your dad's records for you and see what I can find. And we'll send out your email to see if we can turn up anyone who knew him.'

Putting the phone down I collapsed into a chair.

As I chopped carrots for the minestrone soup for dinner that night, my mind returned to Andy's moment fixing the bike. In some war veterans, PTSD is triggered by dramatic incidents, like finding out someone they fought with, and thought had come home, had actually died in Vietnam. For other veterans, like Andy, it was an insignificant event that marked the exact moment when they no longer had the energy to stay one step ahead of their trauma.

Dad was a strong, solid guy: almost as wide as he was tall. With that large vessel came a lot of energy. If the trauma inside him was pushing to get out, he would have been fighting that bastard back with all his might. But if he hadn't been fighting so hard, might all those memories from Vietnam he kept at bay have come bursting forth from the place he kept them hidden? Under their weight, might he have crumpled and softened, giving us a chance at a real relationship?

DIFFERENT COLOURED MOMENTS

On a Saturday afternoon in September, after a morning spent climbing in and out of our newly created cubby house in the boughs of the huge mango tree at the side of the house, Kerstin, David and I were playing separate games on the floor of our bedroom. David was seeing how quickly he could change his Transformer car to robot, Kerstin was dressing and undressing her Barbies and I was making a potion for the chickens in a bowl I had taken from the kitchen and filled with flower petals. Dad's feet thumped down the hall and we all froze, checking ourselves to see if we were doing anything that might annoy him.

I hadn't asked Mum if I could pick the flowers, and wasn't sure if I was meant to have flower petals in the house, so I quickly shoved the bowl behind me and tried to position myself so he wouldn't see it. I began some really intense drawing on the sheet of paper in front of me, hoping to distract Dad from the bowl.

He peeked his head around the corner, and we all looked up, ready to do his bidding.

'Ruth,' he said.

My heart hammered in response.

'Go and wash your hair and then come into the lounge room.

I'm going to comb the knots out.'

Huh? I felt Kerstin's and David's eyes move in my direction as I scanned Dad's face for some further clue about his weird suggestion. Except for running a comb through his own every couple of days, to my knowledge Dad had never touched anyone else's hair. I was not keen to be his hairdressing guinea pig.

'C'mon,' he said, 'I'm gunna do something about that rat's nest.'

Dad had dubbed my hair 'the rat's nest' for about the last year. I don't know why, but for some reason the fact I got knots in my hair really annoyed him.

I had seen a woman on the street once who had hair right down to her bottom and I was growing my hair like that. I didn't care if it was a bit knotty at the same time.

Still, I didn't move, wondering why Dad wanted to do this. Was it a trick? Was I really in trouble? My stomach tightened as his face grew more impatient. 'C'mon. Do you want me to do this or not?'

Umm . . . not. Removing knots from my hair hurt at the best of times. I couldn't imagine what Dad would be like on the end of a comb. I knew I wasn't allowed to say no though, so I got up.

Grabbing my blue summer dressing gown with the brown flowers on the pockets, I headed to the bathroom and undressed. Once under the spray, I tried to let the warm water distract me from the tumbling thoughts in my head. Why had Dad singled me out? He had never shown interest in anyone's grooming before. Was he doing this because he hated me or because he was being nice to me? Though I longed for special attention from him, something about this felt too risky. There were so many mistakes I could make.

I found Dad with a bottle of leave-in conditioner and a comb set up next to a pale pink towel draped over the big brown corduroy cushion on the floor of the lounge room. The TV was off but Mum, Kerstin and David were all sitting in the lounge chairs ready to watch Dad comb my hair. It seemed I was going to be the afternoon's entertainment.

Dad kneeled down beside the towel. 'Just lay down and fan your hair out on the cushion.'

My heart pounded and my cheeks grew warm. We all kissed Dad before we went to bed every night, but apart from that we weren't very touchy-feely. Now he was going to brush my hair. I had no idea how I was meant to respond, especially with everyone watching me.

As I lay down in front of Dad and spread my hair out, I realised it would be impossible to run away from him from this position if I made him mad. It would be nothing for him to reach his arms out and hold me down. What if my hair didn't respond the way he wanted it to? What if I made a noise he didn't like? What if I moved the wrong way?

Everyone was silent as they watched Dad pour on the leave-in conditioner and begin combing. His touch was soft and gentle but my body jolted from the shock of the contact.

I told myself to relax, but my shoulders stayed scrunched up near my ears. The repetitive sound of the comb scraping across the towel sounded very loud.

I looked up at Mum. She was sitting on the edge of her seat, watching Dad comb my hair with an expression of longing on her face. Her eyes flashed to anger when she noticed me looking at her. 'You're lucky to have a father be kind to you.'

What was it with everyone telling me how lucky I was? I could tell she wished she was the one lying here, like it should be her getting this special attention. If I was allowed, I would happily swap places. In fact, I would pay good money to be part of the audience instead of the main attraction. I hated it when Mum was mad at me.

I wanted to tell her the only reason he was doing this was because he hated my hair. It didn't mean he loved me.

I lay as still as I could, barely breathing, while everyone continued to watch in total silence. Dad kept combing until my hair was dry: shining and gleaming. 'There. That looks very nice.'

Dad didn't usually say anything good about the way any of us looked in case we got big heads. I wasn't even sure whether he was complimenting me or his combing ability so I just muttered, 'Thanks, Dad,' to be on the safe side.

I touched my hair. It did feel lovely and soft. I wanted to cry from the tension of lying there, and from the knowledge that I had got it wrong again. Dad was actually being kind to me and I hadn't enjoyed it for a minute. I wished moments like these came in a different colour so I would know it was safe to enjoy them.

Less than a week after Dad's comb-through, my hair was unable to keep itself in the state of untangled perfection he expected and I arrived home from school to Mum saying, 'C'mon. I'm taking you to get your hair cut.'

'I don't want to get my hair cut. I'm growing it.' Mum preferred silent martyrdom to conflict and mostly never forced an issue so I was sure I could convince her to change her mind.

'No. No. Your dad is sick and tired of looking at it all messy.'

So this was about Dad. My heart sank. Why did my hair have anything to do with him? Apart from three days ago, he had never brushed it or looked after it in any way. He didn't have to have it on his head. It was my hair. If he didn't like it he should just not look at it.

'I'll brush it more,' I pleaded, trying to catch her eye. She looked anywhere but at me.

'No you won't.' She drew in a lungful of smoke.

'I will. I promise.'

'No.' She blew her smoke out with enough force that it was almost a raspberry, then stubbed out her cigarette in the nearly full blue glass ashtray. Moving silently around the kitchen, she put her Winfield Blues and a packet of Wrigley's chewing gum into her brown leather handbag. She then grabbed the circular brush that was part of the general table debris and ran it through her short dark hair. Her hair was wavy, and the brushing made it stand up all over her head in a dark brown helmet. I did not want hair like hers. I wanted hair like the beautiful woman on the street.

'Please, Mum. Please don't make me get it cut. I like long hair. Short hair will make me look like a boy.'

She hunted in her handbag, pulling out a compact. Resolutely avoiding my gaze, her eyes stayed on the mirror as she spoke between bouts of lipstick application. 'I'm sorry, but Dad wants it cut. I've made an appointment this afternoon.'

I cried. It was so unfair. What did he expect? That he would brush my hair once and then it would never have knots again? Maybe he thought because Mum was the one who did my hair, she just wasn't doing it right and once he did it, it would fall into line. Part of me was at least happy my hair had proved him wrong.

Oh God. What would everyone in my class think? Tears streamed down my face as I pictured the girls at school in my mind. All the rich, beautiful girls had long hair. I might not have had many things the same as them, but at least up until this point I'd had long hair. Now I wouldn't even have that. I was going to look like some poor, ugly boy-girl.

On the way to the hairdressers, I kept begging Mum not to make me do this, but she just ignored me, her eyes on the road.

As I was still crying when we got there, the dumpy, blonde hairdresser asked if everything was all right.

Mum's orange lips spread into a fake smile. 'She's not sure she wants her hair cut —'

'I *don't* want to cut my hair,' I said loudly, trying to catch Mum's eyes. She still wouldn't look at me. I imagined her relishing my suffering: punishment for the extra attention Dad had given me.

The hairdresser grabbed a magazine from the stack in the shelf underneath the mirror, and said I should look through it to find something I liked. I didn't pick it up. Mum talked over my head. 'It needs to be quite short. Something that doesn't need much brushing.'

After another minute of me sitting with my arms folded, the hairdresser picked up a magazine and began flicking through it herself. She pointed to a picture of Lady Di. 'Lady Di looks lovely. I bet that hair would really suit you.' I looked down at my hands. 'Do you want to look like Lady Di?'

No. I don't. I want to look like the woman on the street with the long, swishy hair. But I'm not allowed to have what I want. I'm only allowed to have what Dad wants.

'It's all right. It'll make you look pretty.' Her kind eyes caught mine in the mirror. I nodded.

Mum went outside to smoke and I kept my eyes tightly closed for the rest of the haircut. With every metallic ripping sound my head grew lighter. All the time I had spent growing it was for nothing. I would never look like that beautiful woman.

When she was done I forced myself to look in the mirror. A stranger stared back. My hair did look a bit like Lady Di's: straight and short with flicks. But I didn't have blue eyes, just stupid brown ones that looked like they belonged to a cow. I tried to say thank you, but the words came out as a sob.

In the car on the way home I looked out the window, trying to ignore the way the wind shot tingles into my scalp as it blew my new, too-short hair. I thought about turning up to school tomorrow and how everyone would look at me, laugh and tell me I was ugly.

I was always in the bottom couple of people picked for teams, and one of the last two girls picked during our term of bush dancing. I was in no doubt where I stood. I was one rung above Cherryl-Lea, the girl who wet her pants. But I knew for certain this haircut would tip me over the edge and I would officially be thought of as the ugliest, smelliest, most disgusting girl in the class.

FROGMARCH

My hair had grown about an inch by the time the whole family gathered in the lounge room a couple of months later watching David Attenborough speak in a hushed voice about the eating habits of the chimpanzee.

Though Kerstin hated sleeping anywhere but in her own bed, and David was not yet old enough for sleepovers, I spent most of my weekends staying over at friends' houses to give me a break from the tension of being at home. It was a novel experience for me to be sitting around freshly showered after a day working in the garden. Flicking my eyes over everyone's relaxed faces and breathing in their clean, soapy smell I was filled with the warm glow of being an actual member of a normal happy family, rather than an interloper.

I wanted to celebrate the Hallmark moment, to show Mum and Dad how much I loved them. 'Mum, would you like me to make you and Dad a coffee?'

'Do you know how to make it?' Mum asked, turning her gaze away from the TV to look at me.

'Yes.' I had watched Mum make it heaps of times.

'Okay then. That'd be very nice.'

I smiled to myself as I headed to the kitchen. Mum and Dad didn't really drink alcohol at home. Their beverage of choice was Nescafé Blend 43 instant coffee and they would have at least five cups a day. It was one of the few non-generic brand items in our cupboard. This made it special and luxurious and I couldn't wait for the day I was sophisticated enough to enjoy its disgusting burnt taste.

After sprinkling a heaped teaspoon of coffee granules into each cup, I added a spoonful of sugar to Dad's. I couldn't believe Mum could drink the stuff without a little bit of sweetness so I added a few grains of sugar to her cup as my 'secret ingredient'. I was sure she was going to say, 'I don't know what you have done to this but it is a really amazing cup of coffee. I don't think I have ever tasted a cup quite this good.'

I managed to pour the boiling water from the kettle into the cups and add the milk with only a minor bit of spillage that was easily wiped up. After a thorough stirring I lifted the cups off the counter and started slowly walking through to the lounge room, where Mum and Dad were in their armchairs still enthralled by David Attenborough.

I had just made it out of the kitchen when I felt Dad move in his chair. I looked up expecting him to be smiling at how lovely I was to make him a cup of coffee, but instead I met eyes burning with rage and disgust. It caught me completely off-guard. Shock vacuumed me out of my body. The physical sensation of this was so strong my torso leaned forward in response, making the coffee sway in the cups.

I snapped my eyes back to the brown liquid, willing it not to spill. I narrowed my world to the cups and my feet so I wouldn't make the mistake that would enrage him.

As unobtrusively as I could, I checked behind me to make sure I hadn't spilled anything, then kept making careful progress toward him. His eyes burned into me, making the hair on my arms stand on end, but I dared not take my eyes off the cups.

'Walk faster,' Dad growled. 'Don't walk around crouching like that. Walk with your head in the air, for God's sake.'

'I'm trying not to spill them.' I picked up my pace a little bit and dared a look up at him to see if I was doing okay, but he was already up and out of his chair.

'Walk! Walk! Walk!' He was suddenly behind me, his hands on mine, gripping the cups as he frog-marched me forward. The coffee spilled all down my legs and onto the floor, burning me through my clothes.

'Walk! Like a normal person!' He wrenched the cups, which by then had sloshed out more than half their coffee, out of my hands, crashing them onto the table. 'What a bloody mess. Go and get a cloth and clean it up.' He shook his head in disgust, as if I was the one who had made the mess, and stalked out of the room.

As I rinsed the coffee off myself in the shower, I let the tears I had been holding in trickle down my face. Even when I tried to do something nice for him, he found a way to turn it bad. No matter how hard I tried it was never good enough.

I knew he hated people being timid, but he also hated people spilling. You had to be confident about what you did, do it perfectly, but not get too big for your boots. It was impossible to skate along the razor edge of his expectations.

Pictures flashed into my head: an angry glance, being ignored in the playground, a reprimand from a teacher. As they started to take form, the deep panic I strived to keep at bay fluttered in my heart like a trapped bird. Did everyone see me the way Dad did?

Bang. Bang. Bang.

The pounding on the wall of the bathroom made me jump.

'You've been in there long enough. Stop wasting water,' Dad's voice barked.

I turned off the tap, nearly slipping on the floor of the pink bathtub in my haste to get out. Towelling off, my heart thumped manically in my chest. Poor heart. Moments ago, it had swelled to bursting at the joy of being part of a happy family; now it was back playing its familiar tune. *Ba-boom. Ba-boom. Ba-boom.*

Each moment of alarm carried its own tone and tempo. The subtle anxiety of being in a room with Dad, the panic of discovery, the heart-crashing terror just before he made contact, the intense pulsing when anger mixed in. But worst of all was the deep, throbbing dread that he might be right. Maybe there was something wrong with me that made me unlovable. Maybe I deserved to be punished just because I was alive.

ically matched my inha-
SHADOW AND LIGHT

A couple of days after my phone call to the Vietnam Veterans Association, I received a call from a veteran called Ollie. He had served at the same time as Dad, but wasn't sure if he had known him. I told him I was interested in anything he could share with me about his time in Vietnam and the impact he felt it had had on his life.

Ollie started talking in a low, urgent mumble. 'Yeah, well I was over there around the same time as your dad but got medevaced back with malaria. My whole platoon was under attack when I was in hospital. One of my best mates got killed but I didn't know about it. I was shipped out the next day.

'I had PTSD for years not really knowing what was wrong with me. I was cranky, crappy, used to snap and yell at my daughters all the time over nothing. They felt very uneasy with me, with my mood swings, so I just locked myself away. It was all part of the PTSD.'

My breathing sped up as I unconsciously matched my inhalations to his. There was no missing the panic behind the rapid flow of his words. I imagined this had not been an easy call to make. I broke in with a question. 'I was just reading about conscription, Ollie. Were you conscripted?'

'Yeah, I got a telegram in 1966. I was just getting settled in a flat. I'd only been married for five months. They told you you had to report somewhere in town for a medical checkout. I'd just broken my foot and it was only just cleared up. Well blow me down, they passed me as medically fit. Even being married I couldn't get out of it. Not that I minded. I thought I was fighting for Australia.'

His words brought tears to my eyes. I remembered Dad telling me the same thing when I was a kid. His grandfather and uncle had fought in World War I and II. He thought the Vietnam War was his turn to do his duty for his country.

I had always liked the idea that life unfolded according to some bigger plan, but during my chat with Ollie I began to wonder about the role luck played.

Like my dad, Ollie was conscripted as part of the National Service Scheme that operated in Australia between 1964 and 1972. Each year, every twenty-year-old man was required to register his birthday with the government. If you didn't submit your name you were fined. If your number came up and you said you didn't want to go, you could be sent to jail for the same period of time as you would have served in the army. If your birth date was drawn out of the barrel you faced the possibility of two years of continuous full-time service in the regular army, followed by three years' part-time service in the army reserve. National servicemen could also be sent for 'special overseas service' including combat duties in Vietnam.

I knew society had changed drastically in the last fifty years, but this whole concept sounded like The Hunger Games to me.

At twenty years of age, some people became the property of the army and were sent to war, while others continued their lives unaffected? My dad's freedom stolen based on nothing more than the luck of the draw.

It seemed incredibly unlucky that Ollie, that my dad, had been chosen to fight in this war when so many others had not. How different would our lives have been if his number had never come up?

My aunt and uncle told me Dad had deferred to finish his apprenticeship before beginning his national service. Dad had hoped that his qualification would give him a chance to stay away from the action. Though he was willing to do his bit for his country, he didn't want to fight.

As a qualified fitter and turner he would have been able to repair guns, tanks, cars – any type of war machinery. And given he won the award for Queensland Apprentice of the Year just before he fronted up for duty, Dad thought he was a shoo-in for a role that used his new skills and kept him away from direct combat.

I looked up information on deferred start times for conscripted soldiers and found this on the Australian War Memorial website: 'The Army was obliged to make effective use of the trade skills of national servicemen. Subject to vacancies, these men were employed in the Army in their civilian occupation.'

The vast majority of the conscripted men I spoke to had trades of equal use to the army as Dad's. They echoed his experience of having their skills overlooked as they were funnelled directly into the infantry. 'Machine gun fodder we called ourselves,' one of them told me. 'We were just meat to them.'

The depth of depersonalisation in those words gave me the shivers. Meat. An image of the foot I had sliced open when I was five flashed into my mind. The trail of blood it had left behind had made it look like the carcass of a butchered animal. Meat. After his experience in the army, had Dad come to regard the value of his life only as a lump of flesh? If he felt that was his inherent worth, it was little wonder he found it difficult to see the worth in others.

It wasn't just the decision by the army to put him into a spare rifle company as 'meat' that showed Dad how little he was worth to his country. Even when his efforts on the battlefield deserved recognition, he received none.

Dad landed in Vietnam only three months after the Tet Offensive, a series of surprise attacks that gave North Vietnamese soldiers control over major city buildings across Vietnam. It was 1968, the peak of the fighting and the year when the largest number of Australians lost their lives. Six weeks after his arrival, he was caught up in the Battle of Coral: the biggest and bloodiest skirmish fought by Australians during the Vietnam War.

The men I spoke to who were at Coral on the first night described how four hundred of the enemy, chanting a war cry, emerged from the darkness, then thundered into the Australian camp, shooting. The flashes of their guns strobed their features so the men could see their faces, their expressions, their weapons. It was intensely up close and personal. Rounds were zinging overhead and everyone was too scared to get out of their pits. The enemy ran through and over the top of the men, managing to take possession of one of their big guns. They were so completely overrun, they had to call an air strike on their own position.

Ollie told me, 'I remember being shelled with mortars and rockets. We were in a pit we had dug out. There was no cover and it had started to rain. I put my raincoat over my ammunition so it wouldn't get dirty. There were explosions every ten to twenty seconds. After every one you'd yell out, "Are you still okay?" to the bloke in the pit next to you. I lit the hexistove up and wrote a note to my wife that I didn't think I'd be there in the morning.'

Even though they were grossly outnumbered, during the night the Australians managed to win back their gun. But on that first night, nine were killed, twenty-eight more wounded. The next day the men gathered up the bodies of their friends and enemies and made repairs as best they could.

With no sleep, they then prepared for another night of fighting. Monday the enemy came. Tuesday. Wednesday. Thursday. Friday. The week of fighting rolled into two and then three. Night after night they kept coming, trying to get the guns. Each night rain poured into the pits, filling them with water so deep it reached the necks of the soldiers.

One of the things Dad mentioned in a brief aside when I was growing up was that his best friend in the army, Shortie, had died in Vietnam. Moments before he was shot down, Shortie screamed his last words to Dad as he ran away from the enemy. 'Dig, you bastard, dig!'

Was that at Coral? What must Dad's experience have done to him? If my own best friend had been shot down after spending his last breath on a warning to me, how would I have lived with that? How were these men meant to return to their lives and have normal relationships again?

Eventually the American forces came in to help, and for the first time since World War II, all parts of the Australian military – tanks, air strikes and armed forces – were used in a planned operation in a time of war.

Soldiers at Coral withstood two major frontal attacks and fifty-seven separate fire-fights. The conflict lasted twenty-six days, with twenty-five Diggers killed and over a hundred wounded. The best known Australian battle of the Vietnam War, the Battle of Long Tan, lasted four hours.

Yet the carnage Dad and all of the other soldiers at Coral endured was barely acknowledged by the country they fought for. What were these men meant to interpret from that? How could they think anything other than their sacrifice was just a total waste of life?

War sends soldiers across the inkiest black shadows of their souls. They cross their most sacred moral boundary, pick up a gun and take the life of another. They do it because they have to. Because it is kill or be killed. But the only reason they really do it is because their government, our government, commands it.

No veteran I spoke to liked the idea of war being celebrated. That didn't mean, however, that their service should go unrecognised, their pain unacknowledged. They should be remembered not because people like war, but as a light to counter the darkness, so soldiers might have a chance of finding their way back home.

SOMETHING TO CRY ABOUT

Every Christmas since our move to Rockhampton we had made the eight-hour journey down the Bruce Highway to see our grandparents in Brisbane. Watching the mostly unchanging landscape of brown grass and dull grey-green eucalypts out of our windows, we feasted on ham sandwiches and barbecue Samboy chips Mum pulled from the esky crammed in at her feet.

On the Callum family road trip there was no stopping except for one petrol and toilet break. Dad thought the pain of travelling with kids was like a bandaid, best ripped off quick.

Any time spent in a moving vehicle made me feel sick. When I wasn't eating, much of my trip alternated between trying to sleep and trying to focus my eyes on the perfect distance to make the whizzing trees a blur that didn't add to the churning of my stomach. If my sickness reached the point where I felt like I was going to throw up, I wound the window down to divert my attention to the fresh air on my face. Occasionally there would be an urgent stop so I could vomit, but normally I got away with just feeling ill for the entire five hundred minutes.

About six hours in to one trip, my face had lost all of its colour and I was coated in the clammy sweat of travel sickness. I twisted my legs one way, then the other, but I couldn't get comfortable in my seat, especially with David sleeping on me with his oversized six-year-old head.

'Get off me!' I shoved him over to Kerstin.

He woke up crying.

'Don't shove him onto me.' Kerstin shoved him back.

'Well, don't put him back on me.'

Kerstin and I ping-ponged him back and forth for a few more times before David cried out, 'Why do I have to sit in the middle?'

'Because you're the littlest,' I told him. 'Stop putting your head on me.'

'It's not fair.' His voice was a balloon squeaking out air.

Mum's arm snaked slowly over the back of the driver's seat, where Dad sat very still, his eyes on the road. She gave us some desperate hand signals, waving and hitting and punching the air while keeping her head forward and her eyes straight ahead. This was her warning to cut it out or there would be trouble from Dad.

I put my head on the window and closed my eyes. But the next minute David put his head back on my shoulder. I was tired and nauseated and I just wanted to sleep.

'Get off me!' I yelled.

Before David had a chance to respond, Dad swerved the car off the bitumen onto the gravel at the shoulder of the highway. We all jerked forward as the car came to an abrupt halt, engulfed in dust. Dad jumped out of his seat, dragged out Kerstin, then

David, before coming around to get me. He lined us up in the brown grass and hit each of us, a few quick slaps each.

'Stop your bloody carry-on! Get back into the car and don't say another word!'

He opened the door, shoved me back in, then Kerstin and David.

We were all crying.

He turned around to look at us, face pulled tight at the edges, eyes sparking green fire. 'You had better stop that noise right now or I'll give you something to really cry about.'

We swallowed our sobs as fast as we could, but squeaks and hiccups escaped.

'I mean it.' His lip curled.

There was a pain in my chest like a stuck burp as I held it all in.

He started the car and we drove off again. Only two more hours to go.

BIG SPILL

When we arrived at Dad's parents' house it was dark. At the crunch of tyres on the driveway I let out the breath I had been holding for the last hundred kilometres.

The light at the top of the stairs shone sudden and yellow into the night, and I opened the car door and ran straight into Grandma's squashy cuddle, breathing in her sunshine soap smell. The house was full of the aroma of the crispy on the outside, juicy in the middle roast chicken she always prepared especially for our arrival. We had made it. We were safe.

That first night Kerstin and I slept in crisp sheets on tall soft beds in the front room with the dark polished boards while Dad, Mum and David slept in the double room at the back. Dad's brother and his family would arrive tomorrow. That meant in the morning we would have to set up the army tent near the macadamia nut tree in Grandma and Papa's huge back garden so they could take our spot inside the house. But tonight the beds were ours.

The scrappy assortment of crayons and colouring pencils Grandma kept in a drawer for the grandkids were spread out in front of me on the section of dining room table I had claimed by moving back the woollen blanket that protected it from getting scratched and dusty. As I worked on getting the petals of the rose I was drawing just right, my attention was diverted by the gasps and shouts erupting from the lounge room.

Grandma, Papa, Dad and his brother were sitting in the four upright armchairs in the small dark lounge room watching the West Indies versus Australia in the cricket. Our three cousins and Kerstin and David sprawled in front of the TV, sometimes watching, sometimes playing with the plastic army men and farm animals spread out on the wooden floor.

Behind me in the kitchen, Mum and my aunty put away the remaining dishes and finished sweeping the floor. Grandma and Papa had very established ideas about the roles of men and women. From what I could understand, this meant the girls did everything – shopped, made all the food, did the dishes, wiped down all the counters and swept the floor after every meal or snack – and the boys watched cricket.

'We're going to get some groceries,' Mum said, poking her head around the doorway. 'Does anyone want anything?'

'Can I come with you?' I asked.

'No, it's just a quick trip. We only need a few things. So, nothing?'

A couple of murmured 'no's floated back at her from the lounge room and I returned to my drawing.

During the next ad break Grandma asked, 'Does anyone want a cup of tea?'

'Yes, thanks.' The men spoke in unison. 'Can I have a cup?'

asked David.

'Okay,' Grandma replied. At Grandma's house we drank proper grown-up tea with lettuce sandwiches on wholemeal bread.

Grandma got herself up off the armchair with a heavy breath and headed to her faded, spotless kitchen. I got up and followed her. The cricket commentary was replaced by a sports announcer calling horse races on the old radio sitting on the sideboard in the corner.

'Can I help you make the tea?' I asked as Grandma disappeared into the pantry. When we were in Rockhampton, making tea involved putting a teabag into a cup of hot water. But at Grandma's, you had to heat the pot, measure out the tea, tip in the water, stir it around, wait a while, then turn the pot around three times and put the tea cosy on top. It was almost like cooking.

She came out of the walk-in pantry and handed me the rusted metal tin with the faded flower pattern that contained the looseleaf tea.

'Okay. Let me warm the pot first.'

As soon as the kettle screamed out its high-pitched whistle she turned off the gas and brought it over, splashing a little water into the pot.

'I can swirl it,' I told her. I swished the water around and then tipped it down the sink.

'Now measure out three level spoons.'

Once I had done as instructed she tipped boiling water over the leaves. I grabbed the spoon and stirred. The leaves spun helplessly in the whirlpool. I imagined them screaming.

'I can pour out the cups,' I said.

'I don't think so, Ruth. It's pretty heavy.' 'I can do it. Please.'

I stood up taller so she could see I was ten – practically a grown-up.

'I do it all the time at home,' I lied.

She gave me a long look. 'Okay.'

She arranged the fragile teacups onto their saucers and went back to watch the cricket. 'Just give it a couple of minutes to draw,' she said.

I counted to sixty in my head three times, and went to move the teapot off the counter. It was way heavier than I had thought. I couldn't lift it with one hand. I wrapped one hand on top of the other around the wooden handle, but even with two hands I still couldn't raise it up. I put my hand under the spout to help lift it instead. In the same second I managed to raise the teapot off the counter, I also registered the aluminium spout I was holding was the same temperature as the boiling water inside. I quickly pulled my hand away. The movement unbalanced the teapot and I poured a big steaming splash onto my stomach. I lunged forward and managed to put the pot down again on the bench.

My clothes were wet and there was a big spill of tea on the floor. I was so panicked by the thought that someone was going to come in and find me surrounded by such a mess, after I had lied about making tea at home, that at first I didn't realise my stomach was on fire.

'Kerstin?' I yelled, trying to keep my voice as calm sounding as possible. 'Can you come in here, please?'

I lifted up my shirt. The whole left side of my stomach was red and pink and splotchy. There was a series of pale blisters coming up, like islands out of the red sea. One of them was about the size and shape of a mandarin. Every second that ticked by, my stomach got hotter.

I wanted to scream but I couldn't let anyone find out I had made a mess so I clamped my jaw down tight.

Kerstin walked in and I could see the fear on her face as she stared at my exposed stomach.

'Don't tell anyone,' she said quietly, meaning Dad.

Tears trickled down my cheeks. 'It really hurts,' I whispered.

'I know. It looks sore.' She wet a tea towel and handed it to me. 'Put that on it.'

The burning made me want to crawl out of my skin. The tea towel didn't make it feel any better.

I was so stupid. If I hadn't been such a show-off I wouldn't have tried to help make the tea and this would never have happened.

'It's still hurting,' I said.

Kerstin grabbed a big handful of paper towel from the pantry and started mopping up the tea on the floor.

'Go and run it under the tap in the toilet.'

I checked to make sure no one was coming out of the lounge room and went into the toilet just next to the back door. I tried not to look down at what was happening on my stomach, but the biggest blister took up half the flesh to the left of my belly button.

The pink sink was only tiny and it was difficult to position myself in a way that let the water get onto the spots that needed cooling. The areas I couldn't get to flamed and burned; water splashed onto the floor. The second I turned the water off, my stomach felt as if I was pouring the boiling water on it again. Tears trickled out of my eyes as I mopped up the mess I had made on the toilet floor.

The sliding door rolled back and Kerstin handed me some ice she had snuck out of the freezer, wrapped in paper towel.

'Go and change your shirt,' she whispered. 'I'll do the tea.'

I went down to the tent, keeping my back to the opening in case anybody came to check on me. I gingerly held the ice on the burn until it melted, but my stomach still thrummed with painful heat.

The whispered touch of my new shirt on my now taut blisters shot pain from my stomach into my jaw. I practised smiling in the small mirror that hung off the central pole of the tent, but my lips looked wobbly at the edges. I couldn't go upstairs. Better to get in trouble for not telling them where I was than to have them find out what an idiot I had been to try to make tea by myself.

I made my way to the strawberry patch next to the crumbling tennis shed. Now I just had to figure out a way to not let anyone see my stomach for the next month.

HIDDEN

When I asked some of Dad's family and friends what he was like before he went to Vietnam, they described him as bright, bubbly, cheeky, always up for a good time.

I knew the Dad they described. It was the part that made him impossible to resist. When he shone his light on me, something in me uncurled and grew. It felt like the best parts of him were the best parts of me. Those good places where we met outshone the bad, so no matter how much I wanted to punish him, I wanted to bask in his light more.

But I knew the other part as well, the one he kept hidden. As I did more research into the psychological impacts of war, I discovered the person I knew was often a lot more like a list of symptoms associated with PTSD: easily angered, often detached, hyper-vigilant, cut off from friends and family, numb, lacking in empathy, suffering flashbacks and nightmares, difficulty sleeping, irritability, restricted emotions, exaggerated startle response.

Certainly a few of the veterans I spoke to said they thought everyone who came back from the war probably had PTSD, even if they weren't aware of it. But as a kid, I didn't know Dad was exhibiting the symptoms of a disorder. I thought those symptoms were just who my dad was.

*

The more reading I did, the more it seemed that the Vietnam War had been specially designed to create the symptoms of PTSD.

In Vietnam there wasn't a series of major battles like in World War I and II. There was no front line. No large units fighting from trenches.

Ollie described his experience to me this way: 'In Vietnam mostly you were wandering around the bush and they were looking for you and you were looking for them.

'In WWII you fought horrendous battles but you might have a month on a boat to get to the next battle. We fought for weeks at a time and then were helicoptered to the next fight.

'You didn't speak much. Being in a jungle on patrol you were in a silent world. You were aware of your friends. You had to look at the trees. You were careful where you put your feet and took one step at a time because bullets might come flying from anywhere.

'There wasn't an enemy you were advancing on and you could see where they were. Half the time you couldn't see a thing. You couldn't see anyone to shoot at so you just shot in the general direction. On those missions we were just trying to keep our mates alive and not run into any trouble.'

When I spoke to Tim back when I was pregnant with my daughter, he told me how during the night, when the dense blackness of the jungle made it impossible to maintain good visual contact, you tied a rope between yourself and the other men in your group. If you saw a North Vietnamese soldier you pulled the rope to grab their attention then used hand signals to communicate where and how many, hoping the others in your group could make out what you were saying in your silence.

I asked Ollie if he had experienced this silence as well. He spoke more about the blackness. He told me how, once night hit, the patrol would set up in a well-camouflaged spot in the jungle then the men would stay awake all night, listening. Any sleep was caught in snatches for an hour or two at most. 'It was that dark you couldn't see a hand in front of your face. You had to run a string line from each machine gunner to the gun so they could find it.'

My childhood had left me with my own form of hyper-vigilance: small noises in the night startled me fully awake; I still tracked people for danger, making sure their words matched what their body was telling me; and I noticed minute changes in environments I visited regularly. It was difficult to imagine how extreme that vigilance would be if I had spent long periods of time sitting in complete silence in a jungle, blinded by the dark, listening to every movement as I waited for someone to come and kill me. Even thinking about it from the safety of my quiet neighbourhood revved up my pulse.

My stress response made me think about something else I had read about PTSD. It is classified as an anxiety disorder. Was it possible that some of Dad's behaviour had less to do with rage and more to do with anxiety?

Since having kids of my own, I knew that nothing I had ever experienced in my life even came close to how anxious they made me feel. Where before I had felt more or less invincible, now that I had these breakable little creatures in my care I saw injury and death everywhere.

As I delved further into the world of Dad's experience and filtered it back through myself, trying to feel what he felt, I wondered if he might have had fears for us as well. Was it possible that he loved us, but the nature of being a child – taking risks, making mistakes, falling over, getting hurt – triggered his anxiety, which triggered memories of his war experience?

It was impossible to imagine what it would be like to have the memories of war in your cells, hunting you in your dreams. Could it be that the unconscious response when his anxiety was triggered was to either shut down into disconnection or tip over into rage? Did the unrealistically high expectations he had of our behaviour come from a misguided desire to protect us? In war, everything was life or death. If that idea had stayed with him, might he have been trying to teach us how dangerous it was to make mistakes so he could make sure we stayed safe?

ENEMY

SURPRISE

One afternoon in January I made my way around the dining table, placing butter knives in exact lines on the side plates. As I pulled gently at the 'special occasion' lace tablecloth to remove a wrinkle, the smell of roast lamb made my stomach growl. I stepped back to admire my handiwork.

I would have liked white plates with gold around the edges like the ones I had eaten off at my friend's house, but tan with brown geometric patterned edges were all we had. The flowers I had picked were mostly daisies and fern fronds, not the pink roses I would have chosen, but Mum didn't grow roses, so daisies would have to do. At least everything was lined up perfectly.

'Mum, should I blow up some balloons?' I yelled across the bench that divided the dining room from the kitchen, where Mum was cutting beans.

'I don't think we have any. But get the candles out of the sideboard if you want. The ones in silver candleholders.'

The first cupboard I opened contained the fragile red tea set Dad had brought back with him from Vietnam. I gently picked up one of the tiny cups and held it up to the sunlight pouring in through the kitchen window. The hidden pattern of a lady's face—

came to life in the bottom of the cup. I wished we could drink tea out of them sometime, but I wasn't even meant to touch them.

After carefully replacing it onto its saucer, I resumed my hunt for candleholders. Cloth napkins, vases, rolled-up bamboo place mats, glass serving dishes, napkin rings . . .

'I can't find them,' I shouted.

Mum came in wiping her hands on her apron. 'I'd better not find them straight away. I still have to ice the cake. I want everything ready before he comes home so he gets a surprise —'

'I know. I know.'

She opened a cupboard I hadn't got to yet, grabbed out the candleholders and shoved them into my hands, before hurrying back to the kitchen.

She began slicing again, then looked at the clock. 'It's twenty past five. He'll be here in half an hour. I need to get dressed. Can you chop the ends off these for me?'

'Okay.' I moved into the kitchen and picked up the knife. I had already donned the purple dress with small pink flowers that was my current party favourite. Not that I really went to parties, more backyard barbecues with lots of grown-ups talking. This probably didn't really count as a party either because it was just the family. But it *was* Dad's birthday.

The food was at least party-like. His favourite meal: roast lamb, baked vegies and gravy made from scratch. And a chocolate cake with Smarties on top. He was going to love it.

Mum hurried back to the kitchen dressed in the new striped denim skirt she had found at the op-shop last week with a red button-up blouse, dangly red earrings and red lips to match. Every few minutes she stopped tidying the kitchen to check the clock.

'When you're finished there put these next to the candles.' She handed me a box of matches. 'As soon as we hear the truck pull in we'll light them then go hide.'

The ticking of the clock grew louder as Dad's arrival time drew nearer, cranking the excitement up notch by notch until I wasn't sure I was going to be able to eat. At three minutes past six, the truck pulled into the drive.

'Quick!' Mum screeched. She lit the candles with shaking hands as I hopped from foot to foot.

'Let's hide.' She turned to us with a grin. Kerstin, David and I moved behind her, laughter bubbling out of us at the game of it all.

As we moved down the hallway she turned dramatically and said, 'Lights!'

She ran to the switch. It wasn't yet fully dark, but we all screamed when the globes went black, clutching onto each other, then laughing again. On the table, the candlelight glinted off the cutlery and made the daisies glow. Even pink roses could not have made it more beautiful.

Mum moved ahead of us, a huge smile on her face.

'Where are we going?' Kerstin asked.

'I don't know,' Mum said, then laughed. 'You're the kids here. Where's a good place to hide?'

'Under my bed!' David yelled.

'Okay, let's do it.'

We held onto each other as we walked.

'Wooo,' David said. 'I'm a ghost.' We laughed.

'Shh!' Mum spoke through her giggles. 'It's meant to be a

surprise.'

We tried to keep the noise under control but snorts and chuckles keep bursting out.

'Shh,' Mum said. We couldn't fit under the bed so we crouched in front of it, figuring it would take a while for Dad to find us anyway with all the lights off.

The house vibrated with Dad's steps and we scrunched into each other more tightly, ready to jump up and say surprise as soon as he appeared. The seconds ticked by and we kept waiting for him to start calling out to us.

'Shit.' Dad's voice drifted in from the other room. The giddy, giggly feeling in my stomach was immediately crushed by a clamp of fear. We all fell silent, the whole mood of our group switching to wariness in an instant.

I looked to Mum, but her face was hard to read in the dark.

The light came on in the dining room, spilling a glow into the back of the house so we could see each other's faces more clearly. Everyone had questions in their eyes. When did we say surprise?

'Barbara.' Dad's voice sounded cold and annoyed and I immediately got up to join him. Mum pulled me back down, whispering, 'We still have to surprise him.'

I crouched back into the group.

'Barbara, I know you are hiding. You can all come out now. The surprise is over.' His voice sounded weary.

'I think we better go, Mum,' I said. She pursed her lips and nodded. We slowly got up and walked back down the hallway.

The candles were no longer burning and the harsh light from overhead made everything on the table ordinary again. Dad was standing in an odd position at the foot of the table and the tension in his hand made my heart race.

'Barbara, what is this?' He pointed toward my flowers. As Mum inched closer her face fell.

'Well?' Dad asked. 'What is it?'

'All right, Doug. All right. I see it. You don't have to make a big deal about it.'

'No. I want to know. What is it?' He shifted his weight and folded his arms, raising his eyebrows as if he had no idea what he was looking at. I moved to see what they were talking about.

'It's wax.' Mum's voice sounded so tired I wanted to take her in my arms and rock her like a baby.

'Yes, it's wax. It's dripped onto the tablecloth and ruined it. But more than that, you could have set the whole house on fire.'

Mum looked down at the floor, but Dad crouched down to get his face under hers, demanding eye contact.

'What were you thinking, Barbara? Did you want to burn the house down? Is that it? Did you —'

'We were trying to surprise you, Doug.' I could hear the tears she was holding back. My throat ached for her.

'Well, I don't think it would be a very good surprise if the whole house burned down, do you?'

'No, Doug.' Her voice was small.

I pressed in closer to her, wanting her to know I loved her, even if he didn't.

'I guess we should all sit down. Next time just be more careful.'

We sat in silence as Mum served the roast nobody felt like eating.

DESERTED ISLAND

There was only one thing Dad loved more than camping, and that was fishing. Often taking a day off work when the weather seduced him, he fished with friends and he fished alone; mostly, though, he fished with us.

'Ruth. Kerstin. Get up!' Dad's voice bellowed into the pitch black of pre-dawn. My eyes snapped open, and as I pushed the covers back I remembered I wasn't wearing pyjamas. Everyone slept fully dressed on fishing days to avoid delays.

Though I was still disoriented from sleep, I sat up straight away and said, 'Thanks, Dad. I'm awake.'

Kerstin echoed me. If we wanted to avoid being dragged out of bed, these were the words Dad expected us to say.

In the hallway David staggered toward us clutching Joey, his purple dinosaur. We gathered together in a silent huddle, awaiting our next instruction.

Rockhampton in autumn guaranteed the day would soon turn hot. But at that moment the air was cool after our snuggly beds so we jumped up and down to warm ourselves up. Some giggles escaped into the darkness.

'All right. Don't get yourselves all razzed up. Get down to the car, close your eyes and go back to sleep,' Dad called.

We fell into a silent line and walked through the dark house, past the brightly lit kitchen, where Mum was loading white-bread sandwiches into the esky. Downstairs, the boat was already hitched up, ready to go.

We hopped in our designated car positions in our new-to-us white Falcon that used to be a police car: Kerstin behind Dad, me behind Mum, David in the middle. I put my hands under my legs to create a barrier against the cool vinyl.

Even though a moment ago I had been sure the excitement of being up before the birds had wiped out the possibility of sleep, as soon as I rested my head on the glass of my window, the scratchiness inside my eyes got the better of me and I shut them.

Next thing I knew we were at the fishing ramp and everyone except me was outside stretching, their car doors ajar.

Out of a shimmering half-circle on the horizon, red, pink and yellow streaked into a sky doubled by the mirror of the ocean. It was dramatic and beautiful and everyone's faces glowed with the reflected glory of it all.

The early morning price of sunrise had always made me prefer sunsets, but that day I felt converted. Nothing could be all bad in a world with a sky like this. My heart stretched into the unquestionable rightness of the moment.

Breathing in a heady mix of salt, outboard motor and fish guts, I looked out across the ocean's expanse. There weren't many whitecaps. Maybe it wouldn't be rough. I might even not throw up today.

I leaned against the car, watching first one and then another group backing their trailers into the still water.

As the second car did a dodgy turn and nearly went over the ramp, Dad put his fingers in his mouth and whistled at top volume to catch their attention, then jogged down to give them directions. A commercial by the Seventh-day Adventist church I had seen the night before on TV popped into my head.

> *Do you need a haa-a-and?*
> *Do you need a haa-a-and?*
> *Be the first to say, 'Do you need a hand?'*
> *If you see some trouble coming*
> *Don't look the other way*
> *Step right up and say, 'Do you need a hand?'*

The people in the car smiled and waved as Dad headed back to us. It seemed a lucky start to the day.

It was going to be our turn on the ramp soon. I looked over at Mum, who was smoking and looking at the ground. It was her job to tell Dad the exact moment he needed to stop reversing the trailer into the water.

Mum headed carefully down the ramp to avoid slipping on the slime and leaked-out motor oil. She sloshed into the water up to her knees. By some miracle she said 'when' at the perfect point and there was no yelling. It was going to be a good day.

Once we were all in the boat we jostled to find a handhold on the windscreen, heads over the top. This was my favourite part of the whole day.

'Ready?' Dad asked, and we nodded. 'Hats off.' We put our

hats on the floor in front of us.

Then we were flying. Keeping our knees slightly bent to cope with the dips, we skimmed the tops of the tiny waves. The *boom, boom, boom* sound of the hull on water set the rhythm for the song we sang every time we were in the boat. Mum, Dad, Kerstin, David and I shouted at the top of our lungs so we could be heard over the roar of the wind.

> *Up in the air I fly*
> *Zoom, zoom a zoom, a zoom, zoom*
> *Up in the clear, blue sky*
> *Zoom, zoom, a zoom, a zoom, zoom.*
> *Zooooom, zooooom.*

We were laughing and yelling, huge smiles splitting our faces. After about ten rounds of the song we lapsed into silence, wind roaring in our ears, salt spray stinging our eyes.

I opened my mouth as wide as it would go, teeth exposed, letting the wind fill my cheeks. I kept it that way until all of my spit had dried and I had to duck down behind the windscreen so I could unpeel my lips from my gums.

Only fifteen kilometres from the fishing ramp, our destination was a collection of eighteen white-sand islets called the Keppel Bay islands. They were surrounded by reefs teeming with blue lip, coral trout and red emperor fish.

Once the first hump of land was in sight, Dad slowed the boat. Though it had just inched over the edge of the earth, the sun had already fried the last hints of cool from the air. Without the wind, the heat reflecting up off the ocean felt like a breath.

To protect his arms from the sun, Dad rolled down the sleeves of the army shirt he always wore when he went fishing. As the boat chugged slowly along, we put on caps and sunscreen, with fluorescent pink zinc for our noses.

'Where do you think, kids? There or there?' Dad asked.

The three of us argued for a moment before taking a punt on the perfect fishing spot: the one on the left. Once Dad had cut the engine, he moved quickly to the back of the boat and dropped anchor.

With the sudden silencing of the motor, the lapping of the waves against the fibreglass shell became loud. Apart from the tiny blip of a distant island, the world was blue. It was closest to black where the ocean was deepest: a scary abyss where unseen predators waited to drag you to the eye-popping pressure below. But as the water became shallower it moved into the lightest of transparent aquamarines: safe and friendly.

I leaned forward over the edge of the boat. Where we were, the water was more green than blue, and so clear you could see metres down. Sometimes you could even see the fish you were going to catch swimming below, but there were none there today. The calm stillness beneath the surface called me to it, but there was no swimming on fishing days. I sat back on my bench seat as Dad handed out the lines.

Dad used a proper wooden rod with a super long, bendy pole. David had a little black fishing rod called 'Killer' he had been given for his sixth birthday. Mum, Kerstin and I had hand reels.

From the plastic bag at his feet, Dad pulled out partially

thawed yabbies for everyone's hooks and we dropped our lines into the water. We sat in silence, the faint slurp of water against the boat logging the passing of time as we waited for the first bite. Petrol fumes from the outboard motor clung to the air. I blocked my nose to it, breathing through my mouth. Without the rush of distracting wind in my face, I was acutely aware of my stomach rolling back and forth with the gentle rocking of the boat.

Don't think about how grey and slimy the yabbies are. My mouth filled with saliva.

'I've got a bite,' Dad said, and pulled his rod back. It was a blue lip, definitely legal size, so it went into the bucket. Kerstin, David and I crowded around watching it gasp.

This was as fun as fishing got. Sitting quietly, getting slowly more seasick, watching fish die.

After we watched the fish for a while we all sat back down. Then Kerstin got a bite.

She screamed in panic as the line dug into her finger. 'It's cutting me!'

'Just keep pulling it in! Pull it in! Pull! Pull!' Dad yelled as his strong hands crunched on top of hers, helping her to get the line in.

His extra weight unbalanced the boat, and we all gripped a side to stop ourselves sliding into the water.

Kerstin was rigid, making sure her feet didn't move – with hand lines, if you moved your legs you could tangle the line, which would require minutes of tedious undoing – then the fish was out of the water, flapping all over the place.

'Don't drop the sinker!' Dad yelled as she made a grab for the fish.

The sinker was the one-centimetre lead weight that allowed the line to sink quickly without spooking the fish. Dropping the sinker made tangled lines a certainty and nothing annoyed Dad more.

Trying to ignore the chaotic dance of the slimy wet fish bumping against her leg, Kerstin made a grab for the sinker. It dropped to the floor of the boat with a sharp knock.

There was a moment's silence, then Dad spread his legs wide to keep his balance while he hit her.

'How many (*whack*) times have I told you (*whack*) not to drop (*whack*) the sinker?'

The fish was flapping on the floor and the boat was rocking wildly in time to Dad's beating as Kerstin cried and said sorry. My stomach lurched at the added movement, and my pulsing heart urged me to make him stop. *Leave her alone!* I wanted to stand up to him, but there was nowhere to escape when you were trapped on a boat. Putting all of my hatred into my eyes, I prayed he would see it there and know it was for him.

He moved away from her sobs with a snort of disgust and grabbed the fish off the ground, ripping the hook out of its mouth and throwing it in the bucket on top of the other still-gasping one. As he wound the fishing line back on Kerstin's reel he went on and on about how if she had held on to the sinker, this mess never would have happened, and how she should know better than to move her feet, then back to why she shouldn't drop the sinker.

Yes, Dad. All right. We get it. Don't drop the sinker. Shut up now. The boat gradually returned to a more or less level position and everyone was totally still. I looked away from Dad, past the ocean, to the milkier blue of the sky. The only noise was the slap of waves and the crying Kerstin tried to muffle with a cupped hand.

After ten more minutes of gentle rocking there was no way past the fact I was really not feeling well. *Don't think about the fish bucket . . . or the petrol.* I put my hand into the water. It was only about two degrees cooler than the warm air. I needed it to be colder than that if it was going to divert my attention.

Clammy sweat beaded my top lip and I brought my hand back into the boat. Down by my feet a smear of something gooey slowly baked onto the fibreglass floor. I put my focus on the horizon, but its stillness amplified the rocking of my stomach. I looked into the ocean, pretending I was swimming down there, but spit pooled in my mouth.

'Ruth. Are you all right?' Dad asked. 'You look grey.'

Grey like the yabbies. Blood drained from my face and my hands went completely cold. I leaned over the boat and vomited, my stomach heaving again and again.

After I had finished and sat gasping salty air like the fish, Mum rocked the boat as she went over to the esky and got me a drink of orange cordial. The sweetness shot into me, helping me forget the acid in the back of my throat.

'Do you feel better?' Dad asked hopefully.

'A bit.' I sipped more cordial. If history was anything to go by, I would be vomiting again in fifteen minutes. Everyone watched me.

'Right,' Dad said. 'Everyone wind their lines in. Ruth, how would you feel if I dropped you off on an island? I think ten's old enough, don't you?'

'I think that'd be all right, Dad.' My own deserted island out of Dad's reach far away from fish smells and rocking boats. It was the nicest thing Dad had ever done for me. This wasn't just a good day; it was a great day!

As he helped stow everyone's line he turned to me. 'You won't be allowed to go swimming, but at least you won't be sick.'

'That's fine.'

'Can we go too?' David asked.

'No. You need to stay on the boat and fish. We need to catch as much as we can.'

Dad was feeding a family of five on a teacher's salary. Though he loved being out in the boat, in our family, fishing was not just entertainment. We ate deep-fried crumbed fish and hand-cut chips a couple of times a week. I never grew tired of fish and chips. The same could not be said for fishing.

When the boat picked up speed, I gulped down fresh air from the wind pounding my face. My nausea ebbed, but the twist of guilt in my guts remained. It wasn't fair that Kerstin and David would be making up my shortfall on the boat, while I traipsed about on an island. If I were a better person I would say I wasn't abandoning ship unless they could come too.

We zoomed past the biggest island in the archipelago, Great Keppel, where a horde of tourists disembarked from the impressive white ship we had travelled on for the first time last year. But

I would not be getting wrecked on Great Keppel Island today.

Ten minutes later the boat skidded onto a tiny island with a hundred-metre stretch of smooth white sand. Twenty metres beyond the beach the sand gave way to scrappy shrubs growing gradually more sparse as they embedded themselves into an imposing wall of rock.

We all slipped off the side of the boat into the warm water, then onto shore, marring the pristine smoothness of the sand with our footprints. After a few races up and down the shore to claim the land, Mum gave me a sandwich and an apple and tipped out the rest of the coffee from the thermos, rinsed it and filled it with water. She gave me a hug.

'Right,' Dad said. 'Just stay on this main part of the beach. No wandering too far. Don't go into the water above your knees. We'll be back for you in a couple of hours. Right?'

'Okay.'

I watched the boat bouncing over the sparkling water until it was a speck in the distance, trying to hang on to the excitement of lucking out of fishing. When I couldn't see them any more I looked along the shore of the island. My island.

Apart from our footprints, the perfect white sand gave no hint of how long it had been since anyone had stood here. I had never felt more alone. I had never *been* more alone! My heart fluttered at the light rustle of wind through the scrubby trees up on the hill behind me.

I dug my toe into the wet sand near where the tiny waves lapped the shore. All alone. Deserted on an island. Except for my family, no one knew I was here. What if they didn't come back?

What if this was some Hansel and Gretel scheme to get me off the boat so they could leave me to die here? What if the boat exploded and everyone died and they didn't bother looking for me because they thought I had been eaten by a shark?

I ground the heel of my foot into the hole I'd made. It was too late now to say that I was too scared, too young. There was no one to hear it. I tried to remember how happy I was not to be on the boat, but the wind picked up, making the hollow echoing ooo sound of a ghost. My heart thudded. Don't be silly. There were no such things as ghosts.

I put my food in the shade of the palm tree down the shore, then collected sticks into a little pile in case I had to make an SOS sign on the beach like they did in movies. Each time my heart pumped fear, I looked to the vastness of the ocean for support.

Diamonds danced on the waves, so dazzling they hurt my eyes. Small waves roared back, then spewed forth foamy soft drink that fizzed tiny bubbles into the air. Back. Forth. Back. Forth. I was not alone as long as the ocean breathed beside me.

I wandered up and down the island looking for driftwood, seaweed and shells, but even without competition from other human scavengers, pickings were pretty slim.

Sitting close to the waves, I scooped watery sand and dripped wormy sculptures, suspended in animation at the exact moment where all the water drained away and the sand could finally hold its form. As I piled worm on top of worm a sandcastle took shape.

Though I assumed the posture of a happy girl at play on the shore, all the while I held back the thought. *They're not coming back.*

Once my sandcastle was as tall as the tops of my knees I collected drier sand to sprinkle on top like sugar, then decorated it with seaweed and shell fragments. Just as I laid a driftwood bridge over my moat, the faint buzz of an engine cut across the rhythmic swoosh of the tiny waves.

I rushed to the water, eyes trained on the dot making the sound. It was definitely a boat. White like ours. As it grew larger I made out a flash of green. Our boat had green. The droning grew louder. It was definitely heading this way. The closer it got, the more my twisted insides unravelled, so by the time they pulled onto shore I was so loose with relief I was jumping up and down and flapping my hands.

Now that I knew I had not been forgotten, I rewrote the day to tell my brother and sister. It had been great playing on the island. So much fun. Next time, though, we would have to find a way to make sure they got to stay with me.

NORMAL LOLLIES

I hesitated on the steps of the bus taking us to school camp, deliberating where to sit. Since my best friend had moved away I was never sure where I belonged. I spent a lot more time by myself at school.

But there was no hiding your lack of friends on school camp. I shuffled clumsily past the legs sprawled in the aisle and looked out of the corner of my eye for spare seats.

'Can I sit here?' I asked a pretty, dark-haired girl called Cathy who sometimes bought me a one-cent Jatz cracker with Vegemite from the tuckshop.

'Sorry, I'm saving it for Cilla.' Her face was apologetic.

'That's all right.' I smiled and waved her away like she was the first of my many options, then kept slowly making my way down the bus.

A boy with sandy hair was pushed into me by his friend, knocking me onto the lap of the tallest boy in the class. He shoved me off him, back into the aisle. 'Watch it.'

My heart thumped in instant anger. 'I was watching it. *He* pushed me.' I pointed at the sandy-haired boy, who was now laughing at me with his mate. 'I didn't land on you on purpose.'

'Yeah, well, watch where you're going next time.' His thin lips turned down into a tough-guy frown and his eyes shoved anger into mine.

'Yeah, well, tell him not to shove me.'

'Or what?' A smirk spread underneath his long nose, which twisted to the left.

'Just don't.' I walked past him. I didn't know why I was going on camp. I should have said I was sick. Nobody wanted me here.

A couple of seats ahead, a girl called Kerrie put her hand in the air, calling over the top of the noise. 'Hey, Ruth. This seat's free. You can sit here if you want.'

I smiled in relief and dropped into the chair beside her.

'Thanks,' I said.

'No problem.' Kerrie was the neatest writer in the whole class. She was wearing a cream-coloured skirt and white top without a crease or a wrinkle or loose thread anywhere. Her long, pale hair was held back with a hair tie and finished off with a navy bow that brought out the crisp blue of her eyes.

I was wearing some red-and-yellow tropical print shorts with an elasticised waistband Mum had made. Though they had been perfectly ironed this morning, the heat had helped to crease them to the point where they looked like they had been pulled from the bottom of the laundry pile. My white polo shirt had a brown stain on the pocket.

My hair had a few streaks of blonde, but its colour was best described as mouse brown. My eyes were also brown, and all the time I spent at the beach meant my skin was brown as well. I was one big tonal variation of the most boring colour ever invented.

I longed to be blonde-haired, blue-eyed and capable of keeping white clothes clean.

As we talked about how exciting it was to be going away on camp, I reached into my knapsack for the bag of lollies I had painstakingly chosen from the man at the corner shop yesterday.

'Would you like a lolly?' I asked Kerrie.

The large white paper bag I held was full to bursting with caramel swirls, racing cars, pineapples, cobbers, ripe raspberries, snakes, strawberries-and-cream and freckles. Unfortunately, the heat of the day had not been kind to them. All of the chocolate lollies had melted into the chewy jubes and the white paper bag was now covered in big, greasy spots.

Kerrie's mouth dropped open slightly as she took in the globbed-together mess inside the crumpled packet. 'Umm, no thanks. I've brought my own.' She grabbed an unopened packet of columbines from her bag, quietly unsealed the plastic packet, removed a perfect circle of caramel from its pink foil wrapper and popped it in her mouth.

My throat felt tight and narrow and for an awful moment I was scared I might cry. It was rare for me to have anything to share that other people might actually be interested in. I had been looking forward to having something to offer for once.

It's just stupid lollies. It doesn't mean anything. I dislodged a blue racing car from the top of the pile and shoved it into my mouth.

Keeping my eyes on the grey-uniformed bus driver tossing sleeping bags and luggage into the storage compartment under the bus, for some reason Dad's disastrous birthday dinner sprang to mind.

It had been great fun preparing everything and thinking about Dad enjoying it. But the whole meal he couldn't let go of the spilled wax. He kept bringing it up and bringing it up, pounding Mum over the head with it as we all sat there in silence.

It felt like this stupid bag of lollies. Yesterday I'd had a great time agonising over my selection, picturing a crowd of people wanting to share them with me, laughing and patting me on the back.

The perfect packet of shining blue-and-pink packages resting gently on Kerrie's lap made me see what an idiot I had been. I should have bought a normal packet of lollies. That's what people wanted. Normal lollies.

Being careful not to let the over-full packet lose any of its contents, I reached down and grabbed my knapsack, putting the stained package inside so no one else would see the deformed mess I had brought with me.

Though my stomach felt shrivelled, I shovelled lollies into my mouth, smiling whenever Kerrie said something. Hopefully by the time we got to camp I would have gotten rid of the evidence.

The Sunday after I returned home, David and I were cackling with laughter at the mess we had made of each other's face.

Standing on opposite sides of the bench underneath the wall phone, we had progressed from a game of noughts-and-crosses to scribbling bold streaks of lead pencil onto the paper and smudging it onto our fingers. From there we had turned each other's face tribal with dots of grey.

At the sound of Dad's truck returning home from touchy

footy, I was struck by the idea that this was exactly the kind of thing that would show him we could be as mischievous and crazy as he had been as a kid.

'We should show Dad. He'll think this is so funny,' I said.

'Yeah, he'll love this,' David said.

We raced downstairs, pushing each other to be the first to find him. Dad stood next to Mum as she hung clothes on the line. Still jostling each other, we raced up to him, shouting.

'Look at us! Look at us! Look what we did.' David's huge white-toothed smile was made more hilarious by the grey and I imagined my face looking the same and laughed even harder.

Too late I saw Dad's face, full of tight bones and impatient ticks. I stopped the second it registered, but his fist was already back. With deliberate efficiency, he extinguished the joy of the moment. Three punches each for David and me.

'Don't go making a mess! Get upstairs and clean everything up exactly how you found it.'

It was all over quickly: the rush of shock, the injection of pain. But this time there were no tears, just slumped shoulders as we headed upstairs in silence.

Slipping into the cramped bathroom at the top of the stairs we pulled off our tops to compare bruises.

'My lump's bigger than yours.' The reddened flesh of David's upper arm had swollen enough that his young boy's body looked like it had sprouted a shoulder muscle. I pulled my arm out. Though it was red and mottled and soon to be a bruise, it wasn't anywhere near as big as David's. It felt like he had been punished more than me, which wasn't fair, especially since the whole thing had been my idea.

'Sorry I said to go down there. I thought he'd think it was funny,' I said.

'Don't worry about it. I thought he'd think it was funny too.'

Another attempt to win Dad's love. Another fail.

We put our tops back on, then slid the door back, checking to make sure Dad wasn't in sight before returning to the scene of the crime.

Halfway through paving the backyard later that month, we were making a family outing of driving over to one of Dad's mates' houses to pick up some tools he needed. A long cattle train kept us waiting behind the boom gate, clickety-clacking at a snail's pace as it wafted grass and manure smells into the hot air blowing through our open windows.

Lindy Chamberlain had just been released from prison and everyone was talking about how it looked like she had been innocent all along. Even the kids at school had strong opinions on whether she was guilty or innocent. It wasn't often I heard Mum and Dad discuss anything other than mundane domestic matters, but even they were talking about the case.

'This whole thing has been such a debacle. Just because the woman didn't cry. Why would —'

'— they have put her in jail?' Mum nodded vigorously as if to claim Dad's sentence as her own.

My toes scrunched at Dad's terse snort of air.

'No, Barbara. I wasn't going to say that. I was going to say why would someone go camping if they were going to kill their baby?'

This was the third snort since their conversation had begun – the third time Mum had interrupted him. Dad fidgeted in his seat, making the vinyl squeak. The noise shot a flutter of panic through my bowel. I pulled a strip of skin off my lip with my teeth as I watched his hands flex on the steering wheel. I couldn't see his face clearly but I imagined lips hinting at a sneer.

They were both silent for a moment, focused on the carriages slowly rolling by.

Mum's compulsion to finish Dad's sentences was an ongoing issue in their relationship. Dad was sure it was a sign there was something wrong with Mum's hearing so he had recently made Mum have her ears tested. Though she was sure she didn't need them, she now wore hearing aids.

I thought the problem was more likely that Mum was too terrified to have thoughts of her own. The only thing she dared to offer was what she imagined Dad's next words to be.

I put my hand on the back of her chair, trying to silently communicate with her. *Just let him talk, Mum. Don't say anything until he is done.*

After a few more minutes listening to the rhythm of the slow-moving train, Dad started up again. 'Yeah. It's a bloody shame she got locked up in jail. People were so sure she'd done it. They didn't even —'

'— look for the clothes properly.' Again the nod, as if she were making a point and agreeing at the same time.

'No, Barbara!' he shouted. 'That's not what I was going to say. If you'd just bloody well listen, instead of always finishing my sentences, you might actually know what I thought, instead of just thinking you know. Why don't you turn up your hearing aid? It might help.'

Mum sat back in her seat, silent. I sat back too, making my body completely rigid so Dad couldn't read the thoughts I was sending Mum, letting her know I was on her side.

As the boom gate finally lifted and the car moved forward I added 'Don't finish Dad's sentences' to the growing list of things I wasn't allowed to do.

PERFECT PERSON

'Barbara, I really think it's time you got a job.' Dad looked up from his paper over to where Mum was dipping fish into the milk and egg mixture before handing it to me. Goo from rolling the wet fish in the plate of breadcrumbs had made balls on the ends of my fingers.

This conversation had been cropping up more and more of late. Mum made eye contact with Dad for a long moment. When she spoke, her voice sounded strained. 'I've been trying to find something, Doug. I don't know what to do. Someone still has to be here for the kids when they get home.' She dipped another fish fillet and passed it to me. 'It's been a long time since I've worked, you know.'

'You don't have to tell me that.' His rolling eyes filled his forehead with lines. 'You're being fussy. It doesn't matter what job you get; any job will do. I'm working two jobs to support this family. I think you should do your bit as well.'

His lips went stiff and his head shook slightly as his face moved into the shape that meant: *Why is everyone so stupid? Can nobody figure these things out for themselves?* Then he returned to his paper.

After a few more minutes he pushed the rubber stoppers of his chair back in a series of shuddering jerks. 'Can I have a cup of coffee, love?' He carried the paper into the lounge room.

Mum moved to the sink and rubbed water back and forth over her hands fast enough to splash water onto the red tiles Dad had put up two weeks ago. 'Yes, your majesty. That's right. I just sit around on my arse all day doing nothing. You're the only one who does any work in this house.'

I burst out laughing. Mum rarely got mad at Dad. When she did, it felt like a victory for my team. She turned quickly, catching my eye then smiling as she dried her hands on the blue-checked tea towel. 'Shh. Don't let him hear you. And don't tell him I said anything.' She winked to show me it was our secret.

'I promise I won't say anything,' I whispered back. I loved the hint of a smile that stayed around her lips as she pressed the button down and waited for the kettle to boil.

A couple of months later, I was standing in the spot where Dad had dragged me, surveying the cause of the latest trouble. My room. For once I agreed with him. It was an absolute pigsty.

Nearly every inch of the brown-and-beige carpet was covered in clothes, scraps of paper and half-started bits of art. My bed was unmade, with the sheets pulling away from the mattress. Even underneath my bed, where I usually shoved things when I 'tidied up', was spilling its secrets into the open. I was not allowed to go anywhere, or do anything, until this room was absolutely spotless.

My fingers unconsciously worked their way down to the

slightly smoother texture on my stomach, where the blisters from the tea spill had wept and popped their way down to a cluster of fading brown circles. I hadn't done a very good job of keeping them hidden. Mum had found them during a bath a few days after the incident and asked how they got there. I was forced to tell her I had spilled tea on my stomach.

'Why didn't you come and get me?' she asked. I didn't know how to answer.

Touching the burns had become a habit that was hard to break.

I stood in the doorway for a moment longer, looking at the bright beam of light coming through the small hole in the blind, once white, now yellow at the edges. The dust in the air made the light seem solid. Or was it the dust? Maybe this was not normal light. Maybe this was the Light of God.

The shaft came to rest on my yellow shirt with the ruffled sleeves and rainbow piping. I bent down and picked it up. Maybe God had shone His light on that top as some sort of sign and if I followed His will He would be so pleased He would magic all the rest of the clothes away to say thanks.

When no miracle of cleaning took place, I put the shirt on my bed and sat down beside it to do a furtive bruise check. Three purplish circles rimmed with red were coming up on the underside of my arm – an exact match for Dad's fingers.

The springs creaked as I leaned forward and picked up a pair of blue shorts Mum had made on her old sewing machine.

Sitting upright again, my head spun with the remainders of the achy, rattled feeling from when Dad had shook me. He had said nothing else got through to me, and I always had a smart-arse answer for why I couldn't do something, and he didn't know how else to make me listen to him. I'd wanted to tell him shaking my head wouldn't make it any easier for me to hear him, but I'd figured that would fall into the smart-arse category, so I had kept quiet.

I looked around with a growing sense of overwhelm at the sheer volume of things I had to tidy up. I briefly thought about shoving every piece of clothing into the washing basket and dealing with it when it came back folded by Mum, but last time I had done that she had got really mad at me. Instead, I bent down and picked up a sock and a pair of tracksuit pants. As I added them to the shirt and shorts, I was filled with such a profound tiredness I had to lie down, just for a moment, to get my strength up.

I was sick of Dad's moods. 'Walking on eggshells' didn't cover it. If you stepped on an eggshell, all that happened was the eggshell broke. This was walking on landmines. Make a wrong move and the world exploded.

He thought he was so smart, but half the time he didn't even make sense. When he was in a good mood he liked us cheeky, to remind him of himself when he was a kid. On those days I would be a smart-arse and he would laugh. The next day, like today, I would do exactly the same thing and he would hit me.

It was my flesh on the line every day. I was sure I had thought about his rules for a lot longer than he had. If he actually wrote down each and every thing he expected from us, he would see how impossible it was to do what he wanted.

I kept one ear on the hallway as I made a little pillow from my clothes. These were the current rules of the house as best as I could understand them.

1. Do what Dad says within five seconds.
2. If you can't do it within five seconds, immediately acknowledge the request verbally, drop whatever you are doing and act on it as soon as possible.
3. If Dad calls your name, answer him with 'Coming' and start running to him immediately.
4. If you are asleep, be ready to wake up the second Dad tells you to.
5. Don't wake Dad up when he is sleeping.
6. If Dad hits you, don't cry or he will give you something to cry about.
7. Don't argue back even if Dad is completely wrong; but never take shit from dickheads – stand up for yourself.
8. If you hurt yourself you were probably doing something stupid so you deserve it.
9. Don't fight with your brother and sister, and never hit them, or else Dad will knock your heads together for being stupid.
10. Only stupid people spill things so don't be stupid, except if Dad does it then it is no big deal.
11. Don't go around thinking you are good at anything because there are at least one hundred more things you are hopeless at, so it cancels the good things out.
12. Getting As doesn't mean you are smart; remembering to bring your lunchbox home makes you smart.

13. If you are sick don't whinge about it because no one is interested.
14. If you are going to try something, even if it is your first attempt, you'd better look pretty competent at it straight away or Dad might have to 'help' you.
15. If you make a mistake, expect to be punished.
16. If you try to cover up your mistake, expect to be punished.
17. If you admit your mistake, expect to be punished.
18. Be quiet, or noisy, depending on what Dad wants.
19. Look people in the eye and be confident, but don't show off.
20. Don't be meek and frightened, unless that's what Dad wants.
21. Be up for a bit of mischief, unless Dad wants you quiet and obedient.
22. Whatever you do, when you are fishing, don't drop the sinker in the boat.

Oh yeah, I almost forgot the latest one.

23. Don't finish Dad's sentences or he will think you are deaf as well as dumb.

Thinking of this list made my whole body heavy; sleep seemed unavoidable. I would happily sleep fourteen hours every day, given the chance. I closed my eyes and pulled a corner of the blanket over my arm, snuggling down into the softness of the bed. Just as my mind was wandering down the dark corridor before it faded to black, the floorboard outside my room creaked.

I was immediately on my feet, sending flying the few clothes I had picked up. With hammering heart I went into overdrive, picking up handfuls of clothes and throwing them on the bed. When a shadow fell into the room as someone stood in the doorway, I didn't look up, acting as if I was so absorbed in my task I couldn't be distracted.

'How's it going in here?' Mum asked.

Both my heart and my pretend cleaning frenzy slowed at the sound of her voice. 'All right.'

In her arms she was carrying freshly washed and folded lime-green flannelette sheets and a purple woollen blanket.

'I thought we could change your sheets as well,' she said.

Inwardly I groaned. Not more work.

'I'll give you a hand if you want,' she said. I ran over and gave her a hug. I loved her so much.

With her help it was much easier to put everything away. We dusted and vacuumed and changed the bedding. By the end of it, the room looked much better. In fact it looked good enough that I wished someone would drop by my house so I could casually invite them in to see it.

'My,' they would say, 'don't you keep your room clean.'

'Oh, this is how it always is,' I would reply. 'I don't like mess.'

I surveyed the new room order and felt good and pure and in control. I promised myself I would keep it this way from now on.

Walking to the end of my bed, I pulled a piece of paper off the recently neatened stack, artfully placed at right angles to my school bag, and grabbed a pen from the old beetroot tin covered in stickers on my desk. I sat on the edge of my bed to write a list: the perfect list would turn me into the perfect person.

I immediately made a hole in the paper and stabbed myself in the leg. Not a great start. I put the paper into the wastepaper basket and grabbed another piece off the pile, and a book to rest it on. That was what perfect people would do. If they made mistakes (rarely), they simply learned from them and promised never to make the same error again.

I breathed the way a perfect person would, calmly and slowly, and used my neatest handwriting to write a list.

1. Get out of bed
2. Make bed
3. Eat breakfast
4. Get dressed
5. Do hair
6. Go to school
7. Don't forget lunchbox

I had already been far from perfect today so my list would start tomorrow. Then tomorrow, and every day after that, I would do everything right, and I would never get in trouble, ever again.

NEVER ENOUGH

I have heard war described as a conflict between opposing wills. That description seemed to apply to the war I waged against my father too. Over the years I became capable of contorting myself into the unusual shapes required to meet his exacting standards. Each time I held form, my body triumphed. I grew to relish the feeling of strength from my coiled muscles as I kept myself on a line straighter and narrower. He wanted to control me. I wanted to prove to him that I could control myself.

Because the ground around Dad was always shifting, my efforts didn't mean I avoided punishment. But they did mean I did not have to feel soft or vulnerable. I told myself fear would not control me and searched for ways to prove to myself I was the one who held the power.

After I got my degree in science, I decided to test my courage by doing the scariest thing I could imagine: following my dream of becoming an actor. Once and for all I wanted to prove to myself that I was free to do what I wanted and be who I wanted. Finally, there was no one to stop me.

But of course, lots of people did stop me. Armed with head shots and an agent, I started auditioning. Each time I failed to get a part, I crumpled in despair. When I dusted myself off, I looked around for the things I could control. I took more classes, ate less, exercised more. Falling to my knees and building myself back up had become such a well-worn groove, it was hard to conceive of living any other way. Whenever I failed I was at the mercy of the voice that had been with me for nearly as long as I had been alive. It was a Frankenstein's monster cobbled from my father at his worst, my imaginings of what he, and every other person in the universe, really thought about me, and my desire to correct my every failing to avoid punishment.

Of course they don't want me. I am disgusting. I eat too much. Drink too much. Don't exercise enough. Want it too much. I am too much. But not enough. Never. Ever. Enough.

After eight years of waitressing and temping to subsidise bit-parts on television and advertisements, I finally let go of the dream. My failure felt like proof that Dad was right. I was not special. I did not deserve to be noticed. I had tried to prove I was worth something, but all I had done was confirm I was worth nothing.

I pounded myself with my nothingness, regretting the years I could have been achieving something in a different career. Though it hurt, I had always preferred delivering my own punishment to having someone else do it for me. At least then I controlled when it happened and wasn't taken by surprise.

I kept a vigil, scouting ahead, never leaving room for others to point out anything bad about myself. I catalogued my faults so thoroughly that no matter what insult someone threw at me, I could laugh in their face. 'You think I don't know how shit I am? Ha ha ha!' But the thing was, most people didn't insult me or tell me how bad I was. Just me.

Though it often did more harm than good, I couldn't let go of my need for control. When everyone else abandoned me, it remained, giving me something to cling to as the world around me crumbled. Control kept me together, so I didn't fall apart.

But once I had my own family, I saw how much it ruled my life. When my kids made mistakes the voice in my head told me to pounce, to help them get it right, because mistakes were not safe, and punishment was sure to follow. When they screamed or cried for reasons I couldn't comprehend, the crashing agitation in my cells screamed at me to shut them down, shut them up, do what it took to make them stop, so I didn't have to feel so wound up. I flashed back over and over in my head to the way Dad was with me, finally understanding how crazy it must have driven him to have so much unpredictability and chaos all around him.

As I tried to make sense of Dad's war, I began to wonder at what stage his need for control started to intensify. Was it the moment his number had come up, when he realised he had lost autonomy over his own life? When he discovered the army had no intention of using his skills as part of the war effort, that it was only his body they sought?

Or did his need for control harden later, when he came to understand the fog and uncertainty of war, after he saw lives risked on dubious information and best guesses? Was it when he helplessly watched his best friend die? Did he think that if only he, or someone, had done something better, stronger, faster, things might have turned out differently?

After the constant shocks of war, it was little wonder he came back with a need to keep the things he could, including his wife and children, under control. I didn't want to repeat his mistakes. I didn't want to control my children the way I had been controlled. But it was so hard.

The times I slipped, lost patience, took over, ripped things from their hands and said 'Just let me do it' filled me with remorse. I remembered what it felt like as a child to know what I was meant to do, to lack the necessary skill, but to not even be given a chance to fail so that one day I might succeed. How could I do it to them? Always in the back of my mind a question burned. Was this it? Was this the moment I handed down the legacy and scarred them for life?

ACCIDENTAL GIRLFRIEND

As I headed up the back stairs after the last day of school before the Easter break, my feet dragged. For the last few weeks, I had done an excellent job of completing my list. I hadn't been in any further trouble with Dad. I had remembered to bring my lunchbox home every day. I'd even had one night where I went to sleep in a perfectly made bed and moved so little I didn't have to remake it in the morning. It felt like I had finally found a way to get it right.

But tonight I was going to be working a new list: the one I ticked off to tell me what to take camping. We would be leaving in the morning.

As I was grabbing some cordial out of the fridge I noticed Mum, Kerstin and David all sitting around the kitchen table with solemn looks on their faces.

'What?' I asked.

'Ruth, your dad's been in a serious accident,' Mum said.

'What sort of accident?'

'On his motorbike. A man was driving drunk and he ran through a stop sign and smashed into Dad's leg.' She flicked open the lid of the blue cigarette box, lit up and blew smoke in my direction. 'We were just waiting for you to get home. We're going to see him at the hospital.'

I loved hospitals. All the buttons to press and elevators to ride in. The food on special trays with those sections, as if it was against hospital regulations for meat to touch vegetable. And you got to watch TV in bed. I wished I was in hospital. Focus. I should be thinking about Dad. 'Is Dad all right?'

'I think so, but I haven't seen him yet so we have to go.'

'Can I get changed?' I thought I might best demonstrate the level of my concern by wearing an appropriately serious dress, shoe and handbag combination.

'No. We have to go right now.' Already walking out of the kitchen and down the back stairs, she turned back and said urgently, 'Come on!'

I dropped the school bag from my back onto the floor.

'Can I have something to eat from a vending machine when I get there?' I called after her.

'No. Just grab an apple.' Her voice floated off into nothing as she disappeared under the house.

I wanted to press the point. Hospitals had great vending machines and I had only ever eaten from them two times before, but Mum's face had been a mass of worry lines so I thought it might not be appropriate.

It was five minutes to the hospital from our place – all hills. At the top of the third peak something occurred to me.

'Mum. Are we still going camping?'

'No, Ruth. We can't go camping. This is a very serious accident. Your dad is going to have his leg in plaster with pins sticking out of it. He'll be stuck in bed for a long time. I don't want to hear you going on about camping. You need to show Dad how sorry you are for him, okay?'

'Okay.' I worked hard to control the smile that wanted to spring out of my lips. I knew it was terrible Dad was in hospital, but I was so relieved not to be going camping I felt like dancing. No setting up the tent! And we never got to spend holidays mooching around the house. I wondered how soon I could call a friend to ask if I could have a sleepover.

As we pulled into the hospital my guilt kicked in. I had always suspected I was an evil, selfish person. The fact that I was celebrating not going camping while Dad lay helpless in hospital proved beyond doubt my suspicions were correct.

With Dad in hospital, the first week of the holidays was as relaxing as I had hoped, mostly spent in the garden playing games with the chickens. I forced their beaks into the cups of cordial 'tea' I prepared, rode to the shops with them balanced on the handlebars of my bike and tried unsuccessfully to teach them to sit. In the background, I noticed one of Dad's students, a massive-breasted girl with stick-thin legs called Kylie, had upped her already regular visits to daily.

'She just started showing up. I don't know how to get rid of her,' Mum had told me a couple of months ago when I asked why Kylie came around to our house all the time.

One day, I was lying on the floor of the lounge room watching a *Calamity Jane* rerun while Kylie had a whispered conversation with Kerstin at the dining room table.

'Did you know your dad has a girlfriend?' The question rang out over the top of the jaunty musical number on the screen.

My breath caught. Where was Mum? Was she in the house? I kept my eyes locked onto the TV so Kerstin wouldn't know I was eavesdropping.

'What do you mean?' Kerstin whispered back.

Kylie lowered her voice only marginally so there was no strain for me to hear. 'Everyone knows. He's got a girlfriend.'

'Shh. Don't say anything else,' Kerstin said.

I turned my head to one side so I could see them in my peripheral vision. Kerstin's head flicked up toward me, but I pretended I didn't notice and kept on picking.

'We're just going to my bedroom for a minute, Ruth.' Kerstin pushed her chair back. 'You stay here.'

Once they left I let myself be swept back into the movie.

When Dad returned home, hobbling around on his crutches, I tried to attach the word 'girlfriend' to him, but the picture my mind conjured made no sense. Men had wives; boys had girlfriends.

As weeks rolled into months, and nothing further was said, the whole conversation seemed more and more unlikely. I let the idea slip away into the world of waking dreams.

BEST HOLIDAY EVER

By the Christmas holidays, Dad was off crutches and his walking had returned pretty much to normal. To celebrate, he took us camping at the Cotton Tree Caravan Park in Maroochydore.

One hundred kilometres north of Brisbane, the campsite had fancy bitumen roads and lots more caravans and cabins than where we normally stayed. But it wasn't until we got out of the car and started unloading that I really got excited about staying there.

'You kids can just go down the beach. I'll set the tent up with Mum.'

Was he really saying we didn't have to help set up the tent? None of us could quite believe it, so we all remained where we were, waiting for him to explain.

'Go on. Go to the beach and have a look around. Stay together and don't come back for at least an hour. Actually, don't come back until 3.30.'

I looked down at my latest birthday present: a gold watch with a tiny face and a fake diamond for the twelve. It was only a bit past one.

We scrambled around in bags finding togs and towels, then took off in case he changed his mind. Two minutes' walk away we found the thumping surf of Maroochydore beach, an exciting contrast to the sad little ripples produced by the ocean at Emu Park.

The water was cooler as well, but we were unwilling to face the pounding of the waves without parents there to watch us. Instead we made our way to a calm stretch of water called the Maroochy River, shallow enough that it came pre-warmed by the sun.

When we made our way back to the tent, it was completely set up, our beds made. I wished camping could be like this all the time.

'Where's Mum?' I moved over to test my bed.

'She's gone to the toilet.' Dad was rifling through the esky, getting out some cheese.

'What're you doing?' I asked. Though Dad was a better cook than Mum, and even taught breadmaking, in addition to fitting and turning, to students at TAFE, he rarely prepared food for us.

'I thought you might want a snack.' He sliced the cheese and tipped out some crackers. We ate in silence, trying to process the topsy-turvy way the holiday was unfolding.

'I'm going to the toilet,' I told Dad. Mum still had not returned and I wanted to make sure she really was where he said she was.

I rounded the path to the cement toilet block. On the inside they were much larger and cleaner than our usual campground toilets, with Laminex bench tops and lots of mirrors. Someone sniffed from behind a closed toilet door. I bent down and saw Mum's feet.

'Mum?'

After a small cough and a blow of the nose she spoke with a thick, garbled voice. 'Yes?'

'Are you all right, Mum?'

'Yeah. I've got a bit of a cold. That's all. Go back to the tent.'

She hadn't had a cold on the way down here.

'You sure, Mum?'

'Please just go.'

I headed back to the tent.

'Mum isn't feeling very well,' I told Kerstin and David.

'Just leave her alone.' Dad came up close to my face and grabbed my arm. 'Don't go back to the toilets. Leave her be. If I hear you've been there annoying her, you're going to be in big trouble, hear me?'

'Yes.' It wasn't hard to hear when someone was yelling right in your face.

Mum came back to the tent at around dinner time.

'Dad bought us fish and chips!' I ran over to give her a hug but my feet slowed and my arms dropped as I saw her face. Her eyes were swollen nearly shut and her nose was huge and red.

She looked down at the ground as she spoke in a quiet voice. 'That's nice.'

'Are you okay, Mum? Have you been crying?' Sometimes when I cried, my whole face swelled up and looked the way hers did now. But I had never seen Mum cry, not more than a few tears. Could grown-ups cry the same way kids did? I wasn't sure.

Dad came over and grabbed my arm, spinning me around. 'What did I tell you? Leave your mother alone.'

'No!' Mum shouted at him. 'Ruth's trying to be nice to me. Don't you stop her. She can give me a hug if she wants to.'

I looked from Mum to Dad, then back to Mum again. Her puffed-up eyes were flashing fire, daring Dad to do something. He fell back into the shadows and looked down at the ground like a scolded little boy. It was like being in the twilight zone. I gave Mum a hug and shot Dad a dirty look. Whatever had happened, I was on Mum's side.

While Mum spent the entire holiday holed up in the toilets, and Dad stayed at the tent staring into the distance, we spent all day, every day, at the beach, coming back only when it was time to eat.

Dad gave us money to buy *Footrot Flats* and *Archie* comics. He gave us money to buy drinks. He sent us out at night to the movies by ourselves. Every time we returned to the tent he sent us out again with cash and instructions to stay away. We had never seen as much money or been given as much freedom. Apart from my constant worry about Mum, it was one of the best holidays I'd ever had.

NORMAL, HAPPY LIFE

After we got back from the trip I lay in bed, listening until my body broke out in a sweat.

Slivers of angry whispers exchanged by Mum and Dad floated from the dining room table, weaving in and out of the chorus of the hundreds of frogs who hammered the silence from the jungle of our yard each night.

'— those kids . . .'

Croak, croak, croak, croak, croak.

'— problem with you . . .'

Croak, croak, croak, croak, croak.

'— marriage . . .'

I waited impatiently for the moment of perfect synchronisation, when, as one, the frogs suddenly stopped, leaving the air tumbling in heavy silence. In the pause I gulped down whispers, trying to piece together what was going on.

After a week I was pretty sure I knew what they were saying. After a month it was like listening to the same old scratched record night after night.

Mum: It was my idea to get the mini-mix truck; you never give me any credit for that.

Dad: That was years ago. That's the problem with you, Barbara, always living in the past.

Mum: At least I tried to make something work for this family.

Dad: Always the 'family', isn't it? You love those kids more than you love me.

Mum: I'm not the one who had an affair with that slut.

Dad: What did you want, Barbara? Our marriage hasn't been right for years.

Mum: What should I have done differently? Tell me.

Dad: I don't want to have to tell you what to do. I want you to do something for yourself instead of always waiting for me to make it happen.

Mum: You don't appreciate anything I do do, all the things I do around the house.

Dad: You should've gone to work when the kids went to school instead of always leaving everything up to me. I'm the one who got you a job.

Mum: Washing boats like a slave.

Dad: You should've got something for yourself then. I just wish you did anything, got a life.

Mum: Everything I do is always wrong so I just stopped trying.

Dad: So, it's back to everything being my fault.

Mum: You don't know what it has been like to live with you since you got back from that bloody war.

Dad: So it's my fault again.

Round and round and round it went. The same things said in nearly exactly the same order every night. Still, I couldn't tune it out or make myself stop listening.

Sick of spinning between boredom and anxiety instead of sleeping, I was so close to going out there and joining in, I had prepared a speech: 'You've said exactly the same thing to each other every night for months. Don't you ever get tired of repeating yourselves? You say this. Then you say that. Then you say this and you say that. Can't you just write it down?

'And by the way, the whispering thing, it's not working. Just yell at each other, would you? We're all awake listening to you anyway. Yelling would be blessed relief. At least then we wouldn't have to keep straining to hear you!'

But I never did get out of bed, and eventually the whispering stopped.

Kerstin, David and I were ransacking the kitchen for afternoon tea a few months after it had all gone quiet, when Mum walked in.

'There's nothing to —' I took in her serious, crumpled face. 'Are you all right?'

Kerstin and David froze at the question and turned to face us.

'There's something you kids need to know.' Her voice was barely more than a whisper. As she leaned against the kitchen table, we huddled around her and gave her our full attention. 'Your dad's going away. He's probably not coming back.' She delivered this last sentence without looking any of us in the eye.

Since the whispering had started, I had given serious thought to what might happen, including Dad leaving. But the lack of further fighting or any other definitive action had lulled me into thinking their arguments had been a temporary glitch in their marriage. The shock of Mum's words felt like ice water on my hot skin.

No one moved or said anything in response. I picked at the plastic coating peeling away from the handle of the chair as the words echoed around in my head, looking for somewhere solid to land. *Dad is going away and not coming back. Dad is going away and not coming back.*

Time moved in slow motion and hour-long seconds ticked by without anyone speaking. Still not knowing how to respond, I looked to Mum. She was staring at the table, squeezing her hands so tight they looked strangled. On my left, Kerstin's eyes were welling up with tears. That was probably the right thing to do, but I didn't feeling like crying.

Though he was eight years old, at that moment David's huge bewildered eyes reminded me of how he had looked as a toddler: so young and vulnerable. I wanted to squeeze him, but nobody else was moving, so I kept myself still.

Keeping my face neutral and eyes downcast, I traced the stiff edge of my royal-blue pleated sports skirt with pinched fingers.

There was something about the silent intensity and drama of our circle that made me want to laugh, but I knew that was the wrong thing to do. I stared at the ground and the words kept running through my head. *Dad is going away and not coming back. Dad is going away and not coming back.* As the rhythm of the words filtered through my body, they transformed into a song: 'Ding-Dong! The Witch is Dead . . .'

I knew it meant I was a complete bitch, but I finally realised how I felt. I felt like dancing. Dad was going away and not coming back! He was going to be out of my life for good. No more tiptoeing around the house or being hit for stupid reasons. Just a relaxing, normal, happy life. I couldn't wait.

THE BOMB

In the hour between Mum telling us Dad was leaving and the sound of Dad's truck pulling into the driveway, nobody spoke about the unfolding events. Mum began making noises in the kitchen and we three stayed close, not interacting as we made half-hearted attempts to play or read. But we all knew what we were really doing. Waiting to see what would happen next.

At the sound of the truck coming up the driveway, everyone's game stopped. As the roar of the truck engine silenced, we tensed for the sound of Dad's foot on the wonky bottom step. Still no one moved.

My heart galloped. Were we meant to know Dad was leaving or was it a secret? If he told me he was going was I meant to act surprised or sad or sorry?

Five minutes passed. I heard movement underneath the house and pressed my ear to the floor. The clang of metal coming from the area where Dad kept his tools. There was a squeak and crunch of heavy rubber twisting on small pebbles. Dad's boat? He must be taking it with him. Of course he was. There was no point in leaving his boat here. He was going away and not coming back.

Something about the boat no longer being here made it feel real, and my heart throbbed with deep and unexpected sadness. I squashed it down. I needed to be strong for Mum. I wouldn't let her see I was upset for even a second.

The noises continued under the house and my heart returned to normal, but we all abandoned the pretence of play as we sat listening.

Fifteen minutes later, Dad's heavy footsteps pounded down the hall. I held my breath. This was it. Something was going to happen. But then he made a turn into his bedroom without looking in our direction.

The cushiony sound of one soft thing landing on another was followed by the clicking of wood and scrape of metal as Dad removed clothes from the hangers in his wardrobe. As the minutes ticked by and the sounds became familiar, my body began to ache from the alert pose I was holding. I slumped to the floor. Waiting.

He walked past our room again without looking in. At ten minutes to seven he called out to us from the lounge room. 'Kids!'

We all ran to his voice, glad something was finally happening to break through the tension.

There were two bags beside him: his khaki army duffel bag with the name CALLUM and the number 1732937 written on it in black permanent marker, and the zip-up blue-and-white sporty-looking bag he took with him when he played squash.

The bags seemed real; but the moment didn't. Was today really and truly the last day Dad would live with us? Could things like this actually happen?

Dad stood awkwardly between the two armchairs on the carpet of the lounge room, still dressed in his work shorts and shirt. His hair looked freshly combed. Had we been meant to brush our hair for this? Whatever 'this' was.

We lined up before him silently, not knowing whether to touch him or say anything. I kept my eyes on his face, trying to read the cues. The sadness and defeat etched deep into his features stabbed at my heart. Dad finally broke the moment by reaching over and giving Kerstin a hug. Then me. Then David. He didn't look at Mum, who was a few metres away, watching the situation unfold from the corner of the dining room.

'Sorry about this. You kids be good for your mother.'

'We will,' Kerstin, David and I chorused in demented sing-song.

He looked at us for another minute, picked up his bags and walked out of the room. No one moved. No one cried. Our faces wore confused smiles.

Hearing the loud creak of the truck door opening, we moved to the kitchen window as one, and watched him load his bags into the front passenger seat of his old Land Rover. He then added a heavy metal toolbox to the tray of his truck.

I expected him to follow suit, leaping into the cab and making a dramatic exit into the sunset, but he disappeared under the house, then returned into view lumbering under the burden of the tent. Oh. That's right. I guess we wouldn't be going camping any more. The thought made me sadder than I would have thought.

Next it was a piece of machinery. Then a large box. Back and forth he went until the rear of his truck started to sink under the weight of all he crammed in. Watching his pile accumulate made my chest flutter. How much stuff did we have? Would there be anything left by the time he was done?

As I felt trapped at my window vigil until his departure was complete, eventually my panic switched to resentment. Take whatever you like, but just go already, would you? You want to leave, so leave!

After one final struggle to attach the trailer and boat, he hopped inside the cab and the engine roared to life. In a sudden rush that felt too quick when at last it happened, he was gone.

Watching his tail-lights disappear up the hill, I felt like laughing, crying and going to sleep all at the same time. This afternoon we had been a family of five. Now Dad had gone away and was not coming back, our number was four. It didn't seem possible.

I turned to Mum to see what would happen next. Maybe this was when we all started crying? Mum's eyes stayed dry.

The silence stretched on, long and exhausting. I finally got up the nerve to break it. 'Mum, can we watch a bit of telly?'

'Okay.' Her voice was so hollow it sounded like she was in a cave. 'How about we just have baked beans on toast for dinner tonight?'

'Sounds good.'

As I sat watching *Sweet and Sour* on ABC, I felt a cool rush of relief calming me. My war was over. Dad had left, but we had just had a normal conversation about dinner. The world had not changed. Everything was going to be okay.

Of course I had no way of knowing that Dad's departure

had thrown a bomb into our family, the timer set to go off in a few short days. My next six years would be spent sifting through the wreckage, and I would never be sure if I was finally on safe ground.

SHAMEFUL SECRET

As I attempted to water the threadbare sticks of the hydrangeas in my front garden, my son made a game of running in and out of the spray. Each time the stream touched his body he shrieked and laughed with full lips and a huge smile of large perfect teeth, just like Dad's.

His full-body delight at the freezing, mid-winter thrill melted my annoyance at not getting to water the drooping plants. I laughed along with him. The next instant the screen door slammed open. My daughter appeared, sniffing out a moment of fun that had not included her. She was naked and next to her brother within a minute, jostling for prime position. 'Spray me! Spray me!'

I attempted to deliver to each of them the same millilitres of spray for the same milliseconds, but soon the idyllic moment descended into tears of *he got, she got more than me*.

Once the kids were dressed and playing again, I went to my room and shucked off my sodden boots. Peeling away my limp white socks I was reminded of something Dad had told me about Vietnam during my childhood. He had talked about how wet it was over there. He described sitting out in the jungle on night watch with rain pouring down on him for hour after hour as 'pretty miserable'.

But it was the story he told me about his skin that I had found the most grossly compelling. He had to put rubber bands around the bottom of his pants so the leeches wouldn't get in as he sloshed his way through constant water. But it would sometimes be weeks before he had a shower. When he finally had a chance to take his pants off, there was a mountain of dead skin trapped in there that fell out in a pile. When he removed his shoes he basically peeled the whole bottom of his feet off as well. 'That hurt a bit,' he said.

The other thing I made him tell me again and again was the story of the time he found a spider in his rations. 'I was so hungry I ate him. He tasted good,' he would say, acting out eating a spider from a pretend dish he was holding, then licking his fingers clean.

'Eeew,' Kerstin, David and I would chorus. 'That's disgusting!'

He would keep pretending to eat from his dish in big chews as he rubbed his stomach in circles. 'Mmm . . . delicious spider.' Then he would slyly move closer to us and begin grabbing at our clothes, pretending to pick spiders off us and eating them as well. We would shriek, running away from him. As soon as he stopped chasing we would all cry out, 'Pick spiders off me! Pick spiders off me!'

I thought about his silence surrounding the war. I was sure he was trying to protect us from knowing what he had suffered. Coming up with stories safe to share with his kids must have been hard, and made all the more difficult after so many years of keeping it to himself.

*

Vietnam has often been described as the 'television war'. People were exposed to warfare in a way never before imagined. They saw graphic footage of explosions, shootings, injuries and dead bodies, and screaming children running away from villages on fire.

Though many people were sympathetic to the experiences of those in the armed forces, a vocal minority turned their horror at the disturbing, ugly reality of war into judgement of the soldiers themselves. It was the voices of the few protesters that jeered and called them baby killers that stayed with many veterans.

The more reading I did, the more it seemed that it wasn't just the protests that kept veterans quiet. The way they were sent into and returned home from the war zone made it hard for them to talk about their experience, even with those who had been there with them.

In most cases in World War II, members of the armed forces fought as a team and were returned to civilian life as a team. The weeks or months they spent travelling home by ship gave them time to begin the process of working through their trauma together. As a rule, these men stayed in touch with others they had served with, and caught up with them during Anzac Day celebrations.

In the Vietnam War it was not common for whole units to be sent at the same time. Though soldiers fought together, it was mostly as a series of small groups. To limit a soldier's exposure to the war, individuals were often despatched on an as-needed basis and returned home exactly one year after they arrived in Vietnam. Each man had his own personal countdown from the time he set foot on Vietnamese soil.

Though some men arrived home on HMAS Sydney and were given parades through the streets of the city as soon as they touched home ground, those who returned by plane were not so lucky. These men, a disparate assortment of soldiers whose tour of duty happened to be up at the same time, had often never met before boarding the plane. Thirty-six hours after they were being shot at in a jungle, they arrived back home to re-enter their lives without acknowledgement or recognition of their service.

Back in the safety of Australia, many men were flooded with guilt about the friends they had left behind. Feeling unwelcomed in Anzac Day marches, afraid to know if some of their mates had died, guilty at the thought that they might have stopped it happening, a large number of Vietnam veterans waited decades before making contact with others in their unit again.

Often those who fought in Vietnam kept their service a secret. The ones who were willing to talk found the overwhelming response from their friends was an intense lack of interest.

From the moment he got back, Ollie felt pressure to act like the war had never happened. 'Two years of my life was interrupted. My friends got married, moved on. When I contacted them, when I started to mention Vietnam, they changed the subject. They didn't want to know, couldn't give a hoot. I couldn't offload on anyone.'

'What about your wife?' I asked him.

'You didn't want to offload on your wife. You didn't want to tell your wife and family about the details of what happened over there. We actually hid and didn't tell people we had been to Vietnam. You lose the friends you have. They move on. You come back to nobody.'

Tim too felt like everyone expected him just to slot back into life without a moment's pause. 'We were stuck in a hellhole while the rest of the world was normal. In Sydney they were eating ice-creams, going to the beach. It was like we stepped out of one room and into the other. Then we stepped out of the hellhole back into that room.'

Mum told me that when people saw Dad after he came back from the war, many of his friends asked him if he had been on holiday. He didn't bother to correct them.

Even when they tried to find their place among other veterans at the RSL, backs were turned. 'You blokes didn't fight a real war,' the older veterans told them.

Ollie shared his experience with me. 'I know I had got withdrawn. I couldn't talk to anyone about what happened, so I decided to go to the RSL. I thought I'd get dressed up in my polyesters [dress uniform]. When I went to go in, the bloke on the door said, "Where are you going?"'

'"I'm going in there," I told him. He said, "We don't recognise Vietnam vets." Well I wasn't going to take that, so I went to walk past him but he put his arm out and stopped me. He said, "You're not going in." I couldn't believe it. I got that mad we ended up in a fight and he threw me out into the street. I got the poos on and I never wore army gear after that.'

I had no idea how to make sense of what he was telling me. What made a 'real' war? I would have thought being ordered around by people in uniform while being shot at, shooting back, with bombs going off and friends dying would have qualified.

Even if older veterans thought the Vietnam War was not a worthy cause, didn't they feel any compassion on a human level? These were still Australian men who had just been through the most frightening experience of their lives. Who other than one who had been to war could understand that?

With every door closed to them, Vietnam veterans shut up, swallowing the shame of a nation. They attempted to slot back into their old lives the way society expected, but they weren't the same men, and the holes they had left behind didn't fit them any more.

'When I first came home I used to get really drunk,' Ollie said. 'They kept a job in my department for me. It was a labouring job with less pay. I didn't get that job back. The guys there I knew had moved on anyway.

'I tried to get my own jobs. I had about twenty jobs in the end. I worked in a car yard, a timber yard, in sales, at a rubber plant. I couldn't really settle down.'

Tim said, 'I couldn't settle back to normality after being through the mill. I drank. I smoked marijuana. I ran around. I slept in the back of cars because my mind was in a real fractured state.'

Relatively speaking, Dad seemed to have kept it together pretty well, at least in the job department. But I was sure there were reasons when he first came back why he decided to run his own businesses – the mini-mix truck, then the bakery – rather than working for others. I could imagine he had had enough of people telling him what to do.

The story my aunty told me about Dad's return was that they flew him in under the cover of night, then put him on a darkened bus at the airport in an attempt to protect him from potential civilian abuse. Even though he managed to avoid protesters, I can't imagine hiding him away as though he was a shameful secret would have made him feel much better.

To imagine Dad going through this was utterly heartbreaking. The average age of a soldier in Vietnam was twenty. Twenty! They were barely more than children. And many of these men were conscripted. They were forced to fight, then felt blamed for doing it.

After the way his country had dishonoured him, knowing all he had endured, how could I also place the blame of my childhood on my father's shoulders? His back was already bowed over by shame and grief, it didn't feel right to further burden it. Perhaps if he had been offered a shred of compassion he might have found it easier to treat others with compassion as well.

HOWLING

Five days after Dad left, I entered the house through the back door we never bothered to lock and dumped my bag in my room. The ride home from school in 32-degree heat had set my throat on fire, so I grabbed pre-mixed lime cordial from the fridge, drinking straight from the bottle. I made deliberately loud frog noises as I gulped, so it wasn't until I put the bottle back that I became aware of the strange noise in the house.

My heart pounded as I homed in on it. What was that? A dog whining? I held my breath and listened harder. The noise was quiet and repetitive, but the tone didn't seem high pitched enough for a dog. It definitely sounded like some kind of animal though – maybe an injured one. My eyes skimmed the flecks of orange rust creeping across the front of our white fridge like a disease. Injured animals could be vicious. The hair on the back of my neck prickled.

As I took a step toward the lounge room, a creaking floorboard rang out like a shot. I froze, waiting for the whining noise to abruptly cut off and be replaced by the clatter of claws, but the noise continued its steady rhythm.

I risked another step, then held still. Now I had gotten used to the sound, it seemed more a wail than a whine. It also sounded like it was coming from our side verandah. We rarely went out there. It *must* be some kind of animal. But what? Maybe it was a dog.

What if it was like the dog in *Cujo*? What if it had rabies? There were no rabies in Australia, were there? Looking over my shoulder to the kitchen, I wondered where Mum was. Had she heard this noise? Had this rabid dog attacked her? Telling myself I could run if there was trouble, I tiptoed as silently as I could across the carpet of the lounge room and poked my head around the doorway to the verandah.

Mum lay sprawled facedown on the floral-covered sofa we had for 'guests' who never came. The foam sections of the couch had come unstacked, making her position teetering on the edge, spilling over onto the floor, look even more precarious.

She was crying. More than crying. She was sobbing. Great racking howls of despair from the pit of her stomach. The four-litre cask of Coolabah Riesling on the floor next to her thickened the air with the sweet, rancid smell of fermented grapes.

'Mum . . .' I said.

She lifted her head and turned toward me. Her eyes were slits. Her nose was red and almost twice its normal size. Snot was smeared across her cheek.

She reached out and grabbed tightly onto my hand. Her palm was sweaty in mine. 'I'm so sorry.' Her voice matched her face, ragged and broken.

Tears flashed to my eyes. What was she sorry for? I kept holding onto her hand, twisting my arm into an unnatural position as

I bent down, not wanting to let go. I gave her back an awkward half-hug but her sobbing escalated so I moved to stroking her springy hair again and again.

I was sure this had something to do with Dad, but I couldn't figure out what. During the past few days no one had mentioned him. To me, the house felt the same way it did when he went away on a fishing trip. We had watched extra television, even eating our dinner of frozen pizza and two-minute noodles in front of it – so much more relaxing than chops and vegies at a silent dinner table bang on the stroke of six.

Bedtimes had been less stressful too. The night he left I had taken myself to bed at 7.30 p.m. as usual, but the next night I had pushed it until eight to see what would happen. Nothing. Last night I had stayed up until nearly ten o'clock and Mum hadn't said a thing.

Keeping up the rhythm of pats on her head, I looked at Mum's weeping form. There hadn't been any crying since Dad had left. Why now? I tried to come up with things about Dad she might be missing, but drew a blank. The only thing I could think of was maybe she thought he was coming back.

'Don't worry, Mum.' I used my kindest, most reassuring voice. 'He's not coming back.'

Her crying picked up intensity and she turned her ruined face to me, speaking brokenly through her sobbing. 'I-I-I kn-know that. Th-that's wh-wh-why I'm cr-cr-crying.'

I was dumbfounded. Mum actually *wanted* Dad to come back? Didn't she remember all those times he had hit us kids? I wanted her to be happy, but there was no way he was coming back here – not if I had anything to do with it.

Maybe she thought that now Dad had left she had to do everything on her own. But she didn't. She had me.

'It's okay, Mum,' I told her. 'I'm here. *I* won't ever go away. You cry if you need to. Don't worry about it.'

If I could be supportive enough, she would stop crying. I kept stroking her hair, but I couldn't think of anything more to say. As her crying continued unabated, I grew more and more helpless. I was also getting a cramp in my thigh from the half-crouched position I was in.

'Mum.' I spoke as gently as I could. 'I'm getting a cramp in my leg. I have to get up.'

She released the intense grip she had on my hand and buried her face again in the damp patch she had created. I massaged my leg for a minute watching her cry. I wanted to show her how useful I could be, but I had no idea what to do.

'I'll be back in a minute, Mum.' I aimed my words at her heaving back. Apart from more sobbing, she gave no response.

The tall stilts and concrete slab made it about ten degrees cooler under the house, and I savoured the drop in temperature as I lowered myself onto the small seat of a rusted blue metal tricycle. I would wait until Kerstin came home before deciding what to do about Mum.

Absent-mindedly I pushed myself up and down the sloping walkway, veering at the bottom into the chasm where Dad's boat used to be. I couldn't believe something could leave such a big hole behind once it had gone.

On my seventeenth trip down the slope, Kerstin rode up the cement driveway talking loudly with a friend about what a bitch a girl at school was. I got off the tricycle and leaned against one of the thick wooden poles holding up the house. As soon as Kerstin spotted me she turned to her sidekick. 'Don't say anything else: she's listening.' She motioned pointedly to me. The conversation stopped as she dismounted.

Kerstin was thirteen and going to high school now. Her white-blonde hair with dark roots was arranged across one eye. She was wearing her interpretation of Rocky High's school uniform: white blouse, navy-blue knee-length skirt, two pairs of scrunched-down white men's walking socks and black kung fu shoes. She was very cool, not that I would tell her that.

Normally I acted as if I didn't care and respected the 'leave me alone' vibes she radiated. When I didn't move away she eyed me suspiciously.

'What do you want? You aren't hanging around with us,' she snapped. Kerstin thought I was an annoying, perfume-stealing, eavesdropping, know-it-all, goody two-shoes bitch. She was right.

I shrugged, as if hanging around with her was the last thing I would ever want to do. 'There's something wrong with Mum.'

'What is it?' Her cool act dropped for a second, but by the time she parked her bike in the metal rack Dad had welded together for us, she was back to acting bored.

'She's crying and saying she wants Dad to come back.' I looked at her friend for a moment, not knowing how much to say in front of her, but I thought she might come upstairs if

I didn't say anything. I lowered my voice. 'And . . . she's been drinking.'

Kerstin and the girl exchanged a look and smirked at each other. 'You'd better go,' Kerstin said. Her friend hopped back on her bike and rode off, yelling over her shoulder, 'Call me later.'

'She's around the side,' I said as Kerstin and I headed up the back stairs into the house.

Kerstin slowed and stopped as she rounded the corner and absorbed the situation. She walked closer to Mum, who looked up from her sobbing and said, 'I'm sorry.'

Kerstin stood next to the sofa looking lost. 'Are you okay, Mum?'

'I will be.' Mum reached for the wine and poured some straight from the cask into her mouth. I felt my face flush.

Kerstin stayed a moment longer without speaking then backed away from Mum.

I followed her. 'What're we going to do?'

She looked at me angrily. 'How am I meant to know? Just leave her alone. Leave me alone too!'

She stalked off and I was by myself again. At least David was at football training. Maybe Mum would be all better by the time he got back home.

I escaped to the front yard to visit my favourite tree: a fifteen-metre-high smooth-barked eucalypt with limbs the perfect distance apart for climbing. The higher into the branches I went, the further away from Mum's crying scene I felt, until finally I reached my favourite set of three limbs and settled into their familiar embrace.

In my tree, nothing could touch me. I had often wished I could live in its branches. (I knew I couldn't because one time I came close to falling to my death after I fell asleep up there.) I traced my finger over the pale brown jigsaw of shapes in the white bark. Every time my mind flicked to the image of Mum's swollen face I said out loud, 'La, la, la, la, la.' When that wasn't enough I flooded my mind with fantasies of *Young Talent Time*, imagining a future when I would be famous too.

A little more than an hour later, the first pink flourish appeared in the sky, followed by dabs of gold, burnt orange, blood red. Though at first the colours seemed dotted at random, they unfolded into an ordered canvas so wondrous it called me to become part of it. Floating into the expanse, my body fizzed with joy at being part of something so beautiful.

My thinking too grew clearer and lighter. The world was not just my mum weeping for the man who had beaten me. It was the sun, the sky. The magnificence all around me was the truth in a way Mum's despair was not. The longer I stayed part of the evolving dance above, the more the afternoon seemed to belong in someone else's life. At that moment it didn't seem possible that such things as leaving fathers and drunk mothers could even exist.

Making my way down through the branches with a leg full of pins and needles, I reassured myself that tomorrow Mum would be back to her old self, standing at the stove cooking chops and vegies for dinner.

It turned out I was very wrong.

CAPTAIN

As the weeks in a single-parent household started stacking up, so too did our new daily routine. Mum was either crying on the side verandah or unconscious on the floor of the lounge room. The space I thought I would have to spread my wings after Dad left had almost immediately been filled by my growing anxiety that Mum wasn't getting any better.

I couldn't accept that there was nothing I could do to help, especially since it seemed likely I was at least partly to blame. I didn't want Dad back, even at the price of Mum's happiness. This knowledge slithered in my guts, whispering what a bad person I was. I tried to make up for it as best I could, racking my brains to find something that would take her pain away so she could stop drinking, but so far I had come up short.

One afternoon after school I paused at the bottom of the back steps, listening. No radio. That wasn't a good sign. Before Dad had left, Mum always had the radio on when I got home from school.

I shrugged out of my school bag and kicked my foot back and forward across the sand on top of the bricks. The ants were determined to use it for their own purposes and we were constantly at war with them, sweeping it back into the cracks. Or, we used to be.

I didn't know who we were at war with any more.

I sat down on the wonky first step and rocked myself back and forth. No cooking smells either. Putting my eye to the hole in the step that let you see all the way through to the pavers beneath, I spotted a lone chip packet among a pile of leaves dropped from the mango tree.

Just go inside. You have to do it eventually.

Stepping inside the door, I held my breath, praying for no sound. The now familiar noise of Mum's sobs muffled by cushions percolated through to me. After getting a drink I walked slowly out to the side verandah.

'Hello, Mum.' I faked a light and happy voice, pretending I was just a normal kid saying hello to their mum after school.

Mum pulled her red, swollen face out of the cushion and gripped my hand tightly, shaking her head from side to side as she spoke with a ragged voice. 'I'm so sorry.' Sour air, moist with wine and tears, filled the space between us.

I braved a look into her eyes: black holes of despair that sucked me out of my body into their abyss. 'Mum, I've told you, you don't have to be sorry. *I'm* sorry I can't do anything to help.'

She buried her head and went back to her crying. Though this scene now repeated itself every day, I had in no way grown accustomed to it. A few quick tears slid out of my eyes. I wiped them away so she wouldn't see. Mum needed me strong. I stroked her hair, telling her again and again, 'You'll be right, Mum. I love you.'

*

Six months later I sat staring at the wall thinking about our new post-Dad life instead of doing the maths homework spread out in front of me.

Apart from one time when she had been drunk at a party, Mum had rarely consumed alcohol the whole time Dad lived with us. The speed with which her drinking had replaced him as the central focus in our lives still had me spinning.

I removed the small blue badge announcing to the world my status as school captain, putting it on the edge of the grey Laminex table I used for a desk. The gold-lettering 'Captain' winked back at me. I still couldn't believe it belonged to me. With everything going on at home, the nomination had come as a total shock. I was still sure, months later, they would tell me they had made a terrible mistake.

Despite all the As, I knew I wasn't special. Not to my father. Not to my mother. But it was true that when I had changed schools at the end of year five, people had begun treating me differently. In my old school I had been the poor girl in second-hand clothes the nasty rich girls liked to pick on. At my new school lots of us were poor. The pecking order was established by how well you could stand up for yourself. There was nothing they could dish out that I couldn't take.

By comparison, the school was a bit rougher – the buildings weren't as nice, the boyfriend/girlfriend stuff seemed way more advanced, and swearing proficiently was mandatory – but I was now picked for teams, not first, but not last either. It was hard to wrap my head around the change, and I was sure as soon as they discovered the real me it would all evaporate.

'What a pretty face you've got, love,' the photographer had told me as he squished me beside the boy captain for our shot in the mayor's office, after our official welcome into our new roles. 'And you must be smart as well, to be captain. Bet the boys love you.' I wanted to believe his words, but the ideas rested on my skin, unable to penetrate.

When the photo had appeared in the local paper, a big grin lighting my face as I pushed my badge into the lens for the whole world to see, Mum had smiled and hugged me. But her eyes had still been puffy from crying and they hadn't quite met mine. How could good stuff happen to me when she spent ten hours a day sobbing?

I picked up my blue biro and drew a five-pointed star in the corner of the page. At least being captain didn't cost any money. Though Dad had given Mum the house and car as part of their settlement, Mum was now trying to raise three kids on the sole parent's pension, a bit more than seven thousand dollars a year. Aside from her drinking, money was the biggest issue in our house.

One day Mum had written the words *electricity, petrol* and *food* on the front of a whole pile of envelopes and put them on her desk beside a mountain of bills. I had checked on them a few times, but there was usually only about five dollars inside; most times they were completely empty. I tried not to even look at the desk any more. The fear trapped inside those envelopes felt contagious.

But there was no avoiding the food in our pantry. Now it came in only two colours: black and white; there was not a coloured tin anywhere, not even Nescafé. I suppose it didn't really matter. Mum had stopped drinking coffee. She wasn't really eating either. Her diet was alcohol only.

Over the months she had grown so thin that she felt like a chicken carcass with all the flesh picked off. Where there had once been soft spaces to press into, her skeleton now felt brittle. I imagined it collapsing to dust at any moment. Apart from patting her head as she cried and offering to make her toast, I didn't know what to do to help.

I finished colouring the last of the five stars I had doodled on the corner of my pad. This wasn't meant to happen. Now Dad was gone, life was meant to be easier.

SLUT NAILS

It wasn't until six months after Dad left, on Christmas Day, that we drove to his house for the first time. Though it was only a few kilometres away from where we lived, the area zipping by outside the window was unfamiliar. Hills flattened, and the high stumps and wide verandahs of Queenslanders gave way to cheaper fibro boxes.

'Is Dad's house around here, Mum?' I put my hand on top of the anxious hum in my chest.

'Not-far.' Alcohol loosened her tongue so her words joined instead of holding their shape.

'I wish we didn't have to go.' This was the eighth time I had spoken these words since the phone call from Dad less than an hour ago, demanding to see us.

'It'll be all right. You don't have to stay long.'

'Well, I don't want to see him.'

'I know.' She put her indicator on, taking the corner too fast.

I had seen a lot of movies where, when the father left the family, he kept close ties through a regular routine of weekend visits. Since Dad had left, we had received one strained phone call nearly five months later, and then nothing until the drunken rant at two o'clock that afternoon.

Mum rolled slowly by Dad's house to show us where to go, then drove the car around the corner, out of sight. Once she had parked, she angled herself to look at us. 'Look. Your dad sounded pretty drunk and Brenda's there, so if you want to leave at any time I'll be waiting right here for you, 'kay? You don't have to stay if you don't want to.'

I patted her hand. 'Don't worry, Mum. We won't be long.'

The thought of leaving Mum alone for even a second on Christmas Day was heartbreaking. It was her first year without Dad. We hadn't been able to afford to make our usual trip down to Brisbane, and Mum had not been up for making a roast dinner, or for anything more than a few presents exchanged.

The day so far had consisted of watching TV from the second we got out of bed until we left the house to see Dad, all laughing loudly at the merest hint of humour in an attempt to dodge the tsunami of sadness threatening to drown us. The only way I could imagine the day becoming more depressing was if you were forced to spend it alone.

Anyway, Dad had chosen *Brenda*. If he felt left out of our family at Christmas time, too bad, so sad; it wasn't like he gave a shit about us anyway.

Kerstin, David and I walked up the sagging front steps of the large fibro house Mum had pointed out. The yard was tiny, mostly cement. In patches, white house paint peeled away, revealing the depressing grey underneath. *Sucked in*. Our house was way better than this. Still, this was where Dad would apparently rather be, living with Brenda, the woman he had left Mum for, and her kids.

I had hated Brenda ever since I'd pieced together what had happened. It turned out Dad had been having an affair with her for years before he left. Mum and Dad both knew Brenda from playing squash together and I had even met her a few times. She was the one Kylie had been talking about the day I overheard her telling Kerstin that Dad had a girlfriend.

After Mum told me who she was, I pictured the scene in my mind. Brenda's fake smile at Mum as she zipped her squash racket into her case, pretending to be her friend, then catching Dad's eye when Mum's back was turned, mouthing the word 'later'. The blood burned under my skin to think of them laughing at how stupid Mum was.

I cut my twelve-year-old teeth on a new saying and used it in my pretend arguments with Brenda: 'morally repugnant'. Without her luring Dad away, Mum would not be crying and drinking. She was the reason Mum's life was falling apart.

I knocked on the door. A moment later Brenda opened it. Thin straight hair streaked with fake blonde that looked grey framed a face lacking much bone structure except for a large chin and a masculine jaw. Her eyes were small and brown, lips a thin slash. She looked mean and nasty and a hundred times uglier than Mum. Dad was an idiot.

'Hello. Come in.' She fake-smiled and waved to us, showing off her incredibly long red nails. *Slut nails.*

I hadn't thought much about how it would feel to come face-to-face with Brenda for the first time. Now my heart thumped in fury. I couldn't believe I was being made to leave Mum alone on Christmas Day so I could spend time with *Brenda*! It felt like a betrayal to share space with her. How could she even show her face?

I walked past her without saying hello. I didn't owe her respect. She was not my parent. After so long without any contact, Dad didn't even feel like my parent. No one in this house had any right to expect anything from me.

Dad was in the hallway, smaller than I remembered. The look on his face was sheepish.

I gave him a hug. 'Hi, Dad.' His strong arms crushed me tight to his chest, as if he was afraid I would slip from his grasp. It was a shock. I couldn't remember the last time someone had hugged me back.

He kept holding me as he stroked my hair and swayed me gently from side to side. Each second in his arms chipped away at my brittle façade, and I felt my muscles unwind. His chest felt strong, and I breathed his familiar smell deep into me. Since Mum had started drinking, I had felt adrift. Now, for the first time since Dad had left, I felt safe and protected, anchored to something solid. How could that be? Everything was Dad's fault. I hated him, didn't I? Kerstin and David joined in, and the tsunami finally hit. We all hugged him and sobbed.

'Some presents for you.' Brenda's voice was nasal and drawling: pure Rockhampton. It was fingernails down a blackboard to our reunion. We broke apart as she shoved the gifts at us, moving from the hallway into their tidy lounge room full of shabby furniture.

I pulled off the green paper covered with tiny red Santas to find some lavender body wash and powder in a cane basket filled with shredded paper.

'Brenda bought them for you. She's really good at buying presents.' Dad's voice sounded weird and perky. I looked down at my crappy two-dollar toiletries more suited to someone in a retirement home. Yeah. She had a real knack for nailing the right gift.

'Say thank you,' Dad prompted.

I put on a voice like someone who was a bit slow. 'Thank you.'

I looked at the ground. How could Dad have let Brenda buy the present for me? I didn't want a present from her. I wanted a present from him. I wanted to know I was important enough to him that he would go to a shop and try to pick out something I liked. Obviously I wasn't. And now he expected me to pretend I was happy so *Brenda* could feel good about herself.

I stared into the brown carpet fibres, swallowing against the tears coming up in my throat. An awkward silence hung heavy in the air.

'You kids have to accept me, you know.' Brenda flicked her limp hair and put her hands on her wide hips.

How dare she demand anything from us? She should be grovelling on her knees, begging our forgiveness. She had probably orchestrated this whole visit just so she could tell us we had to like her. Dad didn't even want us here.

I stood up to face her. She was barely any taller than me. *Stupid, short bitch.* I wasn't about to play happy families to make her feel better about herself.

'No, we don't have to accept you. You might *want* us to accept you, but that doesn't mean we're *going* to.'

She put her face right up in mine but I refused to step away. Sometimes girls at my school threw softballs at my head for fun. If she thought I was going to be intimidated by *her* she was delusional. I lifted my chin, our faces so close it felt like we were going to kiss.

'Listen here, lovey, whether you like it or not, I'm part of your dad's life.'

'Ah, terms of endearment. Isn't that nice of you. You listen to me, *lovey*. You might be part of *his* life, but that doesn't mean you're part of *mine*.'

'Tell 'em, Doug.' She stared at Dad, who was leaning forward on his chair with his head in his hands.

'Just leave it, Bren,' he said.

Ha! Dad was on our side.

'Tell 'em I wasn't the first.'

'C'mon, Bren, just let it go, love.' Dad looked ready for a lie-down.

'No. You tell 'em.' She looked at me, squinty little eyes flashing in what she must have thought was an intimidating manner.

I raised my eyebrows. I hadn't realised until that moment that her oversized man jaw made her look like a big, ugly horse. How could Dad stand *doing it* with her? How could he have left Mum for this?

'Did you know your father fucked other women before me?'

Inside I staggered back as though punched, but there was no way I would let her see it. 'Oh, that is charming. Swearing at children. Very sophisticated of you. Did you go to finishing school for that? Dad made a really great choice when he picked you.'

'You tell 'em, Doug. Tell 'em you had affairs with other women before me.'

I looked at Dad and he nodded. 'I did.' His voice was quiet.

'Now you know it wasn't just me.' She sneered down at me like she had just won a major victory.

'That doesn't mean you aren't a slut.' A red film was clouding my eyes. I wanted her to keep talking. I wanted her to hit me so I could smash her in her repulsive horse face.

'Hey, Ruth! Don't speak like that.' Dad stepped forward with his arms out to separate us.

'What? She's allowed to swear at me but I am not allowed to swear at her?'

I turned my face back to hers, injecting my features with contempt. 'This is meant to be our Christmas. Is this what you invited us over here for? To abuse us?'

'Listen here, lovey —'

'Stop it!' Kerstin burst in, tears streaming.

'Now you made Kerstin cry.' I gathered up my basket. Kerstin and David scrambled for their presents as well. 'We don't have to stay here and be abused by you. You can't *make* us like you.'

Kerstin, David and I headed for the door as Brenda said, 'You can't leave —'

'You don't get to tell me what to do.'

'You're such a stuck-up little bitch.' Her voice trailed after me as I walked down the stairs.

'Takes a bitch to know one,' I called over my shoulder.

WALKING ON EGGSHELLS

Facing my son hitting me so many times a day kept my adrenaline pumping, plunging me back into memories I thought I had left behind. The past anger they evoked demanded I rip shreds off someone, but it was getting harder and harder to know who.

Certainly everything I was uncovering about the way Vietnam veterans were treated was making it difficult to point the finger at Dad. The complex psychology of a person traumatised by war could not be boiled down to *bad man hits kids*.

As the child of a veteran I was entitled to free counselling through the Australian Government, so I made a call and organised a session at the Vietnam Veterans Counselling Service in Melbourne's CBD. On arrival I found the walls of the waiting room crammed with brochures about the services available to veterans and their families, and I started snatching the titles that stood out to me: *Parenting Made Easier, Partners' Self-Care Program, Doing Anger Differently, Legacy, The Partners of Veterans Association of Australia*.

The counsellor I saw gathered all the literature she had on PTSD, and the psychological impacts of war, and over the next few days I pored over them.

In *Mental Health and Wellbeing after Military Service* by the

Australian Centre for Post-Traumatic Mental Health, I was struck by its description of the potential impact of a veteran's service on family members. 'Families are complex systems. When one member is not travelling well it will, inevitably, impact on the wellbeing of other members of the family . . .

'Even when a veteran has a supportive and caring family the veteran can still be isolated, especially if they feel their distress will be too much for their family members to bear, and consequently try to keep his or her distress to themselves.

'Partners of veterans and other ex-serving personnel have higher rates of depression, anxiety disorders, sleep disorders, acute stress reactions and long-term difficulty in coping with major stressful change than partners of non-veterans.

'Children can easily become the focus of irritation and anger when a parent is not coping well . . .

'The children in this situation, along with the parent-partner, typically talk about "walking on eggshells", anxious not to do or say something that will upset the parent with a mental health condition. If this situation persists for many years, and the child's anxieties are not addressed, difficulties can persist through into adulthood for these children.'

The pamphlets seemed to acknowledge the shock-absorbing role partners and children played when someone came home from war. But I wasn't sure how knowing it was meant to help. And this brochure wasn't talking only about the families of veterans from the Vietnam War. It related to all wars since the beginning of time. This was talking to the families of current-day veterans. At this very moment little kids just like I was were probably having childhood experiences the same as mine. Did the government, the people of the Australian community, think this was okay?

I couldn't bear the thought of it. I wanted to rescue them all. The kids. The wives. The vets themselves.

I had looked on the Department of Veterans' Affairs website a couple of days ago. It stated that partners and dependent children of veterans up to the age of twenty-six were eligible for counselling. What if people took longer than twenty-six years to get over a childhood spent 'walking on eggshells' or worse? What if they didn't know the extent of their problem until they had children of their own and their buttons got pushed? What if the unprocessed trauma of the children of veterans meant they started dishing out the same style of parenting they had received? Who was going to help look after the grandchildren of veterans?

When I was in grade three, my teacher set an assignment where we had to research the meaning of our names. My name is Ruth. The opposite of ruthless. Ruth. Meaning compassion.

I had always wanted to feel worthy of that name, and as I came to understand more about PTSD, I did feel a genuine unfurling of the wadded-up fist I had been shaking at Dad my whole life. But there was a tug-of-war inside me that made it hard to fully let go. At one end of the rope was extreme empathy for the unimaginable world of pain Dad had gone through in Vietnam. At the other end was fear that relinquishing my anger at him was a betrayal of my child self, and an abandonment of all other children who had childhoods like mine.

With each of the veterans I met, I projected Dad onto them,

trying to get the answers I had never got from him.

When I asked Ollie, 'Do you think your war experience has affected your relationship with your children?' he didn't hesitate in his response.

'When the kids were little, things would push my buttons. I used to be quite aggressive and smack them with a belt. Within five minutes I felt so upset, wondering what the hell I'd done that for, I'd go in and cuddle them and say I'm so sorry. I couldn't control myself. Even though now I am really good with her [Ollie's daughter], she'll still stay in her room if it's just her and me.

'My kids thought I was like that because I was like that. But that wasn't who I was before I went over to Vietnam. It didn't mean we didn't love our kids. We just couldn't show it. A lot of things we did we didn't have any control over.

'Most guys that came back had problems. Their children would have problems until the person realised he had a problem. It was all part of the PTSD.'

I almost wept in relief to hear him so clearly own his actions. Even though it wasn't for me, I stole his sorry and made it my own, hugging it to the part of me that had been waiting my whole life to hear those words.

A few of the men, however, when they spoke of their estrangement from their families, of children who no longer spoke to them, seemed to place all of the blame on others. When I tried to drill down to how they thought the problem had developed, one man told me of a biting comment made by his son that had hurt him so deeply he hadn't spoken to him in over a decade.

Could they really not be aware they weren't the only ones with scars?

Children of Vietnam veterans have a suicide rate three times that of the general population, as well as significantly increased rates of accidental death, depression, and alcohol and drug addiction.

When a 2014 Vietnam Veterans' Family Study I participated in, along with 27000 other Australians, asked whether the service of Australian men in the Vietnam War had had adverse effects on the physical, mental and social health of their sons and daughters, the unequivocal response was yes.

Though the negative outcomes impacted the group as a whole, the depth of the injury was felt more keenly by some. In the report, 23 per cent of the offspring of Vietnam veteran families reported they had experienced harsh parenting, with the three most significant areas being verbal abuse, too much physical punishment and humiliation, and ridicule, bullying or mental cruelty. This compares with the general population, where the figures for those suffering physical abuse in childhood are generally reported at between 5 and 10 per cent.

The Department of Veterans' Affairs Family Study went on to find strictness and regimentation were recurrent themes in the accounts of growing up in a Vietnam veteran family, with comments like 'His whole life he was a disciplinarian and I think sometimes he went too far' and 'He treated us like we were in the Army.'

According to the report, many sons and daughters said these events influenced their view of themselves. They grew up thinking their father's volatility was their fault and they were 'bad kids'.

In normal families love flows from parents to their kids. But that's not how it felt in my family. As kids we were the ones who did the loving. Swallowing our needs came at a psychological cost. The river is not meant to flow up the mountain. I hoped these men who no longer maintained connection with their children knew that. Like it or not, unprocessed trauma gets handed down to the next generation.

I had never been to war, but I knew what it was like to be prepared to face the enemy every day. The difference was, my enemy wasn't a faceless stranger. My enemy was someone I loved.

CROCODILE TEARS

Eight months after my showdown with Brenda, I lay in the darkness with a pillow over my head trying to block out the sound.

Ring. Ring. Ring. Ring. Ring.

Pulling my thin sheet over my arm I turned with a huff onto my side. The lights on my digital clock glowed 12.43. Seriously? Bloody rude.

The shrill ringing suddenly stopped, leaving a heavy silence in its wake. Maybe they had given up. I turned back the other way, trying to bury my face in the darkness of the wall. If I could just get to sleep before the next —

Ring. Ring. Ring.

I growled into the blackness. Each new peal set off a Pavlovian response in my system, compelling me to take the call. My nerves jangled in irritation as I squashed my impulse to get up.

Mum had passed out drunk hours ago, so I knew she wouldn't be awake. But I had always been the heaviest sleeper in the family. If I wasn't sleeping through this, nor were Kerstin and David. All I needed to do was hold out and one of them would take the call. Then I could go back to sleep.

Ring.

Answer the phone, Kerstin.
Ring.
Answer the phone, David.
Ring.
C'mon. Someone answer the phone.
Ring.
Fine! I'll take the bullet this time.

I stumbled out of bed, felt my way down the dark hallway into the dining room.

The white wall phone continued its relentless attack on the quiet. I grabbed it before dropping down into the padded brown vinyl phone chair.

'Hello.' I yawned as I spoke.

'Hello. Who's this?' Dad's voice was thick and slurred.

'It's Ruth.'

'Oh, Ruth.' The sound of Dad crying. 'Ruth.'

'Yes.'

'You know I love you kids, don't you?'

'Yes, Dad.'

'Sorry everything turned out the way it did.'

'Yes, Dad.' I tucked my knees up to my chest and pulled my t-shirt nightie over them, turning it into a little blanket. It wasn't cold, but the warmth of my bed still clung to me. I fought to preserve it so I could go back to sleep once the call ended.

'Really, really sorry.'

'Yes, Dad. I know.'

'I love you kids, you kn—'

I pulled the phone away from my ear and rested my head on

my arms, closing my eyes. I concentrated on slowing the alert pounding of my heart to let my mind drift back to sleep, but part of my attention was tuned to the muttering from the receiver. I put the phone back to my ear.

'— nothing to do with you. It's between your mother and me. It doesn't change anything about how I feel about you. It's very —'

'Uh huh.'

I pulled the receiver away from my ear again.

The phone calls had begun nearly six months after our visit to his house, halfway through my first year of high school. The first time he called I had listened to every word. But after two months of disturbed sleep, my enthusiasm was waning.

For a start, Dad was always drunk when he called. Though initially it had been refreshing to hear a grown-up talk about what was going on, he never covered any new ground. Often, he barely even made sense.

I had no idea if Mum even knew the phone calls were going on, but I certainly wasn't going to burden her with them. None of us kids felt like we were allowed not to answer the phone, but we were all sick to death of being woken up every night.

'Uh huh.' I spoke into the receiver without bothering to listen to what he was saying.

My eyes had adjusted to the darkness and I looked around the room to distract myself from my boredom and frustration.

Piles of paper, baskets of clothes and a random assortment of household items sat on every horizontal surface. It looked as if robbers had ransacked the house. Keeping the house clean and tidy had followed a similar fate to meals since Dad had left.

I put the phone to my ear again.

'— not easy for you kids —'

'Dad, d'you think you could call back some other time? It's really late.' I may only have been thirteen, but even I could figure out calling someone at one in the morning was rude.

'No, no, no. I need you to listen to this —'

I hated his voice when he was drunk: words all slow and mushed together, tone like a whining two-year-old. 'I get it, Dad. You're sorry.'

'Now don't be like that. I never get to speak to you. The least you can do is listen to your dad. I love you so —'

There was a scuffle on the end of the line. The faint sound of Brenda's voice saying 'Let me talk to her' was followed by a muffled response as someone's hand covered the mouthpiece.

I sat up straighter in my chair, charged and ready for a fight at the sound of her voice. Now it was going to take ages to go back to sleep. Bloody Brenda.

I put the phone closer to my ear to see if I could hear their muted argument. A moment later she was on the line.

'Hello.' She was compensating for her slurring by over-pronouncing consonants. Since the day we had been to visit them, the only talking I had done with Brenda, or Dad for that matter, had been these drunken night-time phone calls.

'What do you want?' My fingers shook as adrenaline reached my extremities.

'Now listen. I know you don't like me. This is not about that. This is about you and your dad. He's over here night after night, crying over you guys —'

'Yes. I know. He calls us every night while he's doing it.'

'You don't have to be smart. I'm just trying to say you should know how much he loves you —'

My heart hammered and I pulled the phone away from my ear. Yeah. He loved us – when he was feeling all warm and weepy after a couple of six-packs of beer. Was I meant to sit around begging for scraps of his affection no matter what time of day or night he dished them out? His 'love' didn't seem to extend to him visiting, or calling, once the alcohol had left his system.

Immersed in my inner rant, I had forgotten Brenda on the other end of the phone. I put her back to my ear. '— you should be grateful to have a father who loves you this much. That's all I'm —'

'You don't get to tell me how I should feel!' I was yelling now. 'If Dad loves us so much, why doesn't he ever see us? Why does he only call when he's drunk? Stop calling here. I'm meant to be asleep. I'm sick of being woken up to hear you say the same thing every night. Leave us alone!'

The force of my hang-up made a satisfying ding. I sat back in my chair, jaw clenched and stomach tight, ready for more fighting. There was no use going back to bed until I was sure they weren't going to keep calling back. Most times a hang-up was enough to give them the message, but some nights they were more persistent than others.

I tried to picture them in the house I had visited, adding a nearly finished bottle of Bundaberg rum and dozens of stubbies to the coffee table of the lounge room. I could almost smell their breath, sweetened from the booze.

I thought about Mum, lying alone and unconscious in the bed she had shared with Dad for eighteen years. Maybe she should get a boyfriend. At least then she wouldn't be drinking alone. Dad had got to leave behind the tattered ruins of the family he had destroyed and start a new life with Brenda. Mum deserved a fresh start too.

I got up and leaned over the bench so I could see the clock on the kitchen wall. 1.06. I would give them five more minutes. Then I was going to bed.

Despite all the phone calls, two mornings a week I woke at five to go rowing with a crew of girls from school.

The morning air snapped my cells awake as we made slow, rhythmic progress along the Fitzroy River. At first the water was a confection of strawberry and orange, our oars cutting through it like spoons through ice-cream. But as the sun rose, the river once again turned muddy brown. The sun's progression changed our faces too. We once more became common and sweaty, instead of lit from within.

Sometimes we talked, sometimes we were quiet, the splash of oars, and the smooth glide of the boat slicing through water, the only sounds. Then someone would move out of rhythm or flick water with their oar and we would laugh. We were not a spectacular team.

A few mornings after my phone argument with Brenda, the lapping silence was pierced by a loud siren. No one had any idea what it meant so we kept rowing.

Our coach sped over to us in his dinghy to pass on a message.

'You have to go back into the boathouse.'

'Is this about the siren?'

'Yeah.'

'What's it about? Why do we have to go in?'

'Just row back and I'll tell you when you get there.'

In front of the boatshed, the rolling green lawn leading down to the water was littered with boats and rowers from other schools. Even fifty metres out, I could hear the rumble of muted talking. As we pulled further in, the noise got louder. Some of the girls were hugging each other and crying.

A red-headed girl of about fifteen with blazing blue eyes came up to us as we were hopping out of the boat.

'Do youse know what happened?' Her big juicy lips struggled to wrap around her braces.

'No. We were just told to row back in,' I said.

'One of the girls who was rowing this morning had her arm bitten off by a crocodile.'

I raised my eyebrows and put a look on my face that told her I didn't believe her.

'It's true. Didn't your coach tell you? Apparently it grabbed her oar and tipped the boat and got a hold of her arm.'

The Fitzroy River runs right through the middle of Rockhampton. There were always croc sightings being reported in the newspaper, but normally they happened near the salt-water barrage.

I looked out at the opaque brown of the water. Each ripple became an ancient, gnarled tail ready to break through the surface. In the scrappy eucalypts on the opposite bank I conjured a reptilian body from the fallen stumps. The poor girl.

For months afterward, I dreamed of cold yellow eyes peering over the top of water. I would scream as loud as I could but no sound escaped. The only noise was the splash as he exited the water, then the slithering of scales and a wide-mouthed hiss as he came closer. I ran, but my feet sank into marshmallow ground. Just as he was about to close his jaws around my leg, I would jump and find myself on the tray of Dad's four wheel drive. In the next instant the crocodile turned into Dad. He continued his pursuit saying 'I'm sorry' over and over again.

MORE MINCE

By the time I started year nine, two years after Dad had left, we had mostly settled into our new normal. When Dad was living with us, the afternoons had been a rigid routine counting down to his arrival: homework and one hour of ABC television followed by a silent dinner of impeccable table manners where everything on every plate was eaten without complaint. Now afternoons stretched into evenings, dinner was often forgotten, and the television was always on.

Though the tragedy of Mum's pain and drinking ate away at each of us, Kerstin, David and I didn't talk about it, or Dad, or how our lives had changed. Mostly we just got on with what needed to be done – scrounging up lunch for school, making cereal and toast when we were hungry – before inevitably turning back to the telly to distract us from it all.

One Thursday I arrived home from school to find Mum on the lounge room floor, her mouth slightly agape as she snored. My gentle nudge made no dent in her 'sleep'. I looked at her for a long moment.

Olive skin hung loosely over her broad, elegant cheekbones. A few lines creased the skin to her jaw and radiated out from the corners of her eyes. Her forehead was smooth and high, nose small and refined. Black lashes matched black hair. She was still beautiful.

I lay down beside her, rested my head on my elbow and whispered into her ear. 'Mum. Guess what? I got chosen for the school musical today.'

She didn't stir. Her chest rattled with each in-breath and I wriggled down, pressing my ear against her back. There was an unbelievable amount of sounds going on in there: the consistent wheeze of each breath, a crackling pop when a piece of phlegm caught, and a deeper rumbling gurgle. Her heart thumped slow and strong.

I pressed my nose into her shoulder, wanting to fill myself with her familiar scent. But she didn't smell right. This woman was too sweet: stale wine and port, and a little bit of something else that made me think of rotting flesh. The cigarette smoke clinging to her clothes and skin seemed thicker, more permanent. I wanted to make her get up and have a shower and brush her teeth so I could breathe her in again. I needed to know this drinking thing was a temporary blip, that Dad's leaving hadn't destroyed Mum for good.

The thin carpet was rough against my skin and the floor was hard and uncomfortable. I pulled away and rolled onto my back. How had it come to this?

One day, after staying late at school for rehearsals, I arrived to the sound of cupboards opening in the kitchen and went to investigate.

'I can help you string beans or chop things if you want,' I offered Mum, as I hoisted myself up on the brown Formica bench, beating out a rhythm with my feet on the cupboards.

'I'm not up for making anything like those meals.' Her words had trouble making it past her tongue. 'I used to make that food every night for your bloody father. He never appreciated it. He never even helped do the dishes. Just sat on his arse and treated me like —'

'I appreciated it, Mum.'

'Yeah. Well. I'm not doing anything like that tonight.'

She leaned against a stretch of wall and put a cigarette in her mouth, using two hands to steady the lighter she held. After a couple of failed attempts to make contact, she closed one eye to get better focus on the end of the cigarette. The ferocity of her inhale once it finally caught light sent a wet kiss into the air.

After a moment of closed-eyes focus on the smoke moving into her lungs, she moved toward the fridge, pulling out some mince, and then frozen peas and corn from the freezer.

After crashing around in the pots and pans cupboard, she banged the large frying pan down on the stove, then dumped in the packet of mince. The smell of congealed blood hit the air.

I kept a smile on my face as my stomach flipped in revulsion. Foul, tasteless mince was the only meal we seemed to have eaten since Dad had left.

'Could we have spaghetti bolognaise tonight, Mum?' I kept my voice chirpy and light, showing her I was fine with whatever we had.

'Nah, it's too much work.' She swayed like she was on a boat, jabbing at the mince with a wooden spoon, then leaned on the wall for support. Her eyes were half shut. The ash on her cigarette grew longer and longer and eventually fell to the ground without her noticing.

It felt like someone had waved a magic wand over my life, wiping out the mother I had known before. I wasn't sure which one was the dream – the person she had been when Dad was living with us, or the one she was now.

I wanted to hold on to the tender feelings I had always had toward Mum, but this drunk woman didn't feel like my mum. This drunk woman made me feel something a bit like anger and a bit like disgust. I didn't want to watch her any more. I hopped down from the bench and left the room.

As the months had ticked over into years, Mum's drinking had become more furtive. She would hide in her bedroom or disappear under the house to gulp down her medicine, then slot herself back among us, as though nothing had changed.

'You're drunk,' I said one day after she had tripped, stumbled a few steps forward and reached out toward nothing to right herself again. The fumes she was giving off were overwhelming.

'No-I'm-not.' The slowness of her tongue as it tried to wrap around the words without making mistakes gave her away.

'You *are*, Mum. Stop lying. We know you're drunk. You aren't fooling anyone. You may as well drink in front of us.'

'I haven't been drinking —'

'Mum. We found your bottles in the washing machine, laundry tubs, closet. Right now you can't even stand up. Look at yourself. You can't even talk properly. I've been drunk. I know what it looks like. It looks like you do right now.'

Since Dad had gone and our house had been governed by the monotony of Mum's misery, life had lacked much in the way of surprises. The problem was, my body had grown used to them, or at least to standing on guard in preparation for their arrival. Now that our life was the same depressing thing each day, my persistent alertness had no purpose. I was like a tiger pacing back and forth at the zoo. Though I played netball and was in the debate team, basketball team, rowing squad, rock band, choir and musical, I still jumped with energy that had nowhere to go.

There was very little under-age night-time entertainment in Rockhampton. But since starting high school, I had been going to any parties I could wrangle an invitation to. If no parties were on offer, there was always a crowd of people willing to make their own entertainment hanging out in parks. Without any parental restrictions to stop me, I usually joined in. When we could manage to scrape together enough cash and get someone to buy it for us, illicit alcohol consumption was often a focus of the night.

It didn't feel hypocritical to me to hate Mum's alcoholism while enjoying drinking myself. The way I saw it, there were two types of drinking: fun drinking with friends, and sad drinking you did alone. To my mind, they were wholly unrelated. Besides, staying out until the small hours of the night was a great way to knock the edge off my restlessness.

I twisted in my seat to better observe Mum's face and felt a rush of venom at the small self-satisfied smile playing around her lips. I tutted and narrowed my eyes at her with a small shake of my head.

Holding on to the top of the armchair for stability she pulled herself up to full height, raising her eyebrows and smirking more widely as if to say, *I don't care what you think. If I'm drunk, that's for me to know and you to find out.*

My eyebrows went up too, eyes bulging out of my head as I made my face say in response, *No, Mum. You're not fooling anyone. I did find out.*

Normally I acted like I didn't notice how drunk she was, but I was over it. If she wanted to pretend drinking in secret meant it wasn't really happening, that was one thing; expecting me to put on a show, smiling and nodding as if I believed her, was another.

She smoothed down the black-and-white patterned hotpants she had been wearing for the past four days and made herself more erect. Moving forward in slow, careful steps, she attempted to look nonchalant while at the same time showing me how easy it was for her to walk in a straight line.

'*I'm* going to cook dinner.' She huffed out of the room.

Great. More mince.

ROCK IN HER POCKET

'Ruth, I've just got off the phone to Sasha's mum.'

It was late one Sunday afternoon and I was on the verandah at my desk, catching up on neglected homework after spending the weekend at my friend's house.

I liked Sasha's parents as much as I liked Sasha, but in all the years I had been sleeping over, often both nights of a weekend, this was the first time Mrs Bryant had ever called my house.

'What did she want, Mum?' Maybe I had done something seriously wrong and she was calling to tell me never to come back. Heat washed over my face at the thought.

'She was checking you're all right. She says you were in a car accident.'

'Oh yeah. I was in a car accident.' It had happened only eight hours ago but somehow it felt much longer than that.

'Bloody hell, Ruth. Why didn't you tell me? What happened?'

'Well . . . Sasha and I were in the back of the van with the dogs, and the car went on the gravel, and when it went back onto the road it tipped over.'

I breathed in, testing to see if the weird grassy smell of terrified dog's wee was still trapped in my nose.

'Who was driving?'

'Sasha's sister, Sadie.'

She let out a sharp breath.

'She's got her licence, Mum. She's driven us places heaps of times.' Sadie did have her licence, but this was the first time she had driven us. The last thing I wanted was to give Mum an excuse to tell me I couldn't visit Sasha any more.

'Were you wearing seatbelts?'

'No. We were in the back. There weren't any seatbelts.'

Two lines appeared between her brows and I didn't know if the anger was directed at me, or Sadie or Mrs Bryant.

'It was fine, Mum. Mrs Bryant said it's a problem with these types of cars. They're tall and thin. It's easy for them to get tipped over.'

I kept searching her face, praying she wouldn't crack down on my visits.

'Why didn't you tell me? It was very embarrassing to get that phone call and not know anything about it.'

I looked at her heavy-lidded eyes for a long moment, then down at the stack of paper in front of me. *Because you were passed-out drunk, Mum.*

'I dunno. I forgot. It wasn't that bad.'

She looked unimpressed.

'Really. I'm fine. I just forgot. That's all.'

'Well, next time something like this happens you make sure you tell me, okay?'

'Okay. Sorry, Mum.' She shook her head as she left.

I looked back at the question I had been working on before

Mum had come in. *The lesson behind Romeo and Juliet is that children should not deceive their parents. Do you agree?*

After Sadie had over-corrected, we had been flung first into one car wall, then in slow motion into the other, a tumbling ball of humans and dogs as the car crashed to its side and skidded along. The screeching of metal and glass had filled my cells with electricity that made my hair stand on end.

Hugo was big, even for a sheepdog, and his forty kilos had landed on top of me during the chaos, knocking the breath out of me. I wasn't sure if it was him or the poodle who had wet themselves during the accident.

I pulled my t-shirt down over my shoulder. There was a decent bruise coming up, and one on my hip. But it didn't hurt anywhere near as much as when Dad used to hit me. It was only physical.

Was it deceptive of me not to tell Mum about the accident? Probably. But it genuinely had not occurred to me to tell her. In our new post-Dad life, I wasn't sure when I was meant to slot in talking to her about the things going on in my world.

When Dad had been there, she had always been in the kitchen. I would do my homework on the kitchen table, or help while she started getting dinner ready, and she would ask about my day. Now he was gone, she didn't cook; she cried and drank.

When the divorce had finally come through, nearly two years after Dad left, stealing away her most-valued identity as his wife, she had plunged into her despair with an abandon that made me think of those women who loaded rocks into their pockets before drowning themselves in a lake.

After a lifetime of other people making decisions for her, she was beyond terrified at being left as the sole adult. I had thought I was doing the right thing: taking pressure off her, making all the decisions for myself. Though I had quickly realised my attempts at comfort were as effective as a bandaid on an amputated limb, I couldn't bear to imagine her thinking of me as just another rock in her pocket. Was she now saying she wanted me to lean on her for support?

I couldn't remember the last time I had turned to her for anything even vaguely parent-like. It seemed silly to interrupt her with forms from school, or trifles with friends, when she was so immersed in problems of her own.

I slumped onto my folded arms. Though Dad had been gone long enough for the dust to settle, I could still feel the aftershocks of his leaving disturbing the air. I didn't care what Mum said; I wasn't going to be the one to add any weight to the flimsy structures that remained. Who knew what would collapse next?

FIGHT OR FLIGHT

The stack of information given to me by the Vietnam Veterans Counselling Service included a DVD called *You're Not in the Forces Now* by Nic Fothergill. From the very first second I was captivated.

The DVD opened up with a camera chat with Nic, in which he introduced himself as a psychologist and Vietnam veteran. Though most Vietnam veterans were now well into their sixties, Nic looked the way I always pictured them in my head. It wasn't just his short back and sides or slightly menacing biker moustache. It had something to do with the burning intensity of his dark eyes and the way the body under his clothes seemed layered in muscles made hard by life, the way no number of hours at the gym could replicate. If I was ever in trouble I would want Nic on my team.

The footage then cut to a real-life session in a small conference room where Nic was speaking to an assembled group of Vietnam veterans suffering from PTSD. When he started talking his eyes flashed with passion for his subject. 'A lot of the behaviours you have, and the sorts of stresses you exhibit now, and the ways that you cope now, really had more to do with your training than it ever did to do with Vietnam. Vietnam was just the icing on the cake that embedded it into your system.'

My whole body grew still and the chatter in my brain came to an abrupt halt as if every part of me had looked up at the same time with a collective gasp. *What did he just say?*

Nic went on to detail how cutting hair, removing civilian clothes and getting yelled at by superior officers were the beginning of the process of brainwashing the army uses to get soldiers ready to fight in a war. He asked the collected people off-camera why the army made soldiers do drills over and over again. Then he wrote on the whiteboard the words *automatic, instinctive.*

'If you don't do your drill right, who do I punish? You. If you continue to not do your drill right, who do I punish? Your platoon. If that happens, what does the platoon do to you after knock-off time? They sort you out. So I use not only the discipline, but peer punishment for those who don't toe the line.'

What happens as a result? 'As soon as a command is yelled out, what do you do? You do it immediately.'

The cogs of understanding in my brain began to spin in a completely new way. Dad's requirement of an immediate response. The way he woke us up and expected an answer straight away, or better still, that we sprang out of bed the second he spoke. How, as soon as he called our name, we had to down tools and start running toward him yelling, 'Coming, Dad.' Was that what he had been doing? Training us to be good soldiers?

Nic talked about the process of training in detail I had never before heard, moving from the three months of recruit training, where you learn the basics, to three months of core training, where you are put in a situation of simulated war using weapon fire, flashes and blanks.

I imagined myself going through the training as he described it. I could see how by the end of six months I would know what to do when I arrived at the battlefield. I realised that up 'til now I had not thought of conscripted boys like my dad as trained soldiers. But, of course, they were.

Nic asked everyone to imagine standing next to a busy street. Suddenly two cars smashed into each other. One of the cars ricocheted off the other and careened straight toward you. Then he asked, 'What would you do? Tell me what the rule is in an ambush. You've got to face into the ambush and assault through it. Which is the equivalent of doing what?'

He turned his attention to the partners of the soldiers who were part of the session as well. 'For those of you who haven't been in the military, what you've got to train a soldier to do is to actually walk toward the car that is coming toward you. Because that is what you have to do in an ambush. To turn into it . . .

'Now you tell me, is that a normal, natural thing to do? Your whole body is saying, "Get away! Get away! Get away!" But you have to be so well trained that you override that. This process changes your fight and flight.'

His words brought to mind a recurring dream from my childhood. I was crouched inside an out-of-control elevator that moved faster and faster the higher it climbed. By the time it reached the top of the building, the momentum was so great, it broke through the roof into the dark night sky above. The elevator was mostly destroyed, so I remained curled in on myself, trying not even to breathe. Then, my body started moving of its own accord. It stood and began deliberately rocking the elevator, edging it closer to the precipice of the fifty-metre drop. My heart pounded in terror. Inside my head, I screamed at my body. *What are you doing? You are going to tip us over the edge. We will die. I don't want to die. Crouch down! Don't move!*

But my body was no longer under my control. Acting on autopilot, it now climbed onto the handrail of the elevator, walking along it like a balance beam. *You will fall! We will die!*

Showing me how little it feared death, my body wrapped its legs around the metal bar it had walked along, and leaned back as far as it could go, arching like a diver toward the dark abyss. The elevator swung out with it, teetering on the very edge of the building. Then it started to slide . . .

Somehow that dream seemed related to what Nic was saying. In times of fear I did not run. In times of fear I got ready to fight. Had the training of my childhood changed my fight-or-flight response as well?

On a whiteboard Nic drew a straight line. At one end he wrote the word *flight*; at the other, *fight*. He drew a dot on the whiteboard with a button near the *fight* end of the line. He named that dot *stand-by*, likening it to pressing the pause button on a DVD player.

'Now obviously it is peacetime in Australia and I can't have you operating at this level,' he gestured to the word *fight*, 'otherwise you'd be punching the lights out of everybody. But instead of entering society and finding a middle ground where someone could choose flight or fight depending on situation, veterans came home and stayed right near the fight end of the chart, living in stand-by mode . . . This stand-by button now becomes an anger button.'

This was a portrait of my dad. The shortness of his fuse.

The immediacy he required of us. It all fit this pattern. He was living his life in the way the army had trained him. I should have seen this before! My husband had said my upbringing sounded militaristic, but I had never truly processed what that meant. Dad was training us, the way he had been trained, and now my responses too had become instinctive and automatic.

If my childhood training was still embedded in the way I behaved today, what must it have been like for Dad? During wartime he had to stay switched on, living in stand-by mode so his reaction times were lightning fast. Land mines, sniper fire, artillery fire. He would have exploded out of stand-by into fight mode many times every day. Then he did this for weeks, months, a year.

In his video Nic explained how the training laid down new networks in the brain, which were then strengthened by the most powerful in-built reward system imaginable: follow the training, and you live; fail to do so, and you die.

But what was meant to happen to all of this training when these soldiers came home? While thirty weeks were devoted to training, followed by a year of war to rewire their brain, the reports I read said only two hours were spent preparing these men to return to civilian life. *Two hours*. Programmed to become fighting machines, ready for every danger, but never deprogrammed and shown the world was safe again.

As with so many other veterans, Dad's stand-by button became his anger button. When enough of life's stressors piled up, he did what he was trained to do. Instinctively, he exploded into action. The only problem was he wasn't staring down the enemy; he was surrounded by his wife and kids.

O O O

My eyes snapped open as I listened for the sound that had invaded my dream.

Ears straining, I scanned the shadows of my room, moving from open cupboard door to piles of clothes on the floor. Everything was exactly where I had left it. Was it the phone? Those calls from Dad and Brenda had stopped a year ago. I couldn't imagine it was them.

I listened to the noiselessness of a small town past midnight for another long moment. With my eyes open it seemed much more likely the noise had just been part of my dream. I turned over.

'Aah! Eh!'

I froze, the sleep instantly evaporating from my system. What was that? Who was that? I looked at the clock. Eleven past two. Why was anyone even awake?

'Help! Help!'

I couldn't tell whose voice it was, but someone was in trouble.

I was out of bed and down the hall before I even felt my feet touch the ground. In the darkness I nearly ran into David. Our eyes locked, and I was instantly plunged into his terror. I wanted to ask him what he had seen, but I didn't want to give away our position.

I put my finger to my lips and strained to hear more.

'Help! Somebody help!'

This time there was no mistaking the voice. It was Mum, her voice a muted scream. I streaked past David to the kitchen.

Stopping at the doorway, I took a moment to adjust to the dazzling brightness of the fluorescent light. When they did, I saw that Dad had Mum pinned to the ground. He was kneeling on top of her with the weight of one knee pressed across her thighs, his hand on her shoulder. Her shirt buttons had been popped open exposing the lacy shadow of her bra. The yeasty smell of beer smacked into me and I saw puddles of amber liquid and empty beer bottles strewn over the linoleum floor. How long had I been sleeping through this? Whatever 'this' was.

A hundred thoughts flew into my head. This was the first time I had seen Dad in nearly a year. What was he doing here? It was two in the morning. What was he doing on top of Mum? Dad had never hurt Mum before. Why now?

David had followed close behind and I looked back at him for a moment, wondering how much more he had seen. He was wearing his blue-and-red dinosaur pyjamas and his hair was poking out at crazy angles from sleep. He was only nine. I didn't know how to protect him from this.

'You should go back to bed,' I said.

'No. I'm staying with you.' He moved closer to me.

Dad was looking up at me, his face unrecognisable. Pulled by inner demons, his eyes were smaller and cheeks flattened, emphasising a mouth locked in a vicious sneer. Mum's black eyes seemed to fill her entire face. She was shaking uncontrollably, terror pouring off her in waves.

'Get off her, Dad!' I ran over and furiously hit his shoulder, shoving to try to unbalance him. He braced his position and grabbed my arm, twisting it and pushing me away. Blood pounded in my ears and I immediately went back to him, pushing and punching. 'Leave her alone! Get off her! You don't live here any more! You're not allowed to be here! Get off her!'

He swatted me away and repositioned himself more firmly on top of Mum, then gave me a superior smile. I abandoned my ineffectual assault and turned my attention to Mum.

Kneeling down next to her, I put her head in my lap, stroking her hair and looking into her terrified eyes. 'Are you okay, Mum?'

Before she could answer, Dad sprang out of his position and wrenched me away from her. The back of her head thudded heavily to the ground with a noise that made me feel sick. He picked me up and threw me across the room into the dishwasher. My head smashed into the bench above. His voice was a roar. 'No! Don't you comfort her! You won't take her side when you know.'

He locked eyes with Mum, and the menacing look came over his face again. 'Tell them. Tell them what a slut you are.'

'Yes.' Mum's voice was a rasping whisper. She didn't take her eyes off Dad.

'Yes, what?' The sarcastic tone I hadn't heard for so long was back.

'Yes, it's true.'

'Tell them how you went out with a man you didn't know

tonight, and fucked him at his place.' The sick smile on his face came through in his tone. He was enjoying this.

'Yes.'

'Tell them I'm not the only one who's fucked someone else now.' 'Yes.' It was like we weren't in the room. Their focus was only each other, hunter and prey.

'No . . .' Dad moved his hand up around her throat. 'I want you to say it. Say it. Say, "I'm a slut who fucked a man I just met." And look them in the eye when you say it.'

Mum looked at us, but her eyes dropped down.

'Look at them.' He moved his hand around her chin and forced her head up. She gave a little cry and made eye contact with me. Her voice was shaking. 'I-I'm a slut who fucked a man I just met.' She looked made of porcelain. Like the crush of his strong hand might shatter her face. The deepest part of my heart ached. Tears poured down my cheeks.

I had no idea what to do. I was desperate to comfort Mum, but I didn't want Dad to smash me again. I ignored Dad and looked at Mum. 'It doesn't matter what you say or what you did, Mum. We still love you no matter what.'

Dad threw Mum's face away. 'It's always the same with you kids! Your mum can do no wrong. I'm always the bad one! Always my fault. I'm sick of it!'

He stared into Mum's eyes again, his voice growing cold and quiet. 'I don't care what you say; she isn't getting away with it this time. She's gunna get it this time. I'm going to scoop her eyeballs out with this bottle lid. Then she'll be sorry.'

My eyes bounced from the glint of metal in Dad's hand to

the look on his face. Like nothing in life would please him more than scooping her eyeballs out. As if he had been waiting his whole life for the pleasure of it. What should I do? I couldn't fight him. I couldn't reason with him. I needed someone strong to help me stop him.

Mum and Dad stared only at each other. I didn't want to leave Mum here, but I didn't know what else to do. I had to call the police. I got up off the floor and headed to David. 'You'll be all right, Mum. I promise.'

I grabbed David by the hand and ran down the back stairs. The night air was damp against my t-shirt nightie and my teeth began to chatter.

'I'm going to call the police.' I dragged David toward the phone sitting on the bench in the laundry. Just as I was about to pick it up, I had a thought. 'If we dial from down here the phone will make a noise upstairs. Dad'll know what we're doing. We have to go to Mrs Harper's and call from there.'

David nodded his agreement, and we raced off across the lawn to the yard next door.

I took her front steps two at a time and banged on the door. The noise echoed like a gunshot into the quiet street.

'Mrs Harper!' I yelled as loud as I could and banged on the door again. 'It's Ruth from next door!' The front windows turned yellow as a light switched on, then came the sound of crashing furniture. Mrs Harper opened the door, grey hair in curlers, shin gushing blood.

'Oh no, what have you —'

'I just banged my leg; don't worry. What's wrong?' Her face

was a mask of wrinkles and anxiety.

'Sorry. I know you were sleeping. I didn't want to bother you, but Dad's trying to kill Mum and we need to call the police but we can't call from home because otherwise he'll get us.' The words tumbled out. We were meant to be super-polite to our older neighbours, but I couldn't think of a well-mannered way to convey something like this.

'Oh.' Her hand was still holding the door open, blocking access to her house.

I felt like a switch I didn't know I had in my body had been turned on. I bounced from one foot to the other as the rest of the world moved in slow motion. What was happening to Mum while we stood there?

'So can we come in and call the police?' I prompted.

'Yes, yes, come in.' She stepped back and allowed us entry. I wiped the grass and dew off my bare feet as best I could, before stepping inside her immaculate house.

Limping from the wound on her leg so every step seemed to take an hour, she led us from the front verandah to a tiny room off the lounge room that served as an office.

She sat down heavily on the chair at her work station, and grabbed a couple of tissues from the box on the desk, pressing them against the gash on her leg, before opening the drawer and pulling out her reading glasses.

I could see the phone. I was desperate to grab it, but I didn't want to seem rude, especially since I had made her hurt her leg. My mind flashed up a picture of Dad on top of Mum, bottle top in hand. Had he touched her eyes yet?

She reached down into one of the drawers of her desk. *Christ almighty, was she getting out the phone book? What was she doing? Call the police. Call the police. Call the police.*

She opened the book and began flicking pages.

'Um ... what're you doing?' I kept my voice as polite as I could.

'Looking for the number at the station.'

'I think you can probably dial triple zero.' I tried to keep my voice sounding pleasant, working hard to stop myself from screaming at her, *Mum could be dead by now!*

'No. It's better if you call the station number directly.' She spoke authoritatively. As she got closer to the right section she licked her finger to ensure she turned only one page at a time. I wanted to break that finger, smash her in the face and grab the phone. The police needed to get here right now. Anything could be happening over there. *Oh God, please don't let Mum be dead.*

She finally lifted up the receiver and began dialling. Each number took five hundred years to click back into place. Finally she spoke to someone. 'Hello. My name is Mrs Harper. I'm calling on behalf of a family who live next door to me. There seems to be some kind of domestic disturbance. Do you think you could send someone out?'

Some kind of domestic disturbance? Are you kidding? Her words made it sound as if I had overreacted to someone having a bit of a shouting match. I wanted to drag her over there so she could see what a 'domestic disturbance' looked like.

'What's your address, Ruth?'

'Ninety-nine Wandal Road.'

'Ninety-nine Wandal Road,' she repeated into the phone.

'Yes. That'd be great. Thanks.' She hung up the phone.

'What did they say?'

'They'll send out their first available officers.'

'Do they know he's trying to kill her?'

'Yes, yes, never mind about that. They know they need to come out.'

I had heard her end of the conversation. They might be hours. If Mum died it was my fault for trusting this doddering old fool. I should have called them myself.

'Thanks, Mrs Harper.' I tried to sound polite as I grabbed David's hand. 'We might go back over there now.' I turned to leave.

'I don't think that's a good idea.' She blocked my exit. 'I think you should wait here until the police arrive.'

God, I hated adults. Just because I was a teenager she thought she knew better than me.

'I don't want to leave Mum alone over there.' Tears of frustration streamed down my face.

'Still. I don't think it's a good idea to put yourself and your brother in danger as well, do you?'

Who cared about me? Mum could be dying. 'Maybe David can stay here with you and I'll go back and make sure everything is all right.'

'I'm staying with you.' David moulded himself to my side, and clung on to my hand.

'No. You can both stay here.'

I was shocked into silence by the finality of her voice. What on earth made her think she had the right to tell me what to do? I knew I should be grateful for her help, but in that moment I hated her. I hated her for not taking me seriously. I hated her for trying to control me. But mostly I hated her for downplaying the situation because she wasn't comfortable facing up to reality. Some things weren't polite or nice. Some things were a matter of life or death. In case of emergency you dialled triple zero. If Mum died I would never forgive her.

'Come and sit on the couch for a minute.'

David and I followed her, holding tightly on to each other's hand as we manoeuvred past tiny end tables with lace doilies and sat on her plastic-covered floral sofa.

The thin film of sweat covering my body made my arm stick to the plastic, and I peeled it away impatiently. It was too quiet and dark in her pristine lounge room. I longed to know what was going on in the kitchen less than fifty metres away. I needed to be back over there. At least then I could be doing something.

'So, how's school?'

'Fine.' I could not pretend this was a normal situation. I squeezed David's hand, grateful he was with me, then pulled him over to a window with a view to our house. 'I'm going to watch for the police.'

In less than ten minutes flashing red-and-blue lights strobed through the room.

'Thanks, Mrs Harper, the police are here so we'd better get over there. Don't worry about coming with us. We'll be fine. Thanks.' I raced out the front door and sprinted across the lawn to our place.

When I arrived home the lights were still on in the kitchen, but Mum and Dad were no longer there. I couldn't see any blood. Maybe he had removed her body.

There was a loud knock on the front door. I raced down the dark hallway to open it. Just as I was about to grab the handle, Dad stepped out of the shadows. He didn't look in my direction as he opened the door.

SEEKING SHELTER

Two young men in neatly ironed uniforms stood in front of us. They looked so calm and in control I wanted to kiss them.

I flicked a glance at Dad. His face had lost the sneer. Now he looked like a little boy who had been caught throwing rocks.

The taller officer removed his hat, looking at Dad as he spoke. 'There's been a report of domestic disturbance —'

I jumped in before Dad had a chance to say anything. 'Yes. Dad was hurting Mum and he doesn't even live here any more. He's not meant to be here. I want you to take him away.'

They looked at Dad, who kept his eyes on the ground. 'Is this true?'

He nodded without looking up. At least he didn't lie.

Their attention shifted to me. 'Is your mum here?'

I looked at Dad. 'I dunno. I just got back into the house after calling you. I'll just check... Mum!' I shouted into the darkness. 'Mum, the police are here and they want to talk to you!'

Mum emerged from her bedroom. She was still in the clothes she had worn on her date earlier in the night, but her stockings had a huge hole in them, the pocket on her shirt was ripped and there were three spots of blood near the collar. It looked like her skirt was on backward. My knees went weak with relief when I saw her but I didn't move. I needed to make sure Dad didn't get away with anything.

'Are you okay?' The taller policeman stepped inside the house and walked over to Mum. Her whole body was trembling. She nodded and looked down. 'Do you want to press charges?'

She looked at Dad. He was partially obscured in the shadows, eyes still focused on his feet. She shook her head without speaking.

'Do you want to go to a shelter for a couple of days, to be on the safe side?' The smaller policeman stepped forward, placing himself between her and Dad.

'I dunno.' Mum's voice was completely blank.

'I think we should, Mum.' I moved over, putting my hand on her arm.

She jolted at my touch. 'Okay.'

'All right then, gather up a couple of changes of clothes and your toothbrush. We'll take you there now.' The dark-haired officer turned to Dad. 'And I think you should go home.' Dad nodded and left through the front door without looking back.

I remembered our budgie, Flag. What if Dad came back and did something to him? Or burned the house down? 'We can't leave our budgie here. Can we take him with us?'

'Sure, I don't think that will be a problem.'

I walked into Kerstin's still-dark room and shook her gently through her blankets. 'Kerstin, you have to pack some clothes. We're going to go to stay at a women's shelter for a couple of days.'

'Okay.' She hopped out of bed without asking further questions. I wondered if she had been lying awake, frozen in fear, this whole time.

Not wanting to keep the police waiting, I went straight to my room and changed into some checked blue shorts and a pale pink t-shirt. I pulled down my pink duffel bag with the white Sportsgirl logo on the side from the top of my wardrobe.

What did you pack for a women's shelter? Shorts and t-shirts, I guessed. As I moved around my room, picking up clothes off the floor, I spied the box of chocolate bars I was meant to sell to raise money for school. My mouth watered. I could really do with some chocolate. They were ridiculously expensive, but I guessed I could afford to buy one. I ripped open a bar, had a big bite then shoved the rest of the block back into the box.

The sweetness in my mouth was the first awareness I'd had of my body in what seemed like a long time. I still felt like I stood outside myself, but my feet were inching closer to the ground again. I decided to take the chocolates with me, just in case Dad came back and something happened to them.

I retrieved my toothbrush, then returned to the front verandah and removed the cover from Flag's cage. 'We're going away for a couple of days but you're coming with us. It's okay. Yes it is.' He chirped at me. I grabbed his food and dropped him at the front door next to the policemen.

Mum was standing talking to one of the officers in a muted voice. She hadn't changed out of her clothes and her bra was showing. I walked over to button her top and she jumped back. 'Just me, Mum.' I touched her arm gently and she drew in a quick breath.

'That's a bit sore there, love.' Embedded in a purpling bruise, a deep scratch ran from her wrist halfway up her forearm.

'Sorry, Mum.' My stomach curled into a ball as I imagined how the scratch had got there.

Kerstin and David joined us and we all huddled together until the taller policeman asked, 'Are you ready to go?'

We followed the men to their car. The four of us, the birdcage and our bags were all crammed into their backseat so we couldn't put on seatbelts.

'We won't tell anyone if you don't.' The officer in the passenger seat turned around and winked at us. We all laughed like it was the best joke we had ever heard.

As we drove he continued to make small talk, asking us what grades we were in at school and the name of our budgie. Somehow I had expected things to be all serious. I thought they might want me to give them a report on everything I had witnessed. It already felt like I was looking at the last few hours through a sheet of dimpled glass. I guessed that was what we were meant to do. Put it behind us. Not dwell.

After ten minutes we pulled up in front of a white weatherboard house on a main road on the other side of town. It looked like any of the other houses on the street. Normal. Suburban. I was expecting something a bit more *Prisoner*. Perhaps with armed guards.

A woman opened the door and stepped into the light flooding the landing at the top of the stairs as we piled out of the car.

Marjory ('we only use first names here') was businesslike as she led us down the hallway. She was fifty-something, or looked like she was. Her unruly hair was dyed a brassy red and the roots were spiked with grey. She had the tired, drawn face of someone who has smoked ten thousand cigarettes.

Our home for the next two nights was a small bedroom crammed with four single beds. The mottled grey carpet failed to disguise the stains. The door of the battered cupboard in the corner stayed ajar for the duration of our visit.

Marjory remained outside the door continuing her run-down as we claimed our beds. 'There's no smoking in the rooms. You can use the bedding already provided if you haven't brought your own. There are tea and coffee making facilities in the kitchen, which is just down the hall to the right. There's only one bathroom. It's not the next door, but the one after that, on the left. There's another toilet at the end of the hallway.

'There are currently two other women and two children staying here, but most people like to keep to themselves so you probably won't see them much. Also, this is a safe house, as well as being a women-only shelter. That means you can't tell anyone where this place is. And no visitors. Especially men. Any questions?'

No.

'Good.' She breathed out, breaking into a smile for the first time. 'I'll leave you to get settled.' And with that we were left alone.

The wonky blinds had started to let the sun in, so it must have been after five. It felt scary and serious to be in an actual women's shelter. No one said anything, but we exchanged small nervous smiles. At least we were in this together.

My bed was in the far right corner of the room. I flopped down on the thin lemon-yellow sheets. A waft of the bruised, stressed bodies that had sweated there before me hit me in the face. I shoved my bags underneath the bed, but the remainder of the chocolate bar I had begun eating at home caught my eye. I surreptitiously grabbed it out of the box and slipped it into my sleeve. This chocolate bar was going to cost me a ridiculous amount of money. There was no way I was going to share. I pulled the covers over my head and took a huge bite.

The chocolate was intensely smooth, with tiny almond fragments, though not as sweet as I would have liked. I took my time, letting each bite melt to nothing, but too soon it was gone. Moving my tongue around my mouth to soak in the last remnants, I shoved the empty wrapper underneath my pillow.

I lifted the covers off my head to survey the scene. Mum was gone, out having a cigarette in the cement area with the Hill's hoist out the back. David was facing the wall, trying to sleep. Kerstin was in the bed nearest the door reading a magazine with a cover torn off from the stack next to her bed.

Surely one more chocolate bar would be all right? I kept my eyes trained on Kerstin, and slowly moved my hand into the cardboard box, withdrawing another chocolate bar as silently as I could manage. My hand made it back under the sheet unnoticed and I pulled the covers back over my head and turned to face the wall. I faked a coughing fit to cover up the noise of crinkling paper, then sank my teeth into the firm, brown block.

I commanded myself to go slow. After ten minutes the bar

was gone and my eyeballs felt like they were covered with sand. I shoved the wrapper beside the other one underneath my pillow and fell asleep in seconds.

Sunlight was streaming through the blinds when I woke. My mouth and teeth were covered in a thick coating of fur. I threw the tangled covers off my sweating body and stumbled out of the room and down the hall in search of water.

The hallway lacked any artwork or pictures, the only point of interest the lightly striped wallpaper that lifted in some sections. There was a blonde woman wearing an old pink tracksuit standing in the kitchen. She had a black eye and a swollen nose. She didn't look up as I entered. I assumed this must be shelter etiquette, so I pretended I hadn't seen her.

I grabbed a flowery mug that was missing a handle from the brown Laminex cabinet overhead. I checked it for cockroach poo, but it looked relatively clean, so I shoved it straight under the tap. One cup. Two cups. Pink tracksuit lady walked out, so I took my time on my third cup, opening drawers lined with orange-flowered wallpaper. Tea towels, utensils, some takeaway shop menus. I'm not sure what else I thought I was going to find.

Mum, Kerstin and David were all awake when I returned to the room. I walked past them and headed straight for my chocolate box, grabbing out another bar. Kerstin and David chorused, 'I want chocolate too!'

I put on my sweetest voice. 'Sure ... only $2.50 a bar.'

They both grumbled and Kerstin asked me how I could afford them. I hadn't quite figured that out myself yet so I lied and said I had some money saved she didn't know about. She didn't believe me, but I didn't care. I needed that chocolate.

The chocolate tasted even better now that I could eat it out in the open. I chomped away happily for another couple of bites before I felt guilty.

'Want a bite?' I handed the chocolate to David, hovering over him as he bit into it. 'Not too much.'

He passed it to Kerstin, who took a bite before handing it to Mum. She declined.

Mum came from a family of sweet teeth. Her father ate Arnott's Assorted Creams for breakfast and snacked on a mountain of lollies every day. Mum could devour a family-sized block of chocolate in approximately four point six seconds. Things were really bad if Mum was refusing chocolate.

'You okay? You can have a whole bar for yourself if you want.'

'No thanks. Just a bit sore. I think this scratch on my wrist where Dad ripped the watch off me is going to scar. And my thighs are really hurting where he kicked me. But I'll be all right.'

The chocolate taste in my mouth felt too sweet. I wished I had something wholesome inside me. I wanted chicken soup. 'Is there anything we can do, Mum?'

'No. I'll be okay.' She stared silently at the carpet.

I grabbed a magazine and flicked through it, thinking about last night as I watched her.

Four hours later Mum spoke. 'I might go and visit a friend of mine in a little while.'

'What friend?' Mum didn't have any friends. And if she did, she certainly didn't drop by for visits.

Her eyes darted around the room and her voice sounded

deliberately casual. 'You remember that man I went out with last night? He lives just around the corner from here.'

'Oh.'

Last night Mum had gone on her first date since Dad had left. After the night we'd had, I hadn't thought to ask her anything about it, but it was obviously still on her mind. I wanted to stay supportive, but I was horrified that she expected us to stay in a safe house with a bunch of strangers for even a moment without her. Was it even legal to leave children at a shelter? What about if some psychotic wife-beater found the place and started shooting people? If she was going, she had to take us too.

'We can come with you then.'

'No. I think it would be best if I went by myself.'

Best for who? I could not believe she was thinking about doing this. Dad had been Mum's first and only boyfriend. I agreed it was time she moved on. But she could wait until we went back home, couldn't she?

Besides, what was she going to say to him? Look how terrible it is. My husband beat me up. It was so bad I had to go and stay at a women's shelter. Poor me. Save me. Make it all better.

I wanted to scream at her, *We are only at this women's shelter because I thought of calling the police. I have already saved you. And while I am at it, why is it that when Dad beat you up it was important enough for all this, but when he beat us up you didn't do anything? He hit me hundreds of times and you never once tried to drag him off me. You never once called the police for me. Why is that? What makes you so important?*

She lifted up some clothes and put them down again, then

shook her cigarettes before putting them in her brown leather handbag. As I watched her my head started shaking out a no. She wasn't seriously going to do this, was she?

The finality of the sound the zipper made as she closed her bag set my teeth on edge. She was actually going to leave us here.

'Well, what are we meant to do?' I put bile in my voice and willed her to look at me so she could see the depths of my rage.

'You'll be safe here. I won't be long.'

I grasped onto one last straw and prayed. *God, make her stay. If she stays, she loves me. If she goes, she doesn't love me and neither do you.* She walked out of the room without making eye contact.

With that, everything solid was now officially rubble. Dad wanted to kill Mum. Mum had a boyfriend. We were all alone.

I kept staring at the door, expecting her to walk back in, but after three minutes I realised she had really left us. She had always put Dad first. But this man she had met only last night? Was he already more important to her than us?

The angry heartbeat thumping in my ears triggered images from last night. Dad's reptilian sneer. Mum appearing from the bedroom with her skirt on backward. The beer smell. The way he looked at her with the bottle top in his hand.

A groan escaped my throat. I tried to convert it into a hum to drown out the images. I needed a book. I couldn't believe I had forgotten to pack a book. But then Mum hadn't packed very well either. When I had returned from a trip to the kitchen earlier that morning, I had been surprised to hear Mum, Kerstin and David laughing.

'What's going on?' I had asked.

'I was just telling Kerstin and David that when I looked at what I had in my bag, I realised I mostly packed pantyhose. I found twelve pairs in there but no toothbrush. I don't know what I was thinking. It's too hot to wear pantyhose!'

I had forced a laugh though I didn't think it was funny. It just set off a deep ache in my chest I didn't know how to ease.

Unwrapping another chocolate bar now, I bit down on it, no longer registering much more than a vaguely cloying sweetness. The thrill had worn off after the sixth bar and it now felt like some joyless inevitability that I would make my way through the whole box.

I would be turning fourteen in four months, but by the end of the stay at the shelter I felt a million years old.

At school four days later, I finally mustered up the courage to talk to my homeroom teacher about the chocolates I had eaten.

I decided to tell the truth. Well, parts of the truth, plus a lie I thought would be likely to get me out of the $37.50 I now owed.

I pulled Mrs Mann aside after English class. 'Sorry to tell you this, but my father tried to kill my mother on the weekend and we had to stay in a women's shelter.'

She let out a gasp.

'Yeah, it was pretty bad ... and the worst thing is while I was there someone stole the box of chocolates I'm meant to sell. I'm not going to be able to give you any money for them.' My face went hot at the lie, but I acted like I hadn't noticed, and looked her in the eye the way all good liars know to do.

Her mouth hung open. She stared at me a few seconds too

long then her eyes darted to the windows overlooking the walkway between buildings, like she thought they might offer a way out of the situation. I counted the strands of grey in her jet-black hair, waiting for her to call me a liar and tell me I was going to have to pay for the chocolates anyway.

'It's all right, Ruth.' Her voice was small and her face had lost all of its colour. Her green eyes didn't meet mine.

'So I don't have to give you any money for them?'

'No. It's fine.'

I thanked her as I walked away.

COURAGE

After watching the Nic Fothergill documentary, I felt down to my bones that the impact of Dad's army training was core to many of his actions. How we set up the tent, running around like it was dusk and the enemy were approaching; the way he taught us how to march, so when we walked along as a family we often did it in left, right, left procession; the military precision he expected in even mundane life tasks like carrying a cup of coffee. If he was still hair-trigger sensitive to danger, it made sense that the smallest thing could set him off. How sad that he had been released from the army so primed. What had they expected would happen?

The film got me thinking about my own 'training' too. I was sure it was a big part of the reason I had survived my childhood so intact. It didn't matter how many times I got knocked down; I had been trained to shake it off and stand back up ready for more. If I felt scared, I had been drilled to override my fear, stand my ground and fight back. People who had been to war talked about the incredible mateship they felt with those they fought alongside. I couldn't imagine it was any different from the ferocious protectiveness I felt toward my mum, my sister, my brother.

Growing up, Dad had always been a fierce competitor, excellent at any sport he put his mind to. With his life on the line I was sure he would have been an intense and focused soldier. He was certainly a good sergeant. Under his command, I had been shaped into a brave warrior. How could I hold on to my anger at Dad if it was his training that had rewired his brain? How could I feel fury, when by teaching me all he knew, he had allowed me to become resilient enough to withstand anything life threw at me, including him?

As a parent, I had thought a lot about this concept of resilience. Though part of me longed to protect my children from the harsh realities of life, I knew this wasn't possible, or even healthy for them. They had to go out and face the world for themselves. But I wished I could teach them what I knew.

I wanted them to know that another person did not have the right to tell them whether they were good enough, and that screaming *fuck you* to the world was not only okay; it was sometimes the only possible way to keep themselves intact.

I wanted to teach them that 'faking it 'til you make it' actually worked. So that even if they didn't feel strong deep inside, by acting as if they did often enough, one day they would discover they had convinced even themselves. And that they should never give up. Because if they pushed hard enough, for long enough, they could move mountains, or climb them, or paint them, or whatever the hell they wanted to do with them, because it was their life to live and it belonged to nobody else.

I wanted them to know that getting hurt was part of life, and that scar tissue was stronger than ordinary flesh could ever hope to be. But I also wanted them to know that if they did get knocked over, there was someone here to help them as they struggled to their feet. That I would always have their back.

I especially wanted them to know that sometimes it was okay not to be strong. That resilience was a suit to wear to get you through a moment, not a place to live. I would know.

I wore my resilient suit so long it became like a Teflon coating, keeping me separate from the world – untouched, disconnected – so it took me a long time to realise that the war was over. When I finally dared to take it off, I found it wasn't just the scary things it had been keeping at bay. It was the gentler, kinder things too. Every good trait has its shadow side.

Yes, there were times to be resilient. But there were also times to be sad. Tears were not a sign they were damaged and weak. Maybe if more people cried, more often, instead of hiding their hurt, we could stop having so many things we had to be resilient about.

I wanted to warn my children against people who expected them to get over their hurts and move on without a backward glance, because it was these people who were so scared of their own darkness and pain they couldn't bear it in another.

I wanted them to understand that not everyone was born with the same amount of elasticity. And that sometimes, when a load became too heavy, the rubber band could simply break. That's when they needed to have compassion for the pain of others, rather than blaming victims for their lack of ability to bounce back.

Maybe the quality they should be seeking was courage: the ability to act *despite* feeling fear, strength *in the face* of pain and grief. It certainly felt more inclusive to me. Sometimes they would find the most courageous thing to do would be to feel the vulnerability, helplessness and fear underneath the armour. I wanted to teach these things, but I didn't know if they could be taught.

SCREAMING PRACTICE

A few months after our weekend at the women's shelter, I was lying on the carpet in front of the telly reading my dog-eared copy of Stephen King's *Carrie*, with *The Breakfast Club* on for background noise.

I had begun reading all the time: as I got ready for school, when I walked to school, and any time I finished my work in class. As long as I kept cramming the words in, I could keep the picture at bay. When I ran out of books, I just started back at the beginning of whatever I had in my hand. Stephen King. James Herbert. Dean Koontz. I made myself face the monsters in people's imaginations so I could be ready if a real one ever came back to my house.

My eyes returned to the start of the sentence I was reading, but my mind drifted to the conversation I'd had with David earlier in the day.

'You were so smart not to dial the phone downstairs,' he said. 'I don't know how you even thought about that. I couldn't think of anything that night.'

I nodded along, but it was that moment I felt most guilty about. I should have hidden David, dialled the phone from downstairs myself, drawn Dad off Mum and down to me. If I had stayed at the house, maybe I could have stopped him sooner. Instead I had abandoned her and run next door to save my own skin. But then, I couldn't have lived with myself if I had done something that meant David ended up getting hurt.

I pressed my face deep inside my book, wrapping it around my cheeks and breathing in the dusty smell of its yellowing pages.

Maybe Dad wouldn't even have come downstairs. As lost as he was in his deranged mind that night, maybe the tinkling of the bell wouldn't have penetrated. Then the police would have got there sooner, because I would have dialled triple zero like a normal person.

I felt terrible for feeling angry at Mrs Harper. She had worn a large bandage for nearly a month after the attack. She must have needed stitches from where she knocked her leg in her hurry to answer the door to me. She was very kind to have helped us. But those missing minutes, while she got the phone book out and kept us trapped in her lounge room, haunted me.

A picture of Mum walking out of her bedroom with her skirt on backward slammed into my brain. Heat spread from my stomach to my knees. I buried my face further into the book, before a voice in my head yelled *No!*

I tried to block the images threatening to pile on top of me, saying out loud, 'La, la, la, la, la, la, la.'

Dad would *not* come back again. I would *not* be like Mum. If any man tried to attack me, I would be ready. I dog-eared the page of my book, got off the floor and headed out the front door.

Not bothering to put on shoes, I walked across the road to

Jardine Park. After the recent week of rain, the oval was dotted with green patches of clover as tall as my knees. Walking through them released the mouth-watering green smell that reminded me of the hours I had spent searching for four-leaf clovers here over the years. But I wasn't looking for luck today.

I had heard somewhere men were less likely to attack if you looked ready to fight, and weren't afraid to make noise. But I had seen the way Mum's throat had frozen when she was scared. I knew screams could come out as whispers. I wasn't going to let that happen to me.

I headed toward the most central part of the oval, as far away from houses as I could get, to continue my regime of screaming practice.

I looked around to make sure no one was coming, then leaned my head forward and focused on the painted white line on the grass which defined the running track. I looked around again. A red ute rumbled past on the road. This was so embarrassing. But then, that was what they said. Often women had a sense someone was going to attack them and they were too embarrassed to make a noise. Not me.

I imagined a man, face emerging from the shadows, ready to hold me down and rape me. As he inched closer to me, quickening his pace to match mine, I pictured myself kneeing him in the balls, then sucked in a deep breath and let rip. 'Noooooo!'

The high-pitched noise set my body alight and shot pain deep within my ears. As soon as the scream was finished I drew another breath and screamed again. There was no word this time, just the loudest noise I could make.

After four more screams, my eyes felt ready to explode. I squeezed them tighter to make sure I didn't burst a blood vessel like last time, then took another deep breath and pushed harder from my gut. My throat ripped, but I kept at it, claiming my savage roar so I could call on it when I needed it.

After a few minutes, my legs were wobbly and I was covered in a sheen of sweat. I lay in a patch of clover that loomed over me like a miniature forest, and stared at the sky. Fine white clouds stuttered in stripes across the endless blue; but I would not escape into light and air today.

Instead, gravity pinned me to my place, a reminder I was merely a tiny speck on a planet hurtling in a vast universe. I tried to picture darkness and stars all around me, but the bright sky and light breeze tickling my hair were too distracting. I focused on the planet beneath me instead.

Though the cushion of grass felt firm, deep in the bowels of the earth I knew there were movement and heat and lava. I imagined its energy pulsing upward into me. People could see whatever they wanted to see on the outside, but if they scratched the surface they would find I too pulsed with dangerous power. This was my secret. This was my weapon. This was what would get me through.

NOBODY'S VICTIM

It was twelve past nine on Friday night when I hit the brick paving of the open-air East Street mall.

A couple of straggling shoppers lingered on the seat a few doors down from the shoe shop where I had started part-time work nearly three weeks earlier. Apart from them, the mall was pretty much deserted. Many of the shops were dark after either closing up early for the night or shutting down altogether and standing abandoned.

The humidity had been building up for the past four days, but despite an occasional flash of lightning and far-off roll of thunder, the rain they kept promising hadn't arrived. After the crisp air-conditioning of the past four hours, it felt like swimming in soup.

The click-clack of my low-heeled silver court shoes, from the latest season's range, echoed off the hard edges of the buildings. A friend from school had laughed at their middle-aged uncoolness when I'd worn them out to a party after work last week, but what did I care? I lived in Rockhampton. My whole life was uncool.

As I rounded the corner past Stewarts department store, a crowd of people came off a side street. One of them shouted something I couldn't make out. I froze, acid dripping into my stomach. My breath moved up to the top of my lungs, ready to help me run, but they moved off in the opposite direction.

Years of living with Dad had given me a good antenna for danger, but ever since the night he had come back it had been ultra-sensitive. Mum never spoke about what had happened and I didn't ask, but images from that night still flashed into my head, and I spent lots of time imagining what I would say as I hit Dad with a baseball bat and made him get off Mum.

Apart from that, our lives had gone on as normal. It was just now the house didn't feel safe and sometimes my heart raced at the smallest thing, making it hard to breathe. The unreasonable humidity didn't help.

Crossing the road, I paused in the light blazing out of the police station, debating what to do. There were a few taxis lined up at the rank, and I did have seven dollars in my purse. Each week since I had started work, Mum had given me money to get a cab home. (Booze buses were out in force on Friday nights and she was too drunk to drive.) I had pocketed it every time and walked. But tonight for some reason I felt a prickle of fear at the thought.

I checked my watch. Surely the later it got the more dangerous it was. I couldn't just stand here. I reached into my bag, wrapping my hand around my wallet. I wouldn't get paid until next Tuesday, and apart from the taxi money I had only three dollars left. I needed every last cent for booze for tomorrow night's party.

I started walking. For the next block I counted my steps to try to push the feeling of being watched to the back of my mind.

Thirty-six, thirty-seven, thirty-eight . . . Don't be paranoid. No one is interested in you.

I let my walk speed up to time with the pounding of my heart, telling myself this was how assured people walked. I was only five feet seven and fifty-five kilos, but I imagined myself bigger, and felt instantly stronger. *C'mon, you rapist bastards, I dare you.*

As if I had conjured my foe, a small gang of guys fell into step behind me. I didn't look around, but by their voices I guessed there were three of them, my age or a bit older.

Keeping my pace the same, I made my stride longer and more purposeful, then clenched my fists and pulled my shoulders back. People were less likely to attack if you didn't hold yourself like a victim.

The sound of a bottle shattering came from the direction of their footsteps, and my body gave an involuntary flinch I hoped they didn't see. They laughed. Had they dropped it, kicked it or turned it into a weapon? Fuck. I really didn't want to be raped.

I crossed to the other side of the street. One of them called out to me, 'Hey. Where're you going?'

I kept my eyes straight ahead. Was there a service station nearby? Where was the nearest public place? Should I go back to the police station? They might intercept me. What was open at this time of night? I racked my brain, but all the places within running distance I could think of were closed. Stupid Rockhampton.

I picked up my pace. The hurried clip of my shoes sounded like that scene in a suspense movie where the woman was being chased through an abandoned car park. Was this the moment I was meant to scream?

Don't be stupid. They're just drunk idiots. They're not interested in you.

I turned down one of the larger streets I usually avoided, hoping to see a light on.

'Hey!' one of them yelled. 'Don't go!'

I kept walking, deliberately not increasing my pace. *If you run, they will chase.*

They laughed at something I couldn't hear. I imagined them doing the same as they held me down and took turns. My heart hammered.

For a moment their footsteps seemed to fade and I thought they had broken off in a different direction, but then the scrunch of shoes on bitumen started up behind me.

'Where're you going?' one of them called out. More laughter.

'We won't bite. Not unless you want —'

I turned around and faced them. It was three guys, about fifty metres away on the other side of the street. It was time to put my practice into action. I screamed as loud as I could, 'Leave me alone! Go away! Leave me alone! Don't follow me any more! Leave me alone!'

The noise shattered the eerie silence of the street. I sounded as psychotic and unhinged as I had hoped. If they thought I was going down without a fight, they had another thing coming.

Their bodies went rigid, then a short, dark-haired guy at the back (shorter than me, olive complexion, couldn't see the eye colour, kind of a hook nose, no distinguishing features I could make out, officer) reached forward, pulling at the arm of a spiky-blond one in front. 'C'mon,' he said quietly. 'Let's go.'

I stood my ground, watching them until they turned back around the corner they had come from. The second they were out of sight I flicked off my shiny granny shoes and bolted.

ADULT DECISIONS

'Sir, *please* can we have a year-ten formal?' I flashed my brightest smile and put my head to one side in a way I hoped was endearing.

The smile our school principal, Mr Choden, had given me when I first entered his darkened office drooped.

I pushed on. 'A lot of people are leaving at the end of this year. I don't think it's fair they miss out on having a prom just because they're not going all the way to year twelve.'

He picked up a pile of papers and knocked them into alignment on the desk, not looking at me.

'Please, sir.'

'No, Ruth.' He continued his stacking. 'We've decided not to do it.'

'Why?' I stared at him, willing him to meet my gaze.

Beady little eyes buried within an overly fleshy face looked resolutely at the table. 'It's too much work and the teachers have to give up their time to supervise —'

'But for the people who are leaving —'

'— and the numbers of students leaving in year ten is dropping so it is no longer an important school function.'

'It's important to the people who are leaving, sir.' *And to the people who are bored out of their minds in this crappy little town.*

'No. Too much work. We decided against continuing —'

'But I will organise the whole thing, sir! I promise you won't have to do anything! It seriously won't be any work for the school. All you need to do is give me permission. I'll do the rest.'

'No, Ruth. We're not having a year-ten formal. The decision has been made.'

At last he looked at me. In his eyes, I could see the gleam of satisfaction that came from having the final word.

My ears rang and blood pounded into my fists. I looked down at the desk, feeling tears thickening my throat. Since Dad had left no adult had pulled rank with me. Mr Choden wasn't even listening. He must think I was so beneath him, he didn't even have to come up with a decent explanation for his decision. All of his reasons boiled down to *because I said so*. He just wanted to prove he was the one with the power. Well, screw him.

I had never been in trouble at school, and my bowel twisted in deep clenching knots of fear, but my anger slammed in my chest, egging me on. I struggled for a moment to push my heavy chair back. 'Okay. That's fine. If the school doesn't want to do it, I'll organise it anyway. Thanks very much for your time.' Though I tried to make my voice sound light and breezy it slid all over the place with the effort to keep the tears at bay.

My legs wobbled as I walked out, pretending deafness as he said my name. I closed the door to the entrance foyer with the middle finger of my right hand raised. *Fuck you, motherfucker.*

My voice was still shaking as I shared the news of my meeting with a few people as keen for an excuse to dress up and go dancing as I was. They promised to back me and help however they could. I got out a pen and paper and started planning. We were bloody well having a school formal.

That afternoon Mum came with me to the reception centre near the school, where Kerstin had had her prom. I asked them how it worked and got them to put together a package. A thin boy from school with a big mouth and an eagerness to stick it to Mr Choden came along to help. Over the next few weeks we booked a date, printed tickets and gathered money.

As the prom took on a life of its own, Mr Choden began calling me into his office more and more. Initially it was once a week, but soon my classes were regularly being interrupted by a knock at the door announcing the principal wanted to see me.

'I'm very disappointed to see you're still going ahead with this event,' he said in his office eight days before the function.

I didn't respond. There was nothing left to say. I cleaned dirt from underneath my fingernails.

'You're not allowed to use the name "Rockhampton High" in any of your materials.'

I raised my eyebrows and rolled my eyes at him. 'You already told me that. We're calling it an end-of-year formal. Rocky High is not mentioned.'

'And the school is in no way respon—'

'I know!'

He paused for a moment, leaning back in his chair. 'You know, if people die on the way to your event their families will sue you.'

I stared at him. 'What're you talking about?'

'People have car accidents all the time. If they have one on the way to your event, you're responsible for their deaths. You know that, don't you? They can sue you for lots of money. You might even go to jail.'

My legs filled with water. Was that true? It felt like a trick he was using to try to scare me. I sat up straighter in my seat as I scrabbled frantically for a comeback to show him I wasn't intimidated. 'If people die, and sue me, and I wind up in jail, that has nothing to do with the school. It's none of your business. But I tell you what is your business: school.'

He didn't say anything.

The red mist came over my eyes and I shifted forward in my seat. 'Sir, d'you know what kind of student I am?'

'Yes.'

'Have you seen my records?'

'Yes.'

'So you know I'm one of the best students in my year.'

'Yes.'

'Yet you continually interrupt my learning, dragging me out of class to scare me into stopping this prom.' My whole body pounded. 'It's on in less than two weeks. Everyone's bought tickets. I've paid the venue. It's *going* to happen. There's nothing you can do to change that, so you may as well stop pulling me out of class.'

He tapped his hand on the edge of his desk, and his eyes followed the movement. I kept at him, willing him to grow balls big enough so he could meet my gaze.

'You're a principal. Your interest should be in my education, not whether I'm organising a party that, *as you say*, has nothing to do with the school.'

I stopped talking and catalogued his faults as I waited for him to speak: he wore suits in forty-degree heat so everyone knew he was the big man on campus, grew a bushy beard to hide his weak chin, was barely able to string an argument together. He was obviously covering up all manner of physical and intellectual insecurities. Did this pathetic man actually think he could break me?

My legs were shaking so much I could barely stand up, but I managed to drag myself erect before moving behind the chair and leaning on it for support. 'If you keep pulling me out of class I'm going to report you.'

Finally he looked at me. I stared back. Could he really not see past his ideas of what it meant to be young and female to see me as I truly was? I was more powerful than he could ever dream of being. He would never win against me.

After a long moment he dropped his gaze.

'So can I go back to class now, sir?'

'Yes. You can leave.'

I would show him how strong I was. I would show them all.

The next time he dragged me into his office, I made good on my promise. At home, Mum helped me scroll through the phone book, figuring out who to report him to. After a few false starts within the Department of Education, we ended up at the right person. I told him what was happening. He said Mr Choden shouldn't be acting that way and he would look into it.

After the phone call ended, I climbed my tree, trying to distance myself from the pulsing stress in my gut. I didn't want to bring more conflict into my life, especially at school. I liked school – the order of it, the learning, the thinking about bigger things – and it was nice having somewhere to go each day where I knew what was going to happen. Why did Mr Choden have to keep harassing me? What did he think? That I was going to bow down to his greater wisdom just because he was an adult?

Since the age of eleven, I had made nearly every 'adult' decision in my life. I was now nearly fifteen. I wasn't about to roll over and be treated like a child because some grown-up wanted to exert their authority on me. Why should I?

The grown-ups I knew were at least as flawed as I was. As far as I was concerned, a wanker was a wanker, no matter how old they were. Mr Choden was definitely a wanker.

I shifted in my branch and pressed my fingernail into the bark, leaving behind a dotted trail of semicircles. How dare he try to strong-arm me! I hadn't wanted to dob on him. I didn't want to threaten and intimidate, but if that was the game he wanted to play, I would play it. I had had enough of bullies. If he got in trouble from the Department of Education for his tactics, so he should.

I don't know what happened at his end, but after the phone call he left me alone. The formal went ahead without any problems. No one died. No one had an accident. The only thing that happened was that I realised I would rather organise a function for a hundred people than be told, for no good reason, that I couldn't do something I wanted to do.

FORGETTING

While my understanding of the psychological forces that drove Dad's actions was growing, the amount of time my son now hit me was shrinking. Though he still sometimes gave me a whack, the peak of his physical expression seemed to have passed and I was able to let go of the breath I had been holding for the past eighteen months. I even let myself imagine a time in the future when he might stop hitting for good.

The way I thought about Dad was in a much healthier place as well. But there was still something dogging me. The thing I found most difficult to get my head around: Dad never made amends for his behaviour because he said he had no recollection of it.

In a phone call when I was eighteen I confronted him with his violence, listing incident after incident, trying to make him say sorry.

'Do you remember when I was three years old? When you beat the shit out of me because I stuck a Tic Tac sticker on a wall?'

He made no noise.

'Do you?'

'No, I don't remember that.' His small, hurt voice infuriated me.

'Well I do, Dad. I remember every fucking minute of it! And

do you remember beating the crap out of me for dropping the sinker on the boat? Or not setting the tent up fast enough? Or falling down? Or what about that night with Mum? Do you remember that? Do you? Do you? Do you?'

He told me he didn't know what I was talking about.

His lack of ownership left me so stunned I couldn't breathe. If it wasn't for the countless conversations I'd had with my brother and sister where we corroborated all he had done, I might have thought I was insane. Thank God I wasn't an only child.

His denial turned my molten anger to glass and sharp edges formed around the thinking I'd had since childhood. He was an arsehole: no capacity to look at himself, yet more than capable of seeing my faults. He was completely insensitive to the way his behaviour affected others, but highly tuned to the way their actions affected him. He hated people for not being as perfect as he expected them to be yet forgave himself completely for his own imperfections.

I tried to punish his selfishness, withdrawing my love, withholding myself from him. But despite my efforts, I found myself reaching out to him again and again.

Our already fragile connection had been further impeded by geographical distance. While Dad stayed living in Rockhampton, after finishing university I had moved two states away to Melbourne. With more than two thousand kilometres between us, our relationship mostly took place over the phone, and it always felt one-sided.

I would wait to see how long it would take him to call me. I waited and waited and waited, aware of the time ticking by, thinking of him, before finally relenting about every nine months and calling him instead.

I always felt ashamed that I was the one to break our silence. I had never been one of those girls who did all the chasing. I wanted an equal relationship with him, but if I had waited for him to call me, we would never have spoken at all.

When I did call he was always delighted to hear from me and we would have conversations for hours about the bigger ideas of life. Dad was well read and watched mostly documentaries on ABC, so there were very few topics on which he didn't have an informed and well-considered opinion.

Those conversations with him were probably some of the most intellectually satisfying I have had, and I always got off the phone so buzzed it felt like I had chugged ten espressos. *That was such an awesome conversation, I would think. Surely he doesn't have conversations like that all the time? He will want to do that again soon, won't he?*

Then two weeks would turn into a month, one month would roll into two, then three. I carried our last conversation around with me, thinking it over, gathering new things to tell him that might let us pick up where we had eft off.

I imagined coming home to the ringing phone and hearing Dad's voice when I picked up. *I was just thinking about you*, he would say, and then we would laugh and talk again.

But as more time ticked by, and the bounce in my step faltered, then dragged, another voice in my head would grow louder: Maybe he doesn't find you anywhere near as interesting as you find him. It was the eucalyptus project all over again.

To drown it out I would beat my angry drum. *Fuck him. If he can't appreciate me then I won't appreciate him. I am not calling him. Not even at nine months. Never again.*

Then I would call Kerstin. 'You're not allowed to talk about me to Dad,' I would say.

'What?' She was used to my nine-monthly rants.

'Last time I spoke to Dad, he said he knew about something I was telling him because you had told him about it. I don't want you telling Dad anything about me.'

'Why?'

'Because if he wants to know something about me, he can bloody well ask me!' The hoarse desperation in my voice squeezed my words.

I hated the idea that he would be able to act like he had a relationship with me just because I spoke to Kerstin regularly and she passed my information on to him. If anyone asked him about me I wanted him to falter in his narcissistic image of himself as a good father. Then maybe he would realise he hadn't spoken to me in a long time and pick up the phone and call me.

'So what am I meant to say if he asks about you?' I heard the flick of her lighter and breathy exhale as she smoked her Alpine Light sixteen hundred kilometres away in Brisbane.

'You say to him that you haven't spoken to me and that he should give me a call if he is interested in finding out about me. I mean it. Don't tell him.'

'Yeah, okay.' Her voice was full of rolling eyes and I knew she would tell him whatever he wanted to hear so that she could remain the favourite daughter.

Though I loved my conversations with Dad, and luxuriated in his warmth and humour, each time I spoke to him, I was also aware of a part of me that stood to the side, waiting for him to address the accusations I had made. He needed to say sorry for what he had done if we ever had a chance of having a real bond.

It wasn't until he made a drunken phone call to me on the night of his fiftieth birthday that I even considered the possibility that he genuinely didn't remember the violence.

I had been living in Melbourne for two months when he called me.

'I know you weren't lyin', love.' His voice slurred down the phone at me.

Brain still fogged from sleep, I couldn't make sense of his words. 'Dad, what is it? It's four in the morning.'

'It's my birthday, love. Kerstin's here with me. She tol' me you weren't lying.'

'What're you talking about?'

'I know you weren't lyin' about me givin' ya a touch-up. She tol' me it was true. I din' know. Sorry.'

It took me a moment to figure out what he meant. *This* was his acknowledgement of the phone call four years ago when I'd tried to get him to own up to all he had done? The phone call we had never mentioned again? Was he seriously trying to tell me he'd thought I had made it up?

'Right. I know I wasn't lying, Dad. It's nice for you to say so, I guess.'

He cried down the line. 'I . . . sorry, love . . . didn't know.'

I had always believed in the power of words. Calling it a 'touch-up' was weird and wrong on so many levels. Firstly it made the abuse sound sexual, which it had definitely not been.

The only other way I could imagine those words being used was if a couple of good ol' boys were playing a game of rugby and one of them gave the other a clip around the ear. The euphemism felt as if he was trying to diminish his already reduced responsibility.

And why did he have the luxury of not remembering while I got to carry the load? If anything, my childhood memories felt supercharged, like I remembered the details vividly enough for two. Maybe everything that was split off from him got channelled into me. Maybe I was holding the memories for us both.

But the phone call haunted me in a different way.

If he truly didn't remember hitting us, he didn't hold himself to account for his actions. That meant he had been living his life without the horror of those moments while I had carried them around with me every single day. It was hard to believe that level of forgetting was even possible.

LOSING TICKET

It wasn't until my fifteenth birthday that I saw Dad again.

Two years earlier, when Kerstin had turned fifteen, Dad had bought her a ghetto blaster costing over a hundred dollars. It was sleek and silver with levers and dials to adjust the bass, treble and EQ output. It had a radio and two tape decks so you could make mix-tapes. The whole floor vibrated when you turned it up all the way to ten. I could tell by the big smile on Dad's face when he handed it to her that he knew he had chosen well.

Ever since she had got the present, I had been sneaking into her room, secretly playing tapes on it and pretending it was mine. Now I was turning fifteen, it was my turn for Dad to buy me one just like it.

'Happy birthday.' Mum knocked lightly on my door, crossed to where I was still in bed and handed me a box wrapped in shiny red paper.

Peeling away the layers I found a small tape player inside. It was pink and plastic with one tape deck and no radio. I kept a smile glued to my face as I turned it over in my hands. The only buttons on it were the play, stop, rewind and fast-forward ones. The one dial was for adjusting the volume. I swallowed and nodded about ten times in quick succession.

'Thanks, Mum. I love it.' I struggled out of bed and gave her a hug.

I had been telling Mum all about the stereo Dad was going to buy me for weeks now. I'd had no idea she would take it as a hint. After everything he had put us through, Dad owed me a stereo. Anyway, it wouldn't be fair if he bought one for Kerstin and not for me.

During the past few months I had mostly managed to lock the night he had come back inside the vault buried deep inside my brain. This was where I hid the growing pile of things I had no idea how to deal with: Mum's drinking, the chaos in the house, acting normal all the time, having the boogieman for a father. Still, the system wasn't foolproof, and many days I was bombarded with images that left me cringing in a corner.

I dressed in a special birthday outfit: white baggy pants turned up three times at the ankle, and the red t-shirt three sizes too big, onto the pocket of which I had sewed a small turtle, in the hope anyone looking from a distance might think it was the Lacoste crocodile.

I slid 'Kiss Me, Kiss Me, Kiss Me' by The Cure into the tape deck of my new player and turned it up as high as it would go. Crackling drowned out Robert Smith's voice. I turned it down so I could make out the words.

As I sang along, I fluffed up my perm in the mirror, moving my head from side to side as I checked out the dye job I had done last night. Deepest Plum. I was going for a more mature look now I was fifteen.

After playing all the music in my four-tape collection, I found Mum in the kitchen listening to the radio. The light streaming through the window was warm and yellow and the smell of the onions she was chopping reminded me of the times she used to make dinner when Dad lived here with us.

She didn't seem as drunk as usual, and it felt like she was making an extra effort because of my birthday. It was almost like having the old Mum back. I hugged her from behind and gave her smoky hair a kiss to show her how much I appreciated it.

There had never been much money for parties and presents, so birthdays in our house had never really been a big deal. Each increase in age was marked by the arrival of two cards containing ten dollars from each our grandparents, and a small gift from Mum and Dad. At some stage during the day the family would gather and sing 'Happy Birthday'. The one time I had begged for an ice-cream cake like American kids had in the movies, Mum had bought a two-litre tub of Neapolitan, tipped it onto a plate and put a candle in it. Generally I tried to keep my expectations in check.

'Mum. Has Dad called yet?' I asked.

'No, love, not yet. But you know this time of year. Everyone's busy. I'm sure he is going to call.'

My birthday was at the crappiest possible time. Three days after Christmas, three days before New Year's Eve. No one had any money to buy presents. No shops were open. All my friends were on holidays.

But it was two minutes to three. Surely he would have had time to call by now.

I pushed back onto two legs of my chair, first holding on to the table, then letting go and balancing hands-free in mid-air.

'Stop doing that.' Mum glared at me. I locked my knee under the table and brought the chair softly to the ground.

I made a game out of looking at the clock, counting out sixty staccato clicks and looking up at the exact moment the second hand crossed the twelve.

At eleven past three I said the words I had been thinking all day. 'Maybe he's forgotten.'

Mum mixed the sauce she was making in short, sharp jabs. 'I don't think he'd do that.' She moved to the table, hunting for her smokes. 'Give it a bit more time.'

At 3.38 I made a suggestion. 'Maybe we should call to check what time he's coming over?'

'Good idea.' Mum lit another cigarette, grabbed the overflowing ashtray and walked over to the wall phone. 'Hello, is Doug there?' Mum's lips pulled tight and her eyebrows were up as high as they went, making her forehead a series of deep grooves. She must be speaking to Brenda, probably for the first time since Dad had left. I imagined how much it must hurt to hear her voice. I wondered if *Brenda* knew about the night Dad had come back.

'Hello.' There was a pause as she listened to something on the other end of the phone.

'Yeah. You too.'

Another pause.

'There's a reason I'm calling. I was wondering if you remembered what day it is today?'

'The date.'

'Does that mean anything to you?'

'Your youngest daughter's birthday.'

A longer pause.

'Well, she's been waiting to see you all day.' Mum's voice wobbled with anger. I shrank.

'You don't do anything else for them. The least you could do is remember their birth—'

'The government makes you give us that money.'

'Yes. I think it'd be good. I think Ruth would like to see you.'

She looked over at me and I nodded. I still wanted my ghetto blaster.

'Okay. See you then.'

Mum hung up the phone and I smiled at her to show I didn't care. My face felt stretched in weird places. I swallowed the lump blocking my throat so I could talk. 'When's he coming?'

'Half an hour.'

I nodded, went to my room and lay on my bed.

At the crunch of tyres on gravel and the roar of Dad's truck, I looked out my window. Dad emerged wearing grey stubbies and a pale green polo shirt that had seen better days.

Shelly, the dog we had recently inherited, raced toward him, barking.

'Hey. Hey there.' He bent down as if to pat her, but she jumped out of his reach, still barking. As he moved in the direction of the back stairs, she lunged toward him.

'C'mon now. That's enough.' His voice turned harsh. When

he moved, she came at him again, teeth bared, barking escalating. 'Stop it, ya silly dog.' He pushed past her and she followed behind him, barking.

She's not a silly dog, Dad. She knows danger when she sees it.

I raced out to the kitchen, throwing myself into a chair and striking a relaxed pose to demonstrate how much I had not been waiting.

Two knocks on the open back door and he poked his head around the corner and smiled weakly. 'Sorry I forgot your birthday, love.'

I got out of my chair and walked into his outstretched arms. 'That's all right. It's a stupid time of the year to have a birthday.' We held each other for a long moment. This man was not the same one who had come back to our house that night.

We broke apart and stood awkwardly for a few seconds.

'Now, I didn't have anything in the house to give you. This is all I had.' He pulled a white plastic bag, the kind supermarkets put groceries in, out of his shorts pocket.

I looked at him for a moment trying to figure out what he was doing. I didn't quite understand the joke, but I put on an expression that let him know I wasn't fooled. 'Ha ha. Very funny.'

'There's a TAB ticket in there for a horse I put a bet on this morning. I hope it wins for ya, love.'

I kept my voice light. 'Are you joking with me?'

'No, love. Sorry. This was all I had.'

Looking at the scrunched-up ball of white plastic in my hands, I teetered on the edge of a deep hole that was opening up in front of me, my head spinning as I tried to make sense of what was happening. I knew he had lost track of today being my birthday. I hadn't known until that moment that he had forgotten about me entirely.

In Rockhampton at that time, the shops were always closed between Christmas and New Year's Eve. If he hadn't bought me a birthday present, it meant he hadn't thought about me for the whole time leading up to Christmas.

Kerstin's birthday was 5 January. It was part of the craziness of Christmas holidays as well. He had never forgotten her birthday. What did it mean that he remembered her but forgot me?

I knew that since he had started living with Brenda, she had done most of the shopping. But the year Kerstin turned fifteen, *he* had chosen the stereo for her. If someone was important enough to him, he could make the effort.

I tried to keep my face in a neutral position but my chin moved up and down under aching cheeks. I looked out the window.

Clothesline. Fence. Tree. Truck.

Water roared in my ears as a wave of worthlessness threatened to lift me off my feet.

There could be no other way to look at it. Kerstin was worth a ghetto blaster. I was worth nothing. Less than nothing. To Dad, I was a piece of rubbish and a ticket destined not to win.

'Okay, Dad. Thanks for coming by. I'll see you later then.' My voice was quiet and flat as I strained to keep it under control.

'I thought I might stay for a while.' He sounded surprised and moved toward me as if to hug me again. I dodged him and backed away. I had to get out before he saw me cry.

'I'm not feeling very well. I think I need to lie down.'

I walked quickly down the hall and tried to open the sliding door to my new bedroom. The door didn't budge. After Kerstin and I had descended into a fiery catfight of teenage hormones a couple of months ago, it had been decided we needed separate rooms. Since I was the 'easygoing one', I had been moved into a tiny section of the verandah barely big enough to contain my single bed and wardrobe. Kerstin had kept the large double bedroom with the proper carpet.

Tears blurred my vision as I heaved the door along its rollers, finally managing to open it wide enough to slip through the gap into my stupid room. Footsteps approached, but I managed to slam the door closed behind me just as the wave finally crashed. It spewed out of me in a wail I barely recognised as my own. The hurt flooding through me was worse than any physical pain he had put me through. Every part of me was a bruise and my skin was stretched so thin, the merest hint of someone's gaze would be enough to pierce it and make my insides pour out onto the floor in a useless pile. I didn't want anyone to look at me ever again.

After a while, as my tears ebbed, I thought over what had happened. It was my birthday – the first time I had seen Dad since that night. I was meant to be the one with the power. He was meant to be grovelling for forgiveness with expensive electrical items in hand.

But yet again, he had managed to reduce me to rubble. Less than rubble. Dust. Insignificant and unimportant. I had no power over him, because he didn't love me. He didn't love me, because I was unlovable. Hadn't he been trying to show me that my whole life? Sobs poured out of me again.

When my crying slowed, my eyes roved to the wardrobe I had painstakingly painted two weekends ago. They were made of some kind of plastic that meant the paint had dried shiny. The simple white I had thought would look elegant had turned out cheap and nasty. Everything about my life was cheap and nasty and I was sick to death of it all.

SURPRISE ATTACK

The week after I started year eleven it was hot. My hands slipped in pools of their own sweat on the cover of the plastic ring-bound folder I was carrying as I walked between the grey brick buildings of my school.

Just as my foot hit the shade of the building where I could stow my things, I heard my name being called. I turned in the direction of the voice, and saw Sean, a tall boy with a short back and sides haircut who was in the same year as me, looking expectantly in my direction.

Sean sometimes hung around the fringes of a group of my friends. Or maybe he was part of the core group now. I wasn't sure. My friends had always been good, slightly nerdy types, heavily involved in school activities. But over the years I had begun to feel a chasm between the world they inhabited – mums and dads together, cooked meals, curfews – and my own. I liked them; it just felt like we had less and less in common.

It wasn't their fault. They would have been kind to me if I had given them a chance. But I had no room for kindness in my life. Kindness could break me in a way violence could not. I needed to stay strong.

I checked the faces of the group surrounding Sean. Not my friends. He was in a cluster with six boys who regularly got into low-grade trouble for drinking in school, or vandalism, or petty theft.

'What?' I called over to him.

'C'mere.' He gestured me over. Sean rarely spoke to me unless he was with my friends. Yesterday, the skinny mature-age student with the mullet and multiple earrings who stood at his left had informed me that 'the boys' had been talking about me, and they thought my body was getting better: firmer. I was not going over there to be assessed like a piece of meat.

'No. What do you want?'

He paused a moment then yelled, 'Is your mum a drunk?'

There were twelve metres between us. His question sailed out over the distance and echoed off the edges of the buildings, before landing in the depths of my bowel, where my darkest secrets lived.

Fourteen eyes burned holes into me, and I stood naked in front of all the boys, the way it happened in my dreams. White light flashed past my eyes and my face made shapes I couldn't quite control. I tried to signal him to shut up.

'What?' I managed to eject the word out of my completely dry mouth as I moved closer to him so he could see the pleading in my eyes.

'Your mum. Is she a drunk?'

Shut up, shut up, shut up. 'Why do you say that?'

'I saw her out the front of our shop the other day. She was patting this dog. Then she fell over. She was pretty much lying on the ground next to it. She stayed like that for ages.

Oh Jesus. A swarm of locusts started up in my head. Beyond the angry buzzing, I could hear their hard-shelled bodies rubbing together as they fought and began devouring each other.

How was I meant to respond?

My mouth opened and closed in the way I had always thought of as bad acting when I had seen someone do it on TV. I wanted to say words, but when I opened my mouth none came out.

My vision narrowed into a white tunnel focusing only on Sean's face. In a daze, I scanned his features for signs of malice, but saw none. Could he really be asking this question, ridiculing Mum, without any sense of how much he was hurting me? Could he really be so stupid? After what felt like a hundred years, I finally found something to say.

'You're not very bright, are you, Sean?' I was initially trying to speak to him in code, tell him how stupid he was to bring up something like this in front of a group of people, but once the words were out of my mouth I saw how I could morph this situation into something I hoped would make him shut up about Mum.

'What?'

'Sorry. Maybe I need to speak a bit slower for you.' I exaggerated my speech and gestured with my hands in mock sign language. 'Yooou aaaren't veeery briiight, aaare yoooou?'

'What are you saying that for?' He flinched away from me.

'Well, you're repeating year eleven, aren't you?' I paused and watched as his mouth fell open in a small O of shock, before continuing downward into something like sadness. 'And that's pretty much down to your stupidity.'

His forehead knotted in confusion. 'I don't know why you're saying this.'

The noise of the locusts in my ears was the only awareness I had of my body. Some part of me felt terrible at how much my words would hurt him, but another part of me, the part that had always come out swinging when it felt under attack, didn't care. As long as he shut up about Mum.

I hit my head with my palm as if suddenly struck by an idea. 'Oh sorry. I forgot. This must be confusing for someone with such a low IQ! I'll break it down for you. What I mean is, you're repeating this year . . . but it's not like you are doing any particularly challenging subjects, is it? Vegie maths, vegie science, PE.' I listed them off on my fingers. 'What's the point? I mean I know you probably only got about a four hundred TE score last time. How much more do you think your score's really going to improve by coming back this year?'

His face crumpled. Some of the boys in the group laughed and banged their shoulders into him.

I didn't wait around for him to answer. I walked away, my face bright red.

My legs barely carried me to the toilets less than a hundred metres away. As soon as I banged the door to the cubicle closed, my tears rushed out.

How could I have done that? I might not have used my fists, but I knew how to inflict pain. I was such an awful person. *Exactly like Dad.* The locusts had gone, leaving behind a cavernous void that made my self-recriminations echo. I put my face in my hands and squeezed hard in punishment.

How could he have said that in front of everyone? I thought of Mum, and what Sean must have thought as he looked at her patting the dog. *Ruth's mum's a pathetic, stumbling alcoholic.*

Fuck *him*! She was more than that. She was kind and patient and she loved dogs. So what? He didn't have the right to judge her. She wasn't 'a drunk'; she was my mum.

Anyway, how should I have responded? Joked about Mum being a drunk? *Yeah, it's really funny to have the woman you love more than anyone in the world hate herself and her life so much that she locks herself away and drinks to unconsciousness every day. Ha ha. Glad you found that amusing.*

But then, what right did I have to get mad at Sean? I knew exactly what he felt when he looked at her because I felt the same things. I should be protecting Mum from me. I was her daughter. I was meant to love her, yet I found her drunkenness disgusting.

My lower back burned so I adjusted my position on the lid of the toilet, bringing my feet closer in to my body so no one would see my legs under the toilet door if they came in. I took some deep breaths, then looked at the graffiti on the back of the door. *I love Darren 4EVA!!!! Kylie luvs Craig.*

At least, even if I was sometimes disgusted, I loved her and suffered with her as she drank. When Sean looked, he didn't see the heartbreak and self-loathing she was trying to numb.

I put my cheek on the wall of the cubicle, trying to take some heat out of my face. I was such an idiot! Until he had said those words I had somehow deluded myself, believing I was the only one who could see how drunk Mum was. Her drinking was my shame. My secret. But if Sean could see it, then everyone could. I didn't have enough energy to take on the whole school.

I put my feet on the concrete floor and jiggled my legs up and down to shake away the numbness brought on by my awkward position. Mum didn't need any more pain or judgement. If there was one thing I knew for sure, it was that no one could possibly think anything worse about Mum than she already thought about herself.

I looked at my watch. Ten minutes to one. I had fifteen minutes to pull myself together before I had to go back to class. I grabbed some toilet paper and blew my nose, then went out and ran the cold tap. As always, the water came out lukewarm. Why did everything in Rockhampton have to be such an insipid temperature? Pressing handfuls of water around my eyes, I fanned myself with my hand to try to cool down.

I didn't look in the mirror. I knew it would not be pretty. I would look at the ground, not make eye contact with anyone. Then, the second I finished year twelve I would move to Brisbane, reinvent myself and put this whole mess of a life behind me. All I needed to do was keep my head down and take it for another year.

NOT READY

When I was twenty-four, I came home from a boozy lunch for my then boyfriend's birthday to find a message on the answering machine in our apartment in the beachside suburb of St Kilda in Melbourne. The thrill I felt to hear Dad's voice crashed into despair as I heard what he had to say.

'Hi Ruth, it's your dad here. Listen, I've got melanoma cancer. They say it's malignant and I don't have long to live. Gimme a call when you get a minute.'

I felt a punch in my guts that buckled my legs. Who would leave that message on someone's answering machine?

I called back immediately and found out that Dad was in hospital. Though they had removed a malignant mole from his face a few years ago and given him the all-clear, it had already spread its insidious tentacles and started multiplying in his brain and lungs.

'I was having a bit of trouble with my balance,' he told me. 'So I went to see the doctor.'

I heard him flick a lighter but held my tongue about the wisdom of adding the contents of a cancer stick to a body already fighting the disease. I didn't smoke, but at that moment I wished I did. I felt like I needed a cigarette. I couldn't imagine how he must be feeling.

'The doctor told me it could be a few things. The best-case scenario was I'd had a little stroke. The next was a bigger stroke. The worst, a brain tumour.

'I was pretty sure it was a stroke. Y'know Papa had a stroke. But when I came back he told me it was option three.'

'I'm so sorry, Dad.' I swallowed my sobs but tears streamed down my face.

'Hey, hey. Don't cry. Doesn't matter. That's the way the cookie crumbles. It's all right, love.'

I wailed harder that he was comforting me when I should be comforting him.

It matters to me, Dad. I don't want you to die. I'm not ready for you to go. You don't even know me. I haven't stopped hating you yet. I swallowed harder, trying to make the cries stop.

I had already begun reading self-help books to try to work through some of my past pain, but knowing I was going to fly back to Rockhampton to live in the same house as Dad while he died drove me to them with a fervour. I wanted help, any kind of help, to figure out how I was meant to behave in this situation.

I read about people bringing up their issues with dying loved ones and their last memories together being full of arguments and bitterness that they regretted when their feelings softened over the following years. Though my anger at Dad still ate me alive some days, I hoped I would feel differently one day, maybe in a million years' time. I was determined to go up and say goodbye to him acting the way I wished I felt: as if I had forgiven him for everything that had gone before.

Besides, my stirring up conflict would cause Kerstin and David distress. The whole situation was torturous enough already without me adding to it. And if it was true that he didn't remember hitting us, then there was absolutely no point in bringing it up. Not now. Not when he lay drugged out on morphine, dying.

It wasn't fair. Dad's mum had lived until she was in her nineties. Dad's dad was nearly eighty when he died. Dad was only fifty-two. I had banked on having a few more decades to figure out how to have a real relationship with him.

He told me his melanoma cancer was probably linked to his exposure to Agent Orange. 'It'd make sense,' he said on the phone. 'Us blokes'd all be sitting there in the jungle and this plane would fly overhead and send down buckets of the stuff. It'd drip down on you like rain and you just sat there not moving as it sank into your skin.

'In a week or so you'd watch as all the leaves in the jungle dropped to the ground so the trees just looked like sticks. At the time I thought to myself if it did that to the trees I don't reckon it'd be doing us much good either. It could be weeks before you had a chance to wash it off properly.'

The dissociation. Now his impending early death. One more thing to lay at the feet of that stupid war.

PRETENDING

'Ruth, there's something I need to talk to you about.' Mum struggled with the sliding door before stepping into my room and resting against the wardrobe.

I put the book I was reading to one side and sat up in bed. She had said my name. She never did that unless I was in trouble. I flicked through my internal Rolodex for recent misbehaviour.

I had fallen asleep at a party last week and not come home until six in the morning. But I thought I had lied my way out of that.

'I was home at about half past two,' I had said, after Kerstin had given me the heads-up that Mum was going to confront me. 'It's not that late. And anyway, I didn't know I had a curfew. This is the first time you've ever mentioned it.'

I watched her warily, wondering if Kerstin had finally dobbed me in. Her knuckles were white from the grip she had on the plastic handles of the washing basket she held against her hip. But her eyes, so dark I couldn't tell where her pupils ended and irises began, held no anger. She dropped her gaze to her hands.

'What is it, Mum?'

She took a shaking breath. 'I think I need to go to Brisbane to get my life sorted out.'

'Right.' My voice came out high and girly. 'When?'

'Soon. A few weeks or a month?'

My breath stumbled. I was just about to start my final year of high school.

'I know I made a mess of everything.' Mum's chin shuddered and a tear dripped down her cheek. 'I've been trying to change. But it's hard.'

More tears flowed. I took the basket out of her hands and put it on the floor before pulling her to sit on the bed beside me. Stress burbled noisily in her stomach.

'Mum, you haven't made a mess of things. It's all okay. We still love you.'

'I've done everything wrong.' Her body heaved with sobs now and I put my arm around her bony shoulders, crying along with her. Belligerent drunk Mum made me mad. Sad, self-loathing Mum broke my heart.

'You're a great mum. I love you so much.'

'I'm sorry about this,' she sobbed. 'Sorry.'

'Mum, it's all right. I love you.'

Keeping my arm on her shoulder, I wiped my tears on my sleeve and sat in silence as her crying slowed. She pulled a scrunched-up tissue out of her bra and blew her nose, keeping her eyes down.

'I've been trying to get on top of this drinking thing but it isn't working. I've been to a few AA meetings but they're always full of people who know me. It's so embarrass—'

'I didn't know you'd been to AA.'

'Yeah.'

'It's great you're trying to get help, Mum.'

She shook her head. 'I can't do it. When they come up to me afterwards . . . talk to me. It's awful. I can't go back.'

'It's great you tried though.'

'Yeah.' She pulled at the tissue in her hand, tearing off a strip. 'But it's not bloody working, is it? I can't stop drinking.'

I gulped at her honesty. 'What do you think will happen in Brisbane?'

'I dunno. At least I won't know anyone.'

'Where will you stay?'

'At Grandma and Grandpop's.'

I paused as I digested her words. 'I think it'll be good for you, Mum. To get out of here. At least you'll never run into Dad . . . or *her*.'

'Yeah. There's just too many bad memories here.'

I knew what she meant. Rockhampton rubbed up against me like sandpaper, triggering painful memories that kept ripping the scabs off old wounds.

After she left I lay back on my bed. I'd had no idea Mum had been going to AA meetings, but I could imagine nothing about them would feel anonymous. Rocky was big enough to have its own university, but small enough that we had got our first McDonald's only last year. It was way too easy for people to know your business.

Still. Brisbane. Living with Grandma and Grandpop. Jesus. What would that be like? Grandma would drive Mum nuts.

Forced to wander from town to town doing laundry in country Queensland after her father deserted the family, Grandma had been sent to school only until grade four. By the time she met Grandpop, she'd decided she had done enough work for a lifetime. From the moment she woke up to the moment she went to bed, she sat in front of the TV having one-sided conversations with characters on soaps. If she needed food or drink, she called out to Grandpop to get them.

But that would change if Mum went back. When she was barely big enough to see over the stove, Mum had been made responsible for all the cooking and cleaning in the house. Though she had left school at the end of grade nine to work in a department store, Mum had still gone home each night to do all the household duties Grandma couldn't get to because of her heavy television schedule.

If Mum went back to Brisbane, she would return to her role as dutiful daughter and housemaid, silently resenting the instructions Grandma shouted from her throne in front of the TV.

At least she would be safe. And she wouldn't be alone. I just had to figure out the right way to tell her I wasn't going with her.

Later that afternoon, I sat at my desk watching lightning strobe across the charcoal sky. I hoped a bolt might strike my brain and fill it with a flash of inspiration about how to have the upcoming conversation with Mum, but as the last murmurs of thunder petered out without calling forth even a drop of rain, I realised it was going to be up to me.

I switched on the light and opened a chemistry book I had

no intention of reading as I thought over the situation. I could see why Mum needed to get out of here. But if I left with her, I would be holding her hand as she detoxed, while negotiating a new curriculum, and having to deal with all the stupid *he likes you, she hates you* crap of starting at a brand-new high school. Desperate as I was to get out of Rockhampton, I wanted to get into university more.

A mosquito buzzed near my ear and I smacked the side of my head.

Rocky High was such a shit-hole they probably weren't even teaching us the same curriculum as other schools. If I changed schools now I would move from being in the top ten students. That might be enough to stop me getting a place at uni. There was no way I was going with her.

I started working my way through all the arguments Mum might have against me staying.

'You are not even sixteen.' *So what? I will be sixteen soon and Kerstin will turn eighteen before I start school next year. If someone pushes the issue I can just say she is my legal guardian.* (As long as she didn't think that meant she could in any way tell me what to do.)

'You won't be able to look after yourself.' *As if I haven't been looking after myself since Dad left, Mum. You haven't exactly been an engaged parent.* No. A bit harsh. How about, *I can feed myself and wash my own clothes. What else is there? You tell me what you need to see and I will do it.* Much less aggressive.

'It will cost too much money.' *I'm turning sixteen in a couple of months so I can get the Austudy allowance. I am also working. So long as you let us stay in the house and don't charge rent, Kerstin and*

I can go halves in the costs of the electricity and everything. And you won't be paying to stay at Grandma and Grandpop's so that seems kind of fair. And anyway, you aren't allowed to get an income from rent or it will affect your pension.

'You will have parties and wreck the place.' One thing I was absolutely sure of was that I would not be having big parties when she was gone. It would just mean a big mess for me to clean up. If people wanted parties they could throw their own. *No parties.*

My eyes flicked along the top row of the periodic table. Hydrogen, helium, lithium, beryllium, boron, carbon . . . Focus. What else could she say?

'Someone at school will report you and child protective services will put you in a foster home.' *I have been forging your signature on forms the school has sent home for years. I get myself ready, buy my own lunch, do my own study, get myself to my own extra-curricular activities. I don't see how the school would notice any difference.*

I was actually pretty sure my life would be easier once she had gone. At least no other kids at school could bail me up and ask if my mum was a drunk.

I tapped my pen. I got the lead in the musical and won the prize for theatre every year. I had been lying and pretending my whole life. All I had to do was act as if she had never meant for me to go and see if she bought my bluff. I would pull out the arsenal of arguments only if I needed them. It was showtime.

As I approached the kitchen I heard Kerstin and Mum talking, their sentences interrupted by exaggerated in-breaths as they dragged on their cigarettes. I slunk into the shadows and listened in.

'When did you decide all this, Mum?'

'I've been thinking about it for a while. But last meeting I ran into a man who used to work with your father ...'

Right, they were on topic. Time for my entrance. I plastered a big smile on my face and entered the room, looking directly at Kerstin.

'Have you heard the news?' Kerstin nodded.

'It's great for Mum to move to Brisbane so she can get her life back in order. Don't you think?'

She butted out her cigarette and shrugged.

I turned to face Mum. 'It'll be so good. And as soon as I finish grade twelve I can come down and stay with you.' I kept my face open and smiling, directing all my willpower into making her agree with me.

A look of confusion crossed her face. 'What do you mean? Aren't you coming?'

I made my eyes wide. 'Oh no, Mum. I couldn't possibly move for my final year of high school. I'm already halfway through some subjects and some of my year eleven grades count toward next year. I want to make sure I get good enough marks to get into uni. I really need to stay here. But I think it's really great you're going.'

My whole face felt ready to spasm with the effort of smiling. If I were looking at me, I would be able to tell in a second I was putting on an act, but Mum was a terrible liar. Terrible liars are hopeless at telling when someone is lying to them. They think everyone is as honest as they are.

'Oh right. Well, how will it work?'

'Well, Kerstin and I can stay here, can't we?' I looked over at Kerstin and she nodded. 'And I'll pay for my share of the bills and everything. That'll be all right, won't it, Mum?'

'Yeah. Should be . . .' She nodded, her eyes going huge with fear, the way they always did when she thought about money.

'Yeah, it'll be really good. You'll get better down there, you'll see.' I hugged her into me. Her frailness brought fresh tears to my eyes.

Much as I wanted to be rid of her depressing drunkenness, I didn't want Mum to go. I had never been away from her. And though I was sure she'd never noticed it, I had spent my whole life doing what I could to protect her. I didn't know if she could survive without me. I didn't know who I would be if she no longer needed me to stand guard.

HIDING IN PLAIN SIGHT

'Ruth!' I was heading home early from the first school dance of year twelve, when Mrs Dean, a tiny bird of a woman, who also happened to be my year mistress, called my name and gestured me over.

My heart skipped a beat. *This is it. I have finally been found out.* In the ten-metre walk to her through the dark concreted area outside the school hall, I lined up my excuses. *Mum is on holiday. We're just about to fill in the forms to make Kerstin my legal guardian —*

Her pale blue eyes watered with emotion as she looked deeply into mine. 'I'm a bit concerned —'

You have no parental guardians. You are too young to be living alone. I'm going to have to put you in foster care.

'— you have lost weight lately.'

What? I looked down at her, confused. She was more than a head shorter than me, with red hair and fifties cat's eyes glasses hanging on a chain around her neck. She reached out and gently took my hand. 'A few girls in our year have been starving themselves. I want to make sure you're not one of them.'

My mind stopped in surprise as she turned my hand over,

then squeezed up my arm, checking my fleshiness more thoroughly than the witch in *Hansel and Gretel*.

Seriously? She thought I was anorexic? I wish. I had enough meat on my behind to feed a family for a week.

I laughed. 'Miss, I'm definitely not starving myself. I promise. You don't have to worry about me. Honestly.'

'Are you sure?'

'Seriously, my arms are thin, but you should see my arse.'

She let out a cross between a laugh and a tut. 'Ruth! That's not a very nice word.'

'Sorry. Honestly, I'm not anorexic.' *Living without parental supervision, yes. Going hungry? No.*

She flashed me a smile and squeezed my hand. 'I guess you must just be small-boned then.'

As I began the five-block walk to my empty house, I chuckled to myself. *Anorexic. Ha!*

It was ten o'clock at night on a Friday. The street had no traffic. But just as I moved past the block of shops near the school, a car behind me washed light over the footpath. The engine shifted to a chugging purr as it slowed down, keeping pace with my walking. I kept my eyes straight ahead.

I had travelled this stretch of road every day for more than four years of high school, as well as the five years I had lived here before that. I knew each home, especially the places with the *Safety House* stickers on their letterbox: the government had officially endorsed them as people to run to if someone started chasing you.

I didn't look at the car, but was aware of it continuing to creep beside me. I inched subtly closer to the houses. The car kept pace. Just as I had decided to run into number fifty-five's yard, tyres skidded and the car fishtailed down the road. Another crisis averted. Who needed parents?

Mum had left nearly four months ago. Though I kept expecting some kind of authority figure to pull me aside and tell me they knew I was living by myself and needed to report me to the police, no one had noticed.

As I stepped inside the unlocked back door, into the darkness of the house, I felt a moment of alarm. Kerstin was out again. I was alone in the world. After I turned on a few lights, then the telly, my panic eased.

I hunted through the pantry, but there were never any surprises now I did all my own shopping. Two-minute noodles? I put bread in the toaster instead, warming my hands over shimmering lines of heat.

As I waited for it to cook, I looked at my reflection in the window, pulling my dress tight around my bottom to emphasise its roundness. *Anorexic. Ha!*

As I listened to the ting of the elements expanding inside the toaster, the silence of the house crept up on me again, making my heart flutter. It wasn't like it would have been any noisier if Mum had been there. But at least I would have known if somebody tried to hurt me, there was another person in the house.

Seriously though, what would she have done? She probably wouldn't even have woken up. Besides, weren't most crimes committed by someone you knew? Dad was the obvious candidate, and she could never protect me from him.

I didn't expect to see him any time soon anyway. He had taken Kerstin, David and me to see a show before Mum and David had left for Brisbane, but except for a fleeting moment where we had been forced to visit him at Brenda's family's house at Christmas, I hadn't seen him since the stupid plastic-bag birthday present over a year ago. I didn't think he would launch another surprise attack, but if he did, I would just call the police. And this time I would press charges.

Scraping out the last of the Vegemite for my toast, I made a mental note to buy some more tomorrow. Certainly there were moments like this, where it felt a bit lonely in the house without Mum, but mostly it felt calmer. Calmer not being confronted by her unconscious body in the lounge room. Calmer not fighting with her to get her to admit she was drunk. Calmer knowing I just had myself to look after now.

I was managing to feed myself, wash my clothes, clean the house (sometimes), go to school, work, musical and basketball practice and still finish my homework. Sure, I went to nightclubs most weekends and ate apple and yoghurt for dinner nearly every night, but I had been doing those things when Mum lived with me. And yes, I left the washing in the machine for days on end, opening the lid to find a world of damp smells and mould spores, but I just put it on again and wrote a note on my hand: *Clothes!* It wasn't hard.

I had even secretly started to believe that if, at sixteen years old, I was managing to make all my decisions for myself, when I was finally old enough, I might get the chance to have the life I had always wanted.

It didn't involve a prince. I would be the one doing the rescuing. I would get out of this town and make something of myself. And I wouldn't just survive. I would have a beautiful life in which wishes came true and people laughed a hundred times more than they cried. If other people could have it, why not me?

ENEMY

IMPULSE CONTROL

Up in Rocky, visitors I didn't know started coming through on high rotation. Paying their last respects to Dad. He introduced me to men who had served with him in Vietnam, crying tears of gratitude that they had taken the time to visit him. Then I found out Mum was coming to say goodbye, flying up alone on one of the few trips she ever made on a plane.

Dad had not seen Mum since she left for Brisbane. By now her years of drinking had taken their toll. Her once striking appearance had become striking for all the wrong reasons. Her large eyes looked haunted, darting nervously or dropping to the ground to avoid catching people's eyes. Instead of walking, she hunched and cringed in a body too small and frail.

When she arrived I tried to be as welcoming as I could, to let her know that I was still on her side, always on her side, but she was excruciatingly uncomfortable being in the house Dad shared with Brenda. She didn't stay much longer than a cup of coffee and a quick hello before she went back to the airport.

She had obviously been drinking heavily before she arrived. After she left, the unprocessed booze that clung to her hung in the air, shaming and exposing her even in her absence. Dad turned to me. 'I didn't know your mum was on the turps that bad, Ruth.'

I nodded and looked down. Another fucking euphemism. I wanted to punch him in his cancerous head.

Was this another thing he really didn't know? Could he really be that unaware of the trajectory of Mum's life? For some reason I had naively thought because we were a 'family' he must have had some clue about what was going on in our world.

Though I had lived with her only for a short time after I left Rockhampton, I called Mum every couple of weeks. In marathon sessions where I played phone counsellor, we discussed how hard life was for her and I told her endlessly how much I believed in and loved her. Sometimes I resented her lack of interest in anything going on in my world, but mostly I just felt terribly sad that my mum had ended up in such a desperate situation.

With the help of AA, she did have a few sober years after she moved to Brisbane. But since then, she had reverted to drinking full-time, often locked away alone in her room. Even a recent stint in a locked detox ward, where she was warned she was causing herself irreparable long-term damage, hadn't slowed her down.

Describing Mum's alcoholism as 'on the turps' was like describing Dad's stage-four cancer as 'under the weather'. Her drinking was a slow, deliberate suicide. Drink by drink by drink, wiping herself out so often she was barely more than a shadow.

I wanted to tell him that when he left, he had taken my mother too. Just because there was an adult in the house didn't mean we weren't orphaned. He would have known this if he had bothered to check on us. But it was too late for anything I said to change my relationship with Dad. I swallowed down my outrage alongside my grief. But they were among the few things I did allow myself to swallow.

I kept the reins of self-control pulled tight by deliberately denying myself the pleasure of food. If I could squash my impulse to eat, I could squash my impulse to spew forth twenty-four years of fury. When I stepped on the bathroom scales four weeks after I arrived, I had dropped from fifty-six kilos to forty-five.

On New Year's Eve, only a few days after David had flown back to his job in Brisbane, Dad died at home with Kerstin, Brenda and me.

On the night before his funeral I walked the streets drinking beer with Jacob, Brenda's son. After a few minutes of companionable silence, Jacob spoke into the blackness. 'I'm sorry, Ruth. I know he's your dad. But I hated him. Hated him for what he did to Mum.'

'Don't worry,' I reassured him. 'I hated him too.'

'I can't believe she stayed with him. Did you know he hit her?'

'No!'

'Yeah. He used to hit us boys too —'

'I'm sorry. He never really hit Mum except one time. He beat the shit out of us kids though.'

'He hit you?'

'Yeah. A lot. Sorry he hit you too.'

'He stopped after we beat him up.'

I screeched to a halt, a smile spreading over my face. 'What?'

'Yeah. One day he was hitting one of my brothers and I stepped in and said, "C'mon. Take me on too." Then my other brother came in and all three of us ganged up, started laying into him.'

I laughed. 'That's bloody fantastic. I wish I'd done that.'

'He stopped hitting us after that.'

I kept laughing, imagining the look of surprise on Dad's face when they started punching back.

'Didn't stop him hitting Mum though.'

My laugh died. 'I'm so sorry about your mum. I had no idea.'

A pause stretched between us.

'Why'd she stay with him?' I asked.

'Dunno. I told her to leave him. She wouldn't.'

'Fuck.'

'Yeah.'

We walked along in silence, listening to the small loose stones scattered on the top of the bitumen scrunching under our feet.

'Oh well. Doesn't matter,' I said, trying to lighten the moment. 'He's dead now.' He laughed and I joined in. 'Probably shouldn't say that.' Our laughing increased into hysteria and I doubled over, hands on my knees to draw in breath. Once we quieted down I was walloped with guilty sobs. 'I am sad too.'

'Course you are, Ruth. He's your dad.'

Sometimes I wished I could just hate Dad. But mostly it felt easier to believe I hated him rather than face up to the fact that, despite everything, I had spent my life loving him, longing for him, while he had barely noticed I was alive.

My enemy. My beloved. My father.

SAVING FACE

'What do you mean my balance is twenty-two dollars?'

The frizzy orange-haired woman behind the counter at the bank tapped at the screen in front of her with a fake pink nail. 'That's what it says.'

A strange wind roared in my ears. 'It can't be right. I've been saving money in this account since I was in grade one.'

'Sorry. That's what —'

'But I can't even withdraw anything from the account.' My attention flicked to the silvery-blue shadow caught in the creases of her crepey eyelids, then back to her brown eyes. 'My mum has to sign. She's in Brisbane. There's never been one withdrawal from the account. You can check. It just doesn't —'

'There are some withdrawals.' The triumphant tone of her nasal voice made me feel violent.

'From when?'

'The first one for two hundred dollars a little over a week ago, and four more withdrawals since then.'

'But how could they get money out? They don't know my mother's signature!' My voice was shrill and shaking.

'I'm sorry, that's what it says.'

'Well, it's illegal. The bank has made a mistake. I need to talk to your boss.'

'He's not going to tell you anything differ—'

The sob I had been holding deep down in my gut burst forth, wrapping around my words. 'You're wrong!'

'Now, now, it's —'

'Don't try to comfort me! There's been a mistake. I need to talk to your boss.' The sobs were making it hard to get the words out and I felt the weight of the other tellers' eyes on me.

I tried to bring myself under control, but the effort made it worse, like trying to soothe a baby who has been left alone crying.

Behind the counter, a man with the stomach of a pregnant woman appeared. Despite my tears, I could see his expression of concern was a mask: his mouth was pinched and his eyes were hard.

'Why don't you come with me into my office, young lady?' The thin lips in his polite smile pulled tight. He didn't look like someone who was going to give me my money back. He looked like someone embarrassed by my 'display'. *He thought I was being embarrassing, did he? I would show him embarrassing.*

I screamed, 'No! I'm not going anywhere until you give me my money back. The bank has let someone take my money when they shouldn't —'

'I think this would be best discussed in my office.' He kept his voice low, but his snooty tone revved me up more.

I put on an innocent-girl voice, all tears now evaporated. 'I'm just a young girl. I've been told never to go into strange rooms with men. Why would you want me to go to your office?'

I could feel the eyes of people in the queues flicking from him to me. My body was thudding and crashing with the pounding of my heart. I couldn't make my brain work properly. What did I need to say to make him give me my money back?

'Well, I'm sorry, young lady. There's nothing I can do to help you.' He patted his receding hairline, checking the long strands at the front had remained in place. 'There have been a series of withdrawals from your account over the last few days and your balance now stands at twenty-two dollars and sixty-three cents.'

I stumbled as I hit the oven of Rockhampton heat, falling to the footpath with a heavy thud. Perfect. I didn't look around in case the fat, bald bastard was watching, but kept walking as if nothing had happened.

I could feel blood dripping down from my knee, but pretended I didn't notice as I unlocked the combination of my bike lock with shaking hands.

I cried as I rode home. In dribs and drabs since I was five, I had saved any money Mum and Dad had given me, as well as savings from my jobs. Until a week ago, I'd had over eight hundred dollars.

Mum's signature had activated the account, not mine. It was the one thing that guaranteed my money was safe. But now the money, money to buy a car when I got to Brisbane, had been stolen. I had no idea what to do about it.

'We have to tell Dad,' Kerstin said when I told her about it that night.

'What? No! No way. We're not telling Dad.'

Kerstin shook an Alpine Light out of her packet, holding it between fingers with nails bitten to the quicks. 'Well, I don't know what to do about it.'

Tears trickled down my cheeks and she reached over to put her hand on mine, giving it a squeeze.

'It's all right, Ruth,' she said. She rested her cigarette on the ashtray and came over to hug me. Kerstin didn't like to be touched, so it felt like a big gesture. 'It'll be all right. Dad'll be able to help. He's good at stuff like this. He's helped me heaps of times.'

I knew this about Kerstin and Dad's relationship. She called him just to talk. If she needed help, she asked him. What's more, he helped her. I didn't know how she risked opening herself up to him like that. Needing his help would make me weak and him strong. I never wanted him to have that kind of power over me again.

I looked at the scrawling handwriting where the teller had written twenty-two dollars and sixty-three cents on a piece of paper. Fresh tears sprang up and spilled over.

But I did want my money back. And the people at the bank were never going to take me seriously because I was a kid. Plus the fact I had kind of gone nuts at them. I bet they would take Dad seriously though.

But he wouldn't want to help me. I was a bitch. I was the one who had called the police. I didn't make any effort with him. Besides, after the present he had given me I knew exactly what he thought of me. I wasn't worth the trouble.

'Even if I do call, he'll just tell me I'm an idiot for not taking better care of my bank book,' I said. 'He doesn't like me the way he likes you.'

'He does, you know. You just can't see it.'

Two days later, Kerstin and I walked with Dad back into the main branch of the Rock Building Society.

'Hello,' Dad said to a woman behind the counter with two inches of dark regrowth at the base of her yellow-blonde hair. 'My name's Doug Callum. I've got an appointment to see your bank manager about my daughter's bank account.'

I drank his voice in. He was in his most charming mode, smiling and direct. When I had no contact with him, my feelings about him were crystal clear. In person it wasn't as easy. It had taken me by surprise how warm it had made me feel when he hugged me, like something was melting.

He hadn't even given me any grief when I lost my bank book.

'What happened, love?' he asked on the phone.

'I took my bank book to a school dance. I know. It was stupid of me, but I had put some money in that afternoon and I came straight from work. I think someone must have stolen it from there.'

'But your mum has to sign the account, doesn't she?'

My heart rose. If Dad got it straight away, maybe there was hope. 'That's exactly it! I wasn't even worried about it because I didn't think anyone could access it. I've never withdrawn any money from it in my entire life.'

'Well that doesn't sound right. D'you want me to come down

to the bank with you to sort it out?'

'Would you?'

'Course, love.'

In a small glass room with a view into the main bank, we settled down into chairs opposite the bald fatty. He leaned back in his chair making a loud creak. 'How can I help you?'

His thin, condescending smile instantly pissed me off.

I expected Dad to react to the look with anger as well, but his words came out smoothly. 'Well, it looks like someone has stolen money out of my daughter's account and I wondered what we might be able to do to make it right.'

The smile stretched tighter. 'I'm sorry, but the problem we have is someone forged her signature —'

I jumped in. 'But what does that matter? My signature is not the one that accesses the account. My mother's signature is —'

Dad turned to me, put a hand on top of mine and patted it, giving me a small smile. I quieted myself.

'It's true,' he said. 'She's never taken any money out of this account because her mum's signature is needed for withdrawals.'

'I can see that, but unfortunately there is nothing we can do —'

'Hang on a minute. It looks to me like someone in your bank —'

'It wasn't at one of our banks; the withdrawals were made at one of the outlets attached to a post office on the north side —'

'All right then, one of your outlets, one of the places authorised by your bank, has not done due diligence. No one should ever have been able to withdraw funds.'

Due diligence. *Good one, Dad.*

'Well, the signature they presented matched the identification in the wallet.'

'Yes,' I cut in. 'But my signature is not the one in the back of the passbook so it shouldn't matter even if someone matched it.'

'Sorry, but the person was able to show photo ID. That proved the passbook account belonged to them.'

My heart thudded in my chest. 'Well obviously they didn't look too hard at the ID. No one at my school looks like me —'

Dad put his hand on mine again. His voice was calm. 'Listen, mate, I've banked with the Rock since I moved to Rocky. I've had two home loans, two personal loans and all my bank accounts with you. Ruth,' he squeezed my hand as he said my name, 'has paid money into this account since she was just a little girl.'

He moved forward in his chair. 'Is there something the bank might be able to do to help us out? As a goodwill gesture?'

Fatty's smile was replaced by a look of smug relief. 'Yes, well, even though we are not responsible in any way, I can see this is a hardship.'

He leaned back again, creaking. He put his fingers together in a steeple. 'I think the bank might be able to come to some agreement, simply as a gesture of goodwill, you understand.'

'So she could get her money back?' Dad pushed.

'Yes, I think we could make that happen.'

I jumped up and squealed at the man. 'Thank you!'

I hugged Dad and Kerstin and jumped around the office. After the details were arranged, we exited into the hot, bright afternoon.

I hugged Dad again. 'Thank you so much for your help.' It felt good to be on the same team for once.

He smiled as we pulled apart. 'I wasn't sure the old bastard was going to come to the party, but we got him in the end.' He winked at me and I felt his joy filling me up.

'He wasn't very keen to help, was he?'

'No. Too worried about covering his own arse. He knew they were wrong. Sometimes you've got to give people a way to save face before they can do the right thing.'

'Yeah, I'll have to remember that.' I gave him one of the last hugs I had left before I said goodbye to Rocky for good.

SMART CHOICES

Inside the large school hall where I regularly performed in front of the school, purple vinyl seats for the two hundred and fifty year twelves to sit together were spread over the polished wooden floor.

'Okay, these forms are for everyone who is interested in applying to university.'

My ears rang as people huddled together with friends, whispering about what they were going to choose. I had obviously not been paying attention when they told us we would be doing this today.

My hands grew cold and sweaty despite the warm air being blown across my back from the high ceiling fans. University was going to be the key to my new beautiful life. The only problem was that I had barely given a thought to what I wanted to do once I got there. Wasn't someone meant to help with this? A guidance counsellor or something?

My heart sank. I looked over at the group of quiet girls who got good marks. They had probably had countless conversations with their parents about career options. The last time anyone asked me what I wanted to be when I grew up, I had been in primary school. Why hadn't I thought more about this?

Grabbing one of the pens spilling out of a new box of Bics on a table, I stole a glance at the girl next to me. She had sparkling dark eyes and curly brown hair to match her bubbly, chatty personality, but she was not someone who I thought of as smart. On her form she had written *Bachelor of Arts*.

I stretched forward and looked at the sheet of the girl in front of me. She had put down arts as well. I looked at her long gold hair and green eyes. Beautiful? Yes. Smart? No.

Right, that settled it. Arts were for stupid people. And what was the point of going to university if people could still look down on you?

We weren't meant to get out of our seats, but I kept my head low and crouch-walked my way over to where the nerds were sitting.

'Rita. What're you putting down?' Rita and I sat next to each other in chemistry and had worked together on projects a few times. She was unfailingly friendly and the smartest girl in the school.

'Graphic design.'

'What's that?'

'It's an arts degree.'

Damn. That didn't help. Of course Rita was going to put down arts. Though she topped most subjects, she was also an incredibly gifted artist. She could do anything she wanted.

If I was going to choose a course based on what I was best at, I would do drama. But there was hardly likely to be a career at the end of that, was there? It didn't sound very impressive either.

I didn't want people to think I chose acting because that was the only thing I was smart enough to qualify for. I wanted to do something other people would be impressed by so they would know not to underestimate me.

I looked over the boys' shoulders. Science. Accounting. Science. Medicine. That was more like it.

I was as smart as they were. I slunk back to my chair and put down science. I didn't know exactly what that would entail, but it didn't really matter. It sounded way more intelligent than acting. Besides, I could always try to be a presenter on *Beyond 2000*.

As long as I got into a university in Brisbane, I would be a new person. Then I could forget everything about my past and never come back to this stinking crap-hole again.

YOU'LL BE RIGHT

Two weeks after school broke up I hopped on a train down to Brisbane to join Mum. She met me at the station with David.

'You're huge,' I said as he ran up to meet me. In the year he had been in Brisbane he had shot up way taller than me and a faint moustache was threatening to grow.

He lifted me off the ground and swung me around.

I punched his back. 'Put me down.'

'I could carry you forever, you tiny, weeny, insignificant thing.' He staggered along with me.

'Shut up. Put me down.'

When he dropped me, I walked into Mum's arms, inhaling her deeply. She smelled right: Tabu and cigarettes.

It was too expensive to talk much on the phone, but in the few brief conversations we'd had during the previous year she had sounded better than she had since before Dad left.

'You look great, Mum.' I gestured to her navy silk blouse tucked into a white skirt, white dangling hoop earrings and red lips.

'Thanks. There are some great op-shops down here.' She smiled at me. 'So when do you find out if you got into uni?'

It felt weird to have her ask questions like a real mum. Weird, but nice.

'In a couple of weeks.' I slung my navy leather backpack over my shoulder. 'I'm freaking out.'

'Nah, don't be silly. You're smart. You'll be right.'

GOLDEN LIGHT

Growing up in tropical Rockhampton taught me to love the sun. Each day its warm hands reached out to contain and hold me. Each day it unleashed across the sky a display of colours so wondrous it made my mind grow still. The abundance it offered so freely filled me with a hope I didn't know how to explain. As long as the sun still shone, nothing could be all bad.

But I had learned to value the shadows as well. My journey in the dark had brought me close to achieving the mission I had set myself before I visited Dad in the month prior to his death. It would never stop hurting that we had not come to a place of real relating while he was alive, but at least in exploring Dad's war I had soothed my blistered rage with the balm of understanding.

The image I held of the father from my childhood had now blended with the picture I had of him at twenty-four, fighting in an awful war and returning to a hostile reception at home. His portrait had also progressed beyond his death to blend with the faces of the veterans I had spoken to, the ones who showed the lifelong scars of war.

My dad's conflict had not ended when he left the battlefield. It continued on forever inside him, sending its shockwaves into the hearts and souls of his family. That it happened was a tragedy. But it was not one person's fault. I could never feel it was only my mother, brother and sister who needed defending now. Dad needed me to be his champion as well. By swinging my way from one end to the other I had managed to claim more generous ground. Maybe I could love them all rather than choosing between them.

It would always be part of my lifelong journey to accept that I did not have to be perfect to receive love. But in being more compassionate toward Dad, I had gained the unexpected bonus of being more accepting of myself. I could not say I was all the way there, but in those areas where I fell short, I could do what I had always done: fake it until I made it.

One afternoon on the couch, my son's chubby little hands grabbed my face and he pressed his forehead into mine forcing me to look deeply into his eyes. He sucked his cheeks in to form an extreme pucker and pulled me toward him, slobbering his love onto me with a kiss so wet the lower half of my face swam in dribble.

'You're the best mummy in the world. I love you so much.'

'I love you too, my darling.'

'Me too. I love you too,' said my daughter, twisting her body around and scrambling her long, skinny legs to find a place on my lap alongside her brother. They nudged at each other trying to claim the lion's share of me, knocking me over in the process.

When I fell they launched their attack, covering me in a stream of kisses on my eyes, my nose, my hair, my lips – the way I had done to them a hundred times before. I giggled and squealed. *Feel this*, I told myself. *This is your life now*. I was not perfect. But I was good enough. And so very loved.

Tumbling off, they gave their attention back to the television. I pushed myself forward on the couch breathing into tingling fingertips. At that moment, the western sun hit the spot in the afternoon sky where it lit up the lounge room, highlighting every speck of dust in straight orange lines. The golden light was a nudge, reminding me of all the things I had to be grateful for.

'I can't see the TV properly,' my daughter moaned.

'The sun will move lower in the sky and stop being so bright in a minute,' I said. Closing my eyes and turning my face, I let the glow wash through me.

Mum and Dad before Dad went to Vietnam

Dad in Vietnam

Mum, Kerstin and me inside the army tent

Top: Kerstin, David and me eating cake batter. Bottom: The family standing in front of our boat at Emu Park Caravan Park prior to setting up the tent.

Dad, David and me not long before he left

Matt, Scarlett, Alex and me in Melbourne

Dear reader,

Thank you so much for reading ENEMY. I wrote this book for every child who needed to be protected and wasn't. If you were one of these children, please know the way you were treated wasn't your fault, and that you have always been loveable and worthy of belonging.

It is my deepest wish that the most difficult parts of my story have in some way helped you tend to your own pain, and that the moments of joy and humour, and, let's face it, pure awesome badassary of my younger self, have reminded you that even in your darkest days there are always pockets of light.

I know our stories might be different, but I believe those painful places where we have been most deeply wounded, hurt in the same way. It is in this most human of experiences that we are most vulnerable. It is from this place that we can also feel most loved and connected.

Our hearts heal faster when they beat in the company of others. This book is my clumsy attempt to share my heart with yours so we might both have a chance to remember we are not alone.

Much love,

What did you think of ENEMY?

If you enjoyed this book and think it something that others might benefit from reading, I would be very grateful if you posted a short review on Amazon or Goodreads, or wherever else you review things. I read every single word you write and would love to know what you took away from my story. The personal perspective you offer in your review also has the potential to help others and your support makes a huge difference to how many people know about this book.

I really appreciate your help spreading the word. Thank you so much for your support!

Let's stay in touch

I would love to stay connected. Sign up to my free newsletter and find out more about me at ruthclare.com

Connect with me on the socials

I sometimes go into hiding on these but eventually I get back there!
Youtube: @ruthclareauthor
Instagram: @ruthclareauthor
Facebook: @ruthclareauthor
Twitter: @ruthclareauthor

Watch my TED talk

If you're trying to break the habit of people pleasing so you can be more authentic in your life and relationships, you might like my TEDx talk , 'The pain of hiding your true self', about my painful and hilarious journey of taking my real self out of hiding.

Scan to view the talk:

Don't suffer alone

If this book has brought up issues for you, please reach out for support from one of the free mental health support phonelines in your local area.

AUSTRALIA
Lifeline: 13 11 44
Beyond Blue: 1300 224 636
Blue Knot Foundation: 1300 657 380
Open Arms Veteran and Family Counselling: 1800 011 046

UNITED STATES
988 Suicide and Crisis Lifeline: 988
Veterans Crisis Line: 988 then press 1
Ayuda En Español: (888) 628-9454
Crisis Text Line: Text HOME to 741741

UNITED KINGDOM
Samartitans UK: 116 123
National Suicide Helpline UK: 919-231-4525
SANE: 0 (300) 304 7000
Support Line UK: 0 (170) 8 765200

CANADA
Toronto Distress Centres: 416-408-HELP (4357)
Talk Suicide Canada: 1 (833) 456 4566
Gerstein Crisis Centre: (02) 6311 1

ACKNOWLEDGEMENTS

This book would not have been possible without the love, support and encouragement of my darling husband Matt, who put up with me droning on and on at him about war and trauma and pulled extra shifts with the kids so I could write. Also, thank you for putting your graphic design talent to use creating the cover and interior of this book. You are brilliant.

Thank you also to my children, who have taught me how to love more deeply than I ever believed was possible, and who accepted the third child, this book, competing for my attention. You are the best things that have ever happened to me.

To all the veterans who shared their stories with me, my heartfelt respect and thanks for your honesty and vulnerability. Thanks also to the Vietnam Veterans Association, Vietnam Veterans Counselling Service and to Nic Fothergill for his insightful DVD, *You're Not in the Forces Now*.

Great thanks to the many people who read early drafts of my work and urged me to keep going. Magdalena McGuire, Jeanette Fyffe, Anna Henry, Julie Twohig, Elisabeth Hanscombe, Alyse Mobrici, Dana Wong, Shane Lazzo, Troy Holland, Sarah Oliver. Much appreciation to Tony Wilson for his helpful advice and support. Thanks also to Klaudia Furness for helping me go after my dreams and Sarah Coffey for having my back.

Enemy was first published by Penguin in 2016. Many thanks to my excellent editor, Cate Blake, also Louise Ryan, Rhian Davies and the other Penguins who helped bring Enemy into the world. Also to my agent, Grace Heifetz, for your enthusiasm and belief in my work.

One further acknowledgement: I would like to thank every person who appears in this book. They are all real, though mostly their names, and sometimes the timelines of our exchanges, have been changed, for the usual reasons. These incidents might not have made a mark in their memories, but they have helped forge me into the person I am today. Thanks for being part of my journey.

www.ingramcontent.com/pod-product-compliance
Lightning Source LLC
Chambersburg PA
CBHW032334300426
44109CB00041B/798